D0051022

TO THE OTHER SHORE

TO THE OTHER SHORE

THE RUSSIAN JEWISH INTELLECTUALS
WHO CAME TO AMERICA

Steven Cassedy

WITHDRAWN FROM COLLECTION V2

PRINCETON UNIVERSITY PRESS   PRINCETON, NEW JERSEY

Copyright © 1997 by Princeton University Press
Published by Princeton University Press, 41 William Street,
Princeton, New Jersey 08540
In the United Kingdom: Princeton University Press, Chichester,
West Sussex
All Rights Reserved

Library of Congress Cataloging-in-Publication Data
Cassedy, Steven.
To the other shore : the Russian Jewish intellectuals
who came to America / Steven Cassedy.
p. cm.
Includes bibliographical references and index.
ISBN 0691-02975-X (cloth : alk. paper)
1. Jews—Russia—Intellectual life. 2. Jews—Cultural
assimilation—Russia. 3. Jewish Radicals—Russia. 4. Russia—
Ethnic relations. 5. Jews, Russian—United States—Intellectual life.
7. Jews—Cultural assimilation—United States. 8. Jewish
radicals—United States. 9. United States—
Ethnic Relations. I. Title.
DS 135.R9C34 1997   96-44604 CIP
305.892'4047—dc21

This book has been composed in Sabon typeface

Princeton University Press books are printed
on acid-free paper and meet the guidelines for
permanence and durability of the Committee
on Production Guidelines for Book Longevity
of the Council on Library Resources

Printed in the United States of America
by Princeton Academic Press

1 3 7 5 9 2 4 6 8 10

לזכרון מיין זיידן
יעקב לעווין
(1892–1977)

Contents

1 8 1997

List of Illustrations

Preface

THIS BOOK is about a small but influential group of Jews who immigrated to the United States from the Russian Empire between 1881 and the early 1920s, the era of "mass immigration." The immigrants whose story I tell were intellectuals who became leaders in the labor movement and other progressive political movements in the United States. They were women and men most of whom had become culturally assimilated in Russia and had learned radical politics there before emigrating. For this group, becoming culturally "Russian" and adopting radical political views meant reassessing and often abandoning their Jewish identity. When they became influential members of the community in America, by organizing unions or by writing in the Yiddish, Russian, or English-language press, they often retained their adopted Russian identity and their commitment to the Russian political and cultural theories they had brought with them. I tell the story of these Jewish intellectuals first by describing the process of cultural and political assimilation they underwent in Russia and then by showing the impact of that assimilation on the political and cultural lives they led in the United States.

The emphasis in this book is thus on the role that Russian culture and politics played in the formation of the character of the Russian Jewish émigré intelligentsia in America. Though many books have been written about the Jews who came to America from the Russian Empire in the mass immigration, none has given a primary focus to this part of the story.

Some books tell of the immigrants as one large group. Irving Howe's classic *World of Our Fathers* (New York: Harcourt Brace Jovanovich, 1976) is the best known and the most complete of these. Arthur Hertzberg begins *The Jews in America* (New York: Simon and Schuster, 1989) with the assertion that the history of Jews who came to America from the very earliest times is for the most part the story of poor people, so in his excellent chapters on the mass immigration of Russian Jews, he concentrates on the lives of ordinary people.

Other books have dealt specifically with the Russian Jewish intellectuals. Two of the finest are written by scholars who know Russian and are trained in Russian intellectual history. One is Jonathan Frankel's monumental *Prophecy and Politics: Socialism, Nationalism, and the Russian Jews, 1862–1917* (Cambridge: Cambridge University Press, 1981), which traces the history of Jewish political movements in Russia, Palestine, and the United States. The section Frankel devotes to the Jewish intellectuals in America is immensely valuable, but it is only one part of a much larger project. Ezra Mendelsohn's superb *Class Struggle in the Pale: The Formative Years of the Jewish Workers' Movement in Tsarist Russia* (Cambridge: Cambridge University Press, 1970) treats the growth of radicalism among Jews in Russia.

Several books deal at length with the Jewish intellectuals in America: Nora Levin's very engaging *While Messiah Tarried: Jewish Socialist Movements, 1871–1917* (New York: Schocken, 1977); Ronald Sanders's *The Downtown Jews: Portraits of an Immigrant Generation* (New York: Harper & Row, 1969); and Gerald Sorin's *The Prophetic Minority: American Jewish Immigrant Radicals, 1880–1920* (Bloomington, IN: Indiana University Press, 1985). All these books take account, to various extents, of the Russian political and cultural dimension of the story but do not make it the central object of study.

Finally, I should mention two books by authors who were close to the events they described and who were familiar with the Russian intellectual foundations of the Russian Jewish intelligentsia. Leo Deutsch's *Rol' evreev v russkom revoliutsionnom dvizhenii* (The role of the Jews in the Russian revolutionary movement) (Berlin: "Grani," 1923) tells the story of the Russian Jewish radical movement in Russia, a movement in which he was a celebrated participant. And Elias Tcherikower's *The Early Jewish Labor Movement in the United States* (New York: YIVO, 1961), a book constructed from essays in Yiddish by a number of scholars, is probably the best study of the American Jewish labor movement, but it does not dwell on the cultural life of the immigrant Jews.

The nature of my subject has obliged me to confront some tricky problems of transliteration. My intent throughout has been to serve general readers while also transliterating in a way that will be useful for specialists. These are the principles I have followed:

1. For Yiddish, I have used the "YIVO" system, which has become the scholarly standard. The system is designed in such a way that an English-speaking reader can sound out words with a minimum of specialized knowledge (the knowledge, for example, that *ey* is pronounced like an English long *a*, *ay* like an English long *i*). For personal names in the text, in the case of individuals who lived in the United States and Anglicized their names, I have used the Anglicized forms (Abraham or Abe Cahan for Avrom Kahan, Isaac Hourwich for Yitskhok-Ayzik Halevi Hurvitsh). For others, I have simply transliterated the Yiddish. In references in the endnotes, however, I have given the name, in transliterated form, as it appears in the publication in question and then given the Anglicized form in parentheses (where such a form exists). I have made an exception for Abe Cahan, whose name appears especially frequently. Rather than write "Av. Kahan" every time I have simply written "Abe Cahan."

The spelling of Yiddish had not been standardized at the time the texts I cite were written. Different authors spelled the same word differently, frequently the same author spelled the same word differently on different occasions, and almost every author imitated certain features of German spelling and pronunciation (for example, *ihr*, "her" or "you," spelled like the German *ihr*, instead of the currently standard *ir*; *arbayter*, pronounced like the German *Arbeiter*, "worker," instead of the more "Yiddish" *arbeter*). I have transliterated exactly what the authors wrote, instead of modernizing the spelling.

2. For Russian, I have used the Library of Congress system of transliteration. For personal names in the text, however, I have used Anglicized spellings in cases where such spellings are widely recognized (Dostoevsky and Tolstoy, rather than Dostoevskii and Tolstoi). Some very Russified Jews considered the Russian forms of their names to be the original ones but sometimes published, or were referred to, in the Yiddish press, thus giving us at least three versions of their names. Leo Deutsch, for example, was Lev Grigor'evich Deich (pronounced *dāch*) when he wrote in Russian and Leo Daytsh (pronounced *dīch*) when he wrote in Yiddish. Once again, I have used the accepted Anglicized form except in the notes.

3. For Hebrew, I have normally treated words and phrases as existing in a conversational Yiddish context and have transliterated them accordingly. I have thus based the transliteration on the pronunciation that Yiddish speakers use for Hebrew words within a Yiddish context, not the pronunciation they use for them in prayer. Where it has been necessary to supply the "true" version of a Hebrew word or phrase (for example, as an explanation for one I have given in "Yiddish" spelling), I have used a nonscholarly system whose purpose is to render as clearly as possible to English-speaking readers the pronunciation used by the majority of modern-day Israelis (which is different from the Ashkenazic pronunciation used by most Yiddish speakers). Thus the name of the first blessing in the section of the Jewish liturgy known as the *Amidah* is, in modern Hebrew pronunciation, *avot* (*a* pronounced as in *father*, long *o*, accent on the final syllable). A Yiddish speaker using this name in casual conversation (in prayer it would be different) would probably pronounce it *oves* (*o* like the English *aw*, short *e*, accent on the first syllable). This is the form I have used.

Unless I have indicated otherwise, all translations in this book are my own, and all dates of events occurring in Russia are Old Style.

I began work on this book as an utter newcomer to the field of Yiddish studies and have profited from the advice of many friends and relatives. Janet Hadda introduced me to the professional field of Yiddish studies— in the unlikely setting of a car repair shop in Los Angeles. Chava Turniansky kindly invited me, rank novice that I was, to participate in the Yiddish conference at Hebrew University in 1992. At the conference, I was fortunate enough to make the acquaintance of Leonard Prager and Ruth Wisse, both of whom have generously taken the time to answer questions in the last four years. The YIVO staff has been enormously helpful during my visits to their library and archives. Zachary Baker, the head librarian, has taken time out of his very busy work day to help me with problems and has been patient enough to answer numerous e-mail messages. No name has appeared more frequently in the acknowledgments sections of books on Yiddish subjects than that of a legendary YIVO librarian, who speaks more languages and knows more than many of the most accomplished scholars who seek her assistance: I would like to thank Dina Abramowicz for the help she gave me in 1991 and in 1994.

My colleagues in the Judaic Studies Program at the University of California, San Diego, have taken countless phone calls from me to answer questions about religion, history, and language. Thanks to Richard Elliott Friedman, William Propp, and David Goodblatt. Thanks also to San Diego Chabad Rabbis Jonah Fradkin and Moishe Leider, who gave answers to my questions about Tanakh and Jewish liturgy faster than most people can give their own names. Thanks to Alexander Orbach, John Klier, William Phillips, Daniel Bell, and the late Irving Howe for answering my letters. Paul Buhle, with his encyclopedic knowledge of the American left (and his *Encyclopedia of the American Left*), has been an invaluable source of information. Robert Brown and Mary Murrell, my editors at Princeton University Press, have patiently seen this book through to completion. My colleagues in Russian studies Beth Holmgren and Susan Larsen helped me find just the right way to render a troublesome Russian word or phrase.

Uncle Will and Aunt Manya Levin, Holocaust survivors and native speakers of Yiddish, were always available to tell me what a Yiddish expression "really" means, or what the "proper" way to say something is. They should live and be well.

One aspiring Russian Jewish intellectual who came to the other shore arrived in New York on December 1, 1911, at the age of nineteen, carrying nothing but his *tfiln* (at least, that's how he told the story). His name was listed on the passenger manifest as Jankel Lewin, but after he arrived, he Anglicized his name and became Jacob Levine. He worked as a paper hanger, briefly became involved in socialist politics, put himself through pharmacy school at Fordham University, and ran his own pharmacy until he retired. His fondest memories from his early years in America were memories of an era when Second Avenue in lower Manhattan was lined with lecture halls and young people like him could go every day and hear speeches—could live in a world of *ideas*. His fondest memories of his Fordham University years were memories of the courses in which he studied philosophy and literature. His favorite poems of Goethe and Heine remained in his memory—in the original German—to the end of his life, like the endless pages of Talmud he had committed to memory during his yeshiva years in the old country. The German poems he memorized, together with the books and magazines he read, were a hedge against the drudgery and anxiety of running a small business for a half-century. He had a blessed death, if it's possible to speak of such a thing. One day, at the age of eighty-five, he went to a lecture, as he had done so many times long ago. As he sat and listened, he suddenly slumped over and died.

To him, my grandfather, *olev hasholem*, this book is fondly dedicated.

Introduction

In 1898, after he had been in this country for sixteen years, Abraham Cahan published a magazine article called "The Russian Jew in America." He began with this story:

One afternoon in the summer of 1881, when the Jewish quarter of Kieff was filled with groans and its pavements were strewn with the débris of destroyed homes, a group of young men entered one of the synagogues of the ancient city. They were well dressed, and their general appearance bespoke education and refinement. The rabbi had proclaimed a day of fasting and prayer, and the house of God was crowded with sobbing victims of the recent riots, but as the newcomers made their way to the Holy Ark silence fell upon the congregation. The young men were students of the University of St. Vladimir, and although sons of Israel like the others, their presence at a synagogue was an unusual sight.

"Brethren," said the spokesman of the delegation, struggling with his sobs, "we are a committee of the Jewish students of the university, sent to clasp hands with you and to mingle our tears with your tears. We are here to say to you, 'We are your brothers; Jews like yourselves, like our fathers!' We have striven to adopt the language and manners of our Christian fellow countrymen; we have brought ourselves up to an ardent love of their literature, of their culture, of their progress. We have tried to persuade ourselves that we are children of Mother Russia. Alas! we have been in error. The terrible events which have called forth this fast and these tears have aroused us from our dream. The voice of the blood of our outraged brothers and sisters cries unto us that we are only strangers in the land which we have been used to call our home; that we are only stepchildren here, waifs to be trampled upon and dishonored. There is no hope for Israel in Russia. The salvation of the downtrodden people lies in other parts,—in a land beyond the seas, which knows no distinction of race or faith, which is a mother to Jew and Gentile alike. In the great republic is our redemption from the brutalities and ignominies to which we are subjected in this our birthplace. In America we shall find rest; the stars and stripes will wave over the true home of our people. To America, brethren! To America!"[1]

It's a wonderful, poignant story. The setting is a synagogue. Does the head of the "delegation" realize how much his speech echoes the religious service the congregation has just heard or is about to hear? The traditional liturgy is built around a series of nineteen blessings, each with its own theme and name. When the student spokesman says "like our fathers," he calls to mind the first blessing, *Oves* (*avot* in modern Hebrew pronunciation, "fathers"), in which the members of the congregation present themselves to the "God of our fathers," name the Jewish Patriarchs, and refer to the gracious acts of their predecessors (fathers). The delegation comes to ask *forgiveness*, and we think of the sixth blessing, *Slikhe* (*slikhah*, "forgiveness"), in which Jews implore God to forgive them, cry out that they have sinned, and lightly beat their breast. On Yom Kippur and on special days of fasting like the one called by the rabbi in Kiev, the congregants recite a long list of sins (*Al khet*, "for the sin . . . ") and beat their breast throughout the recitation. The spokesman uses the words "salvation" and "redemption," and we cannot help thinking of *Geule* (*g'ulah*, "redemption"), the seventh blessing, in which Jews beg God to look at them in their affliction and to redeem them speedily.

The fifth blessing is called *Tshuve* (*tshuvah*, "repentance"). It goes like this:

> Return us, our Father, to thy Torah,
> And bring us nearer, our King, to thy service,
> And restore us to complete repentance [*tshuvah*] in thy presence.
> Blessed art Thou, O Lord, Who art pleased with repentance.

This is the central idea in Cahan's story. Before the Jewish young people come to their own *Al khet* ("We have striven to adopt . . . we have brought ourselves up . . . We have tried to persuade ourselves . . . we have been in error . . ."), it cannot be lost on us that they are students at St. Vladimir University—*Saint* Vladimir University, that is—and not a yeshiva. And now they have returned, not precisely to God's Torah, as in the blessing, but to their people. The root meaning of *tshuvah* is turning back, returning.

TO AMERICA

The next step after the "return" was "to America." Millions of other Jews would go, too, between 1881 and the early 1920s, but not all were like the *bale tshuve* (penitents who have returned to their people) who addressed the congregation in Kiev.

Young people like these were in a class by themselves. They belonged to a small, elite minority that had made their way—at least partly—into the Russian intellectual classes. They had adopted the dress, the social conventions, the learning, and, of course, the language of their non-Jewish countrymen. Most had turned their backs on a closely regulated life that Ashkenazic Jewry had led in Poland and Russia for centuries. Many had come to reject the notion that the Jews were a people apart, a "nation" within a larger nation-state. And they had thrown themselves, with the fervor of devout Hassidim, into the radical political movements that swept Russian intellectual life starting in the middle of the nineteenth century.

Circumstances had now led many to make a choice. As throngs of ordinary Russians made their way through the streets of towns in southern Russia, attacking Jews and destroying their property, all Russian Jews, including the intellectual elite, came to see that they were a nation apart whether they liked it or not. Some particularly radical members of the elite group held on to their beliefs, seeing the rioting hordes as a hopeful sign that soon the Russian people would rise up *en masse* and direct their ruinous energies against the tsar. But even doctrinaire believers like these could not fail to see that they themselves would be standing in the path of such a revolt if it ever took place. In the years after the first wave of pogroms, as conditions continued to deteriorate for the Jews, others like the students in the synagogue saw that Russia held out no further hope for them, that they were Jews, even if only in the eyes of Gentiles, and that it was time to leave.

Abraham Cahan, or Abe Cahan, as he liked to be called in the United States, was one of them. He had been born in 1860, into a traditional Jewish family, had learned Russian on the sly, had provided himself with a secular higher education, and had joined the radical left. He ran afoul of the law in Russia at roughly the same time as the students appeared in the synagogue in Kiev. He fled and came to the United States. One could probably say without exaggeration that in the first two or three decades of the twentieth century he was the most influential Jew in America. He was the editor of the *Jewish Daily Forward* from 1902 until his death in 1951, and he is a central character in this story.

THE RADICAL INTELLIGENTSIA

There are lots of books about the mass immigration of Jews to America in the late nineteenth and early twentieth centuries. As other authors know, if we look at all the Jews who came, then the story of the mass immigration is largely the story of poor, uneducated people. The descendants of the Jewish immigrants from this period, a group that includes the vast majority of today's American Jews, will agree with this view. How many Jews in America today, when they are asked about their immigrant ancestors, will tell the story of refined, educated, Russian-speaking ladies and gentlemen who arrived at Castle Garden or Ellis Island full of plans to build a labor movement and a socialist press? No, most Jews who left

Russia did not base their decision on principles like the ones that form the substance of the repentant student's speech to the congregation in Kiev. They based their decision on need.

Not that the educated, assimilated immigrants were rich; they were not. But there is a better chance they came for more purely political reasons: they were in trouble with the authorities and had to leave, they saw America as a better place to carry out the political program to which they had recently committed their lives, or both. Many, perhaps most, immigrants came with the entirely personal goal of making better lives for themselves, their families, and their descendants. The members of the educated, radical group, though, generally came with larger political goals, ranging in ambitiousness from improving the daily lives and working conditions of all Jewish workers to overthrowing capitalism and replacing it with socialism. Almost all immigrants arrived in this country and immediately set about finding work to sustain themselves. The members of the radical elite group were no exception, but they were more likely to stay up into the night working on union campaigns and writing articles for a newspaper or journal they had helped found. Many immigrants were entirely consumed by the rigors of their new lives in America. The members of the smaller group became the leaders who hoped to show their less educated fellow immigrants the way to better lives and a brighter political future.

This book is about the Jewish radical immigrant intellectuals who became cultural and political leaders in the new immigrant community in America. The geographical center of activity for this group was New York City, and I have set the scene almost entirely there. The story runs from 1881, when the mass immigration began, to the early 1920s.

In many ways, the intellectuals were a diverse group both before and after they arrived. Some were born into relatively educated, secularized families, some were born into traditional religious families for which the move of a son or daughter into the intellectual classes was regarded as a form of apostasy, and others were born into families that gave their children a combination of Jewish learning and modern, "enlightened" learning. They represented a range of political views in both the old country and the new. In Russia, some favored a cosmopolitan society with no national, ethnic, or religious distinctions, some saw the Jewish struggle in Russia purely as a struggle for equal rights, and, especially after the pogroms of 1881, some supported the establishment of a Jewish homeland in Palestine. In the United States, the "Jewish question" took a backseat to broader political questions. Some Jewish intellectuals declared themselves anarchists, some signed on as Marxists, others favored a less partisan, mid-nineteenth-century utopian socialism, many floated from one system to another, and a few devised political systems of their own.

But almost all members of this group shared one thing: the legacy of the nineteenth-century Russian revolutionary doctrines known as Nihilism and Populism. "Doctrines" is perhaps the wrong word for what might appear to be little more than a collection of often contradictory, constantly evolving beliefs. Still, it is not difficult to isolate and identify the beliefs that formed the core of the various Russian revolutionary programs in the nineteenth century. One can also document how Russian Jewish intellectuals, while still in Russia, came to be indoctrinated in these beliefs. That is what I have done in the first part of this book. I have also told how these beliefs brought about a crisis of identity for the Jewish radical intellectuals who held them.

The Jewish intellectuals did not leave their Russian politics behind when they came to the United States. Even though Nihilism and Populism (to the extent, of course, that they were consistent doctrines) were elaborated specifically for a Russian political context—Nihilism defining itself by opposition to the imperial autocracy and its many heinous institutions, Populism arising specifically in response to the existence of a rigidly delineated peasant class—and even though social, economic, and political conditions in the United States had little in common with those in Russia, the Jewish intellectuals had cut their teeth on Russian radical ideologies. So when they arrived in America, they simply applied these ideologies to their new context—or they continued to apply them to the old context, because for many immigrants Russia remained the focus of all political activity. This is the story I have told in the second part of the book.

CULTURE AND POLITICS

Radical thinkers in nineteenth-century Russia made a great effort to blur the distinction between different forms of political activity, as well as between political activity and other forms of activity that most of us would not consider political. In a society where literature and literary criticism were often the only forum for a written encounter with political issues, novelists, poets, playwrights, and literary critics came to be social commentators, and literary activity came to be a type of political action. Literary people were thus implicitly political activists, and political activists naturally took a keen interest in literature. That is why much of the story I tell in this book has to do with literature and literary criticism. The Jewish intellectuals who came to America never abandoned their faith in the ultimately political function and the supreme power of literature and literary criticism. That the Yiddish theatre became one of the most important institutions of American Jewish life during this era is testimony both to its appeal among the masses and to the ideological fervor of those who wrote and produced the plays. Jacob Gordin, certainly the best known Yiddish playwright of this time, saw his plays not as a diversion in the dreary lives of working men and women, but as a vehicle for the *truth*.

TRANSLATING RUSSIAN INTO YIDDISH IN AMERICA

The transposition of Russian ideology was thus geographical and cultural. It was also linguistic. Like it or not, the émigré intellectuals, who had "striven to adopt the language and manners" of their "Christian fellow countrymen" in Russia, discovered soon after they arrived in America that their largest audience and readership consisted of other Jewish immigrants, and only a tiny number of these had a decent command of Russian. But they all knew Yiddish, and so, mostly for pragmatic reasons (with few exceptions, even the most penitent Jewish intellectuals were unwilling for very long to place Yiddish on an equal footing with Russian), Yiddish became the principal medium of public discourse for the Russian Jewish intelligentsia in America. Hence the odd spectacle of Russian culture translated into Yiddish and propagated in America.

But émigré intellectuals also discovered English, some later than others. On the hierarchy of languages, the language of native-born Americans occupied a higher position than Yiddish. It became the dream of almost every radical intellectual to acquire sufficient proficiency in written and spoken English to be able to publish articles in large-circulation English-language periodicals (even to publish books in English) and to give speeches in English to large, ethnically mixed audiences. Many realized that dream.

TO THE OTHER SHORE

There is something very Russian and something very Jewish about this diaspora of Russian Jewish intellectuals. When Abe Cahan crossed the border out of Russia, he was following an already hallowed *Russian* tradition. Many Russian intellectuals before him had been forced into exile, usually in Western Europe, and many used the freedom of their new situation to continue the political struggle that had forced them from their homeland in the first place. Alexander Herzen (1812–70), an early, titanic figure in the Russian revolutionary movement, left Russia in 1847 for Western Europe. His primary occupation abroad was to continue the political work he had begun before his departure, and through his publications he remained one of the mightiest voices in the struggle back home, giving it, among other things, a foundation for what would later be called Populism.

All this he did "from the other shore," as he titled a book of essays he wrote in Europe. As he explained it, "from the other shore" was a metaphor for "beyond the revolution."[2] But it was also a simple reference to his new home and to the implications of waging a political struggle in exile. Abe Cahan and others like him set out on a journey to another shore on which they, too, would wage a political struggle. In many instances, Russia remained the focus of that struggle for a time, and the immigrants worked, like Herzen, "from the other shore." But for most, despite the conflicting sentiments they might have had—and in some cases retained—about their own national identity (for example, feeling like Russians, yet loving their new country and wanting their children to be purely American), the American movement *in practice* ultimately had to do with America. Though many looked back continually to the motherland, their journey was "to the other shore," where they would remain and follow their political destinies. That's why I have borrowed and modified Herzen's title.

It was a Jewish diaspora as well. After all, Jewishness played a primary role in the decision of virtually all who left. Even for those who had not experienced a crisis of identity like the one that impelled the penitent students to visit the synagogue in Kiev, Russia was becoming an increasingly hostile place for Jews. And so the intellectuals took part, with their less educated brethren, in a Jewish migration like so many others over the previous three thousand years. In their new home, many of the intellectuals sought as much as possible to avoid identifying themselves as Jews, seeking to establish for themselves a Russian or an American identity instead. But even the most unrepentantly cosmopolitan and secularized Jews were obliged to confront the fact of their identity at some point. Emma Goldman, who in her career as this country's most visible anarchist resisted involvement in specifically Jewish issues, gave lectures in Yiddish throughout her life.

Still, this is mostly the story of a group that outwardly directed its energies toward goals other than such "Jewish" ones as fostering ethnic solidarity, encouraging worship and observance, and discouraging intermarriage. This group, when it was not expressing open hostility to Jewish ritual, attempted as much as possible to ignore it. In theory, at least, its acknowledgment of Jewishness came in response to the reality of having to do political work in the Jewish community. The question is whether there was more to this acknowledgment than just theory.

PART ONE

CHAPTER 1

"We Were Not Jews"

BEING RUSSIAN

ONE OF the great warhorses of the American Yiddish stage was Jacob Gordin's *Mirele Efros*, written in 1898. In the middle of the 1938 screen version there is a very funny scene. The play is set in the old country. Mirele is a well-to-do widow who has watched her in-laws, led by her son's calculating and strong-willed new bride, take over the family business she had carefully built up from the shambles in which her husband had left it at the time of his death. The *mekhutn* (daughter-in-law's father), a stock buffoon character, has lost an entire crop of flax, because he insisted on going to the rabbi for advice on the weather. The rabbi had said there would be no rain, there was rain, the flax has rotted, and now the upstart businessman has to tell a gathering of blank-faced Russian peasants that he has no goods to sell them. The *mekhutn* has been the very essence of farcical, old-world, male *yidishkayt*, from his grossly exaggerated gestures, to his constant, annoying references to the Sages of Israel, to his lightning-fast and completely perfunctory recitation of his morning prayers, to his impotent, whining deference before his wife.

Suddenly, the Yiddish-speaking audience notices that a foreign language is being spoken, as the *mekhutn* (in an absurdly fractured and incorrect Russian) attempts to explain to his disappointed clients why he has nothing to sell. The peasants don't understand. The *mekhutn* repeats his speech word for word, but shouts it this time. They still don't understand. Finally, in a fit of exasperation he launches into his speech a third time at the top of his lungs, breaks off, and gives up in disgust. The peasants stare vacantly.

This failure of communication is perhaps only partly a linguistic matter: it may be that the peasants understand the *mekhutn*'s words but that his explanation doesn't make sense to them. Still, his discomfiture would have been easily comprehensible to immigrant audiences that went to see Gordin's plays in the early twentieth century. Among the millions of Jews who were Russian subjects even at the end of the nineteenth century, only a small minority were sufficiently assimilated to be able to converse with any degree of eloquence in Russian.

The Jewish intelligentsia set itself apart from the masses, and one of its primary marks of distinction—one of its primary instruments of power, too—was its ability (in the best of cases) to speak a fluent, correct, and educated Russian. Most of the Russian Jews who immigrated to the United States and assumed positions of leadership in the cultural, political, and social life of the growing community of Jewish immigrants from the Russian Empire were born between the mid-1850s and the early 1870s and thus came of age between the mid-1870s and the late 1880s. Almost all had undergone a process of "Russification" or came from families that had undergone such a process in the previous generation. This process had taken them—or their families before them—from the closed world of the Jewish ghetto to the urban world of the Russian intelligentsia. For those who came from traditional Jewish families, Russification came at great personal cost, since a break with the powerful strictures of traditional Jewish life was a daring and painful step to take.

But the process often brought great prestige, too. To be a Russian intellectual was to be a member of an elite group representing a few hundredths of a percent of the population. It meant access to Western ideas and to public discourse of all sorts. In a country that was almost entirely illiterate it meant reading and writing; it meant access to books and to the press. It also meant access to the underground world of left-wing political conspiracy, where Jewish and non-Jewish activists routinely laid plots against the life of the tsar and other public officials in the brutal Russian autocracy.

THE OLD LIFE

It is difficult for us to imagine a life as restricted, as closely regulated, as cut off from the surrounding society as was that of the Russian Jews and their ancestors before the middle of the nineteenth century. Before the end of the eighteenth century there were virtually no Jews living in the Russian Empire. In neighboring Poland, however, there were many, and when Russia, Austria, and Prussia divided up that country in the three Partitions of Poland (1772, 1793, and 1795), the areas that went to Russia happened to be the ones with the largest numbers of Jewish communities. Poland effectively disappeared from the map, and the newly expanded Russian Empire suddenly found itself with close to a million Jewish subjects.[1]

But it would be only technically accurate to refer to the Jews residing in Poland before the Partitions as "Polish Jews," since they were hardly more "Polish" than traditional Jews in the Russian Empire were "Russian." These were Ashkenazic Jews, the descendants of those who had settled in the Rhineland centuries earlier and borrowed a local German dialect that would develop into Yiddish.[2] Poland was a land that provided a haven for the Jews when the Crusades and other persecutions drove them eastward from their earlier homes, from the end of the eleventh century to the end of the sixteenth century.

Because Poland provided a relatively hospitable climate for the Jews and because a component of this climate was the considerable degree of autonomy the Jews were granted, the entire social, cultural, and religious character of Polish Jewry developed with minimal disturbance from the authorities or from the surrounding Gentile population. The government allowed the Jewish community to exercise authority over its own affairs, and so long as it properly oversaw the collection of taxes and met other basic obligations, the government had little desire to meddle.

The aspect of autonomy that was undoubtedly most decisive in determining the character of Jewish life was the control Jews were given over the education of their children. In addition to bearing the full responsibility of financing Jewish education, the community had a free hand in deciding what sort of schools there would be, what would be taught in them, and who would be required to attend them. The educational system in which the grandfathers and great-grandfathers of many American Jews grew up, based on the long and intensive study of Torah and Talmud from an early age, had been in force for centuries in Poland before the Partitions. Since such education was compulsory for all males in the Jewish community, complete illiteracy among men was almost unknown in this era, and one could safely assume that any adult male was conversant with the prayers and at least some of the central texts of Judaism, all, of course, in the original Hebrew or Aramaic.[3] Subjects like science, medicine, and, philosophy in their modern form, however, were practically unknown to most Jews.

The Jews who abruptly became Russian subjects at the end of the eighteenth century continued to live separately from their host population, but now it was government policy that kept them apart. No sooner had the initial two hundred thousand come under Russian sway in the First Partition of Poland in 1772, than Catherine the Great, the Empress of Russia (ruled 1762–96), issued a proclamation barring Jews from settling outside the territories they inhabited at the time of the Partition. By the Third Partition, the area where Jews were permitted to dwell was carefully delineated. It was an area roughly corresponding to present-day Lithuania, Belarus, Ukraine, and part of eastern Poland. It came to be called *cherta osedlosti* in Russian, the "Pale of Settlement."

Life for the Jews of Poland and Russia was basically the life of the *shtetl*, or small town, where the great majority of Russian and East European Jews lived throughout the century. There are many descriptions of the *shtetl*, some fanciful and idealizing, some harsh and denigrating. The picture that emerges from almost all of them is of a tightly regulated life with rules that insure the almost complete separation of the inhabitants from outsiders.

One of the most obvious marks of Jewish separateness was linguistic. The Jews had retained their German dialect even when they settled in countries that were not German-speaking. But as all modern-day descendants of Yiddish-speaking Jews know, there was more to the language of the Jews than just this. Irving Howe, in *World of Our Fathers*, describes the linguistic peculiarities of *shtetl* life, where Hebrew is the language of prayer, known almost only to men, and where Yiddish, with its heavy sprinkling of Hebrew and Aramaic words and phrases, is the language of everyday conversation, including intimate "conversation" with God.[4] Leo Deutsch (1855–1941), who became one of the most active leaders in the Russian Jewish revolutionary movement, recalls an almost absolute prohibition in the *shtetl* on using the language of the Gentiles. Deutsch speaks (in Russian) of a time when Jews considered it a sin to study Russian. Only in case of necessity was the use of this language permitted, and then, of course, "only in dealings with Christians (*goyim*)." Deutsch here is distinctly unsympathetic to the Jews, but his description of *shtetl* life is among the most eloquent: "Crowded together by the thousands in wretched townlets and hamlets in which there was neither sufficient work nor sufficient trade for craftsmen, the Jewish masses were condemned to drag out a difficult, half-starving existence, to remain mired in ignorance and prejudice, fanatically clinging to their ancient religion and their old customs and views as well."[5]

Despite what Deutsch says, one feature of Jewish life may have eased the transition, for a small minority, from the *shtetl* to the urban centers in the nineteenth century. It is the very devotion to study and learning that Deutsch holds partly responsible for miring the Jews in ignorance and prejudice. Memoirs of Jewish life in the Pale are full of stories about families that would sell their most cherished possessions or go without food in order to pay for their son's *kheyder* (beginning religious school). The traditional Jewish education was extraordinarily rigorous, starting from a very early age and often involving young boys in study for most of their waking hours. Jewish boys who were sufficiently successful at their studies to attend a yeshiva (higher academy of Talmudic learning) had many years of experience both in the memorization of enormous stretches of text and in the dialectical form of argumentation that was the characteristic method of Talmudic study. Owing to the academic prowess they showed as a result of this training, once Jews were permitted to enroll in Russian universities—and before their admission was officially restricted later in the nineteenth century—the number of spaces they came to occupy was well beyond the proportion they represented in the general population.[6]

RUSSIFIED AND SECULARIZED: A JEWISH INTELLIGENTSIA IS BORN

The Jews who emigrated to the United States in the last decades of the nineteenth century were not the first to be exposed to ideas from outside the sphere of traditional Jewish life. As early as the beginning of the nineteenth century a handful of Russian Jews had made a move toward assimilation into Western culture. These were followers of the Haskalah, or Jewish Enlightenment, that had begun in Germany with Moses Mendelssohn (1729–86), in Germany's own era of enlightenment. Some Russian Jews had even traveled to Germany to study German philosophy at a time when such travel and such study were almost unheard of. The Haskalah had left a legacy of assimilationism among Mendelssohn's admirers in both Germany and Russia. In Russia, the move by Jews to Western, enlightened ways was even encouraged at various moments by the government, which in the early nineteenth century viewed the assimilationist and modernizing tendencies of the Mendelssohnian Haskalah as a possible antidote to Jewish separatism.[7]

But not all Russian *maskilim*, as followers of the Haskalah were called, felt that cultural assimilation and the acceptance of Western ideas necessarily meant a wholesale rejection of Jewish religious practice, as did so many of the future emigrants to the United States. In its early years, the Russian Haskalah tended toward a reconciliation between Jewish tradition and modern culture. Mendelssohn had translated the Pentateuch into German (printed in Hebrew characters) as a way of modernizing and Germanizing traditional Jewish experience, and many of the Russian *maskilim*, in the same spirit, sought to integrate ancient Jewish tradition into modern life, for example, in their efforts to promote Hebrew as a modern, literary language. In the early stages of cultural assimilation, then, the idea was to retain Jewishness and modernize it, rather than to reject it in favor of a modern life that was held to be hopelessly out of kilter with it.[8] That rejection occurred in the generation that took part in the mass emigration to the United States, and it occurred in significant measure because of contact with the progressive ideas of the Russian revolutionary intelligentsia of the mid-to-late nineteenth century.

The Russians coined the term *intelligentsia* in the 1860s, though by that time the group to which the term referred had been around for several generations. The word might be construed as simply denoting all intellectuals. But because intellectual life in Russia in the mid-nineteenth century had its own peculiar character, and since a focus on contemporary national and political issues formed an essential part of that character, *intelligentsia* came to designate a group of intellectuals who were generally of the left-wing political opposition, but whose common feature was their concern with contemporary national and political issues and their involvement with a variety of types of written discourse as forums for those issues. These included literature and literary criticism. To be an *intelligent*, or member of the intelligentsia, was to have the requisite educational and cultural background to take part in this life, which was centered almost exclusively in the cities.

For anyone, Jew or Gentile, who wished to become part of this exclusive club, there was only one avenue, and that was a solid secular education. Often this meant a university education, but the essential thing for Jews was that the education had to be *in Russian*. In the first half of the nineteenth century there were thus several conditions preventing the vast majority of Jews from entering the Russian intelligentsia: Jews were largely unassimilated into Russian life, they did not attend Russian schools and universities, and they were forbidden to reside outside the Pale of Settlement. By the middle of the century, however, these conditions had been removed for some, and it became possible for a small number of Jews to join the tiny, elite social group that included in its ranks Russia's celebrated authors, literary critics, and political activists (though celebrity was by no means a necessary condition of membership in the intelligentsia).

Educational policy in the Russian Empire in the nineteenth century had a profound impact on the lives of a small but important group of Jews. Legally, it had been possible for Jews to attend schools and universities since 1804, but few had availed themselves of the opportunity that early. The entry of Jews into Russian higher education came largely as the result of two measures. The first was a law in 1844 that provided special schools for Jews and ordered the establishment of two state institutes to train rabbis and teachers. In reality, this law was part of an effort to deal with the "Jewish question" by first consolidating government control over Jewish education and the rabbinate. As a secret supplement to the law plainly showed, the government's true intent was to use the "Crown schools" to bring about the conversion of Russian Jews to Christianity. The secret supplement became known, and most Jews showed little enthusiasm for enrolling in the new schools. But a few thousand did attend, and the result was a first, small generation of Jews who received a secular education similar to the one their Christian countrymen were receiving.[9] The second measure had greater consequences. In 1861, Tsar Alexander II issued a decree proclaiming that Jews holding a degree from a university would be permitted to settle anywhere in the Russian Empire. Because of the residency provision, this law had a double impact on Jewish entry into the urban intelligentsia. Permission to reside outside the Pale was an incentive to study at the university, and studying at the university was an important form of preparation for the life of an intellectual.

In addition, starting in 1859, Jewish merchants prosperous enough to pay an annual tax were allowed to reside anywhere in Russia, and starting in 1860, certain Jewish soldiers were permitted, upon retirement, to settle in St. Petersburg. The children of those Jewish merchants and soldiers who took advantage of the newly granted privileges and went to reside in the Empire's urban centers would thus find it easy to come into contact with the attractions of Russian cultural life.[10] Many of these children, born in the decade or so after the reforms, were destined to join the intelligentsia in Russia, become active in progressive political movements, and then take their various Russian ideologies to the Unites States.

It is important to remember that, in proportion to the total Jewish population in the Russian Empire, the number of Jews attending institutions of higher learning was minuscule, just as the number of all Russians attending such institutions was minuscule in proportion to the total population of the Russian Empire.[11] Jewish "membership" in the intelligentsia, of course, included a number of Jewish intellectuals who were self-educated, but even when these are factored in, the Jewish proportion of the intelligentsia was quite small. The entire intelligentsia, in fact, was quite small, comprising in mid-century a few thousand in a total population of some sixty million. Even if Jewish representation in this group was three times its proportion in the total population, as it appears by some estimates to have been, this still means that scarcely one Jew in a thousand could be considered an *intelligent*.

The path to membership in the Russian intelligentsia varied as much as the upbringing of an individual Jewish child. Three basic models, not entirely distinct from each other, emerge. Some prominent members of the Russian Jewish intelligentsia in Russia and the United States were born into families that were already considerably Russified and secularized. In this group, some appear to have had little early experience with the Yiddish language, having been raised speaking Russian or even German. Philip Krantz (1858–1922), for example, who became one of the most prominent Yiddish journalists in the world, claimed to have taught himself Yiddish as an adult, just so he could communicate with ordinary Jewish workers.[12] The claim, to be sure, is somewhat disingenuous, since Krantz was capable of writing Yiddish before he made it a full-time occupation, but there is no doubt that he was not nearly so much at home in the language of the Ashkenazic Jews as he was in Russian. Proletarian poet David Edelstadt (1866–92), the son of a soldier, was born in the city of Kaluga, outside the Pale. His parents spoke only Russian at home and gave him almost nothing in the way of a Jewish upbringing. He apparently learned Yiddish in the United States before becoming one of the most celebrated Yiddish literary figures of his time.[13]

Morris Hillquit (originally Hilkowitz, 1869–1933), who would become a towering figure in the American socialist movement in both its specifically Jewish phase and its larger, national phase, had an extensive career as a Yiddish-language journalist. He was born in Riga to a relatively affluent family and grew up speaking both German, the language of the Baltic community in which his family lived, and Russian, the language spoken in the schools he attended. He claims to have learned Yiddish only after emigrating to the United States.

Michael Zametkin (1859–1935) and his wife Adella Kean (1863–

1931), were among the most Russified of Jewish immigrants to come to the United States. Zametkin had been educated at the Odessa School of Commerce. Though he immediately became active in Jewish labor politics, he did not begin to use Yiddish in the United States until almost ten years after his arrival in 1882. He and Kean eventually earned their living primarily through the Yiddish press, he in his job at the *Forward* and she with steady contributions to many Yiddish newspapers. Their daughter, novelist Laura Hobson, writes in her autobiography that Russian was the primary, though not the first, language of both parents—the language in which they told each other secrets.[14] In the larger community of Russian Jewish immigrants, this was quite uncommon.

A second group includes immigrants who came from families that introduced their children to Russian in the home and, in some cases, injected progressive, Haskalah elements into an otherwise traditional, religious upbringing. This group counts some of the most remarkable, though not always the most influential, of the immigrant Jewish intellectuals among its members. Isaac Hourwich (1860–1924) was born into a family with a distinguished rabbinical pedigree on both sides, yet both parents were freethinkers well versed in modern, secular literature. Hourwich was given a traditional elementary Jewish education, tutored privately in Hebrew and Old Testament, and then educated in a Russian gymnasium and Russian universities. In the United States, his political and intellectual activity was initially carried out in the Russian-speaking segment of the Jewish émigré community, but he went on to combine a successful legal career with an equally successful career as a Yiddish journalist.

Jacob Gordin is another example. His father was an odd combination of Hassid and *maskil* who gave his son a traditional Jewish education together with a progressive and secular one. By the time Gordin grew up, he had already studied Hebrew, Russian, and German, gaining much of his early knowledge of European literature through Russian translations. When he arrived in the United States, he began a writing career in both Russian and Yiddish, collaborating with Hourwich on *Progress*, a short-lived Russian periodical, and contributing to the largest-circulation Yiddish newspaper of the day.[15]

The most extraordinary representative of this type is undoubtedly Chaim Zhitlovsky (1861–1943), one of the most learned and sophisticated of Yiddish writers in modern times. His father, like Gordin's, combined Hassidism with a secular outlook. He traveled widely, indulged a taste for opera, and collected Haskalah literature. Zhitlovsky was given a basic Jewish education but also tutored in Russian and sent to a Russian gymnasium, and because he had taken an early interest in the Yiddish language, he was positioned better than many others from a similar background to use Yiddish and Russian with an almost equal degree of eloquence. In fact, his facility was so great in both languages that at moments of spiritual crisis concerning his Jewish identity, he had the luxury of being able to decide which of the two was the appropriate medium of discourse with his intimate friends.

Finally, there is the group that includes immigrants from traditional, Yiddish-speaking families that provided little or no instruction in Russian and only minimal contact with the Gentile world. Jacob Milch (Yankev Milkh, 1866–1945), a prominent figure for many years in the Jewish labor movement and in the Yiddish press in America, was given an exclusively Jewish education as a boy and never learned Russian until he joined the army at the age of twenty. Z. Libin (Yisroel-Zalman Hurvits, 1872–1955), who became quite popular in New York as the author of sketches and plays in Yiddish, came from a poor family, had an exclusively Jewish primary education, and learned Russian by studying with his older brother. He did sufficiently well that he was able to write stories in Russian at an early age, but this phase of his life did not last long, and after he emigrated to the United States he devoted himself to Yiddish.

Also included in this group are two of the most powerful figures in the entire history of Jewish immigration to America: Morris Winchevsky and Abraham Cahan. Winchevsky (Lipe Ben-Tsien Novakhovits, 1856–1932) had a political career and a writing career that began in Russia and continued in Germany, Copenhagen, London, Paris, and the United States. He received a traditional Jewish education at home and did not learn Russian until he was eleven, when he was sent to a Russian public school for two years. His facility with languages was partly the reason for the wide education he was able to provide himself: he read extensively in Russian, taught himself German, began his publishing career in Hebrew, came to be considered one of the greatest Yiddish stylists of all time, and wrote a respectable body of material in a competent though stilted English.

Abe Cahan's early life illustrates with particular vividness the difficulties facing a child who wishes to become part of the Gentile world surrounding his isolated, Jewish community. In his memoirs and in his novel *The Rise of David Levinsky* (1917), Cahan shows how foreign, unseemly, and forbidden the Gentile world was made to appear to children like himself. He also shows how inviting it was, especially to an adolescent boy, who envied the Russian boys in town for their freedom to stroll in the open air with girls other than their sisters (something that would never happen in a Jewish family).

When Cahan took it into his head to learn Russian, he had to do it on the sly. He tells how, in his ninth year, he struck up an acquaintance with a pupil at a local school. He bought a Russian primer from the boy and hired him as a tutor. Cahan describes how his mother discovered the book her young son had hidden away in his coat pocket. He behaved like someone caught in a forbidden act, his parents stopped giving him money, and he was forced to discontinue his lessons.[16] But he remained determined to learn Russian, so later, without letting his parents know, he enrolled in a government school for Jews, where classes were given in Russian.[17] Cahan's subsequent positions as teacher in a Russian-language Crown school and correspondent for a Russian-language Jewish newspaper based in St. Petersburg testify to the success of all these efforts.

Many Jewish intellectuals became involved in radical politics before emigrating to Western Europe or the United States; in fact, involvement in radical politics was frequently the reason for emigrating. They were thus members of the Russian intelligentsia in an active sense, something that was significant in a group that emphasized the importance of political *action*. A few did not begin a true life of activism until they arrived in the United States (or Western Europe before going to the United States). Some possessed degrees from prestigious educational institutions in Russia; others did not. What they all had before they left Russia was a degree of assimilation—Russification—that allowed them to participate in a politically active life firmly based in a culture of secular reading. Emma Goldman was a sixteen-year-old girl when she left for America, and the extent of her political involvement before that was the strong sympathy she felt for the radicals who assassinated the tsar, Alexander II, in 1881.[18] But her acquaintance with Russian progressive literature and her knowledge of German, together with a moral commitment to social causes, equipped her to adopt an activist role as soon as the occasion presented itself, which it first did in America.

In most cases, especially where the aspiring Jewish intellectual came from a traditional family, Russification meant more than just learning Russian; it implicitly meant rejecting a good many of the practices that had made the Polish and Russian Jews distinctive for so many centuries. For many Jews who became intellectuals, this also meant, by a kind of natural, logical progress, abandoning Judaism altogether. There were Jewish intellectuals who actually converted to Russian Orthodox Christianity, usually in order to gain eligibility for a professional or government post. But these were people who planned to stay in Russia and who generally stayed away from the most radical phases of the political opposition. Far more common than outright apostasy, among those who were active in the radical movement and would eventually emigrate, was a simple rejection of Jewish religion and daily practice in favor of a secular worldview.

In some instances, this rejection occurred as part of a relatively gradual process. Emma Goldman, though she certainly came to be an outspoken critic of organized religion, came from a family that was observant but that did not emphasize religious teachings in the home. To believe her own account of her childhood, Goldman learned about God from the family's peasant servants (Christians, naturally), not from her parents.[19]

In other instances, however, the rejection of religion in general or Judaism in particular was accompanied with astonishing passion. Morris Winchevsky recalls a period in his youth when his hostility toward Judaism had become generalized into an almost maniacal hatred of all religious faith. He reserved his greatest fury for Judaism. "For me," he writes, "and not for me alone in those days, unbelief and hatred for any kind of faith had reached the highest degree of fanaticism. It became hard for me to pass a *bes medresh* [Jewish house of study] without gnashing my teeth in anger, and I could hardly stand to hear the voice of men praying or studying a page of Talmud. My greatest delight consisted in demonstrating that Moses did not write the Torah, that Joshua did not make the sun and the moon stand still, that David was no fine man and his son Solomon was not wise." Winchevsky goes on to say that he adopted, as a motto for a heretical song he wrote, the Talmudic dictum that "the kingdom of earth is like that in heaven."[20]

Even Winchevsky's irreverence pales by comparison with that of his friend Moses Leib Lilienblum (1843–1910). Lilienblum never emigrated to America, but he was a typical member of the radical Russian Jewish intelligentsia of the 1870s and is best known as the author of an early Zionist tract (1881). Before he embraced the idea of a Jewish homeland in Palestine, Lilienblum was among the naughtiest of the newly radicalized young Jewish intellectuals, and thumbing his nose at Judaism was among his favorite activities. Winchevsky describes how Lilienblum would light a candle or roll a cigarette on the Sabbath, in flagrant violation of Jewish law, casually explaining, in the first case, that he needed the light, and, in the second, responding to his companion's shock by calmly striking a match and lighting up.[21]

But nowhere is the connection between the repudiation of Judaism and the fact of Russification clearer than in a passage from the memoirs of Chaim Zhitlovsky. In a chapter that tells of his political "education," Zhitlovsky says that, long before he and his friends had completed this education, "one thing had been settled *completely*. We had already known for certain *that we were not Jews*." He then tells the amusing story of how he had changed his given name from Chaim to the more "truly Russian and truly democratic" name Efim, which he chose because he said he had found it in Gogol.[22]

Some members of this generation succeeded so well in their efforts to join the Russian intelligentsia that they managed to enjoy careers—short-lived, to be sure, in most cases—as published writers *in Russian* before coming to the United States. I mentioned Abe Cahan's position as correspondent for a Russian-language Jewish newspaper, a position that he retained for a brief time after he arrived in America. Philip Krantz, too, contributed to a Russian Jewish newspaper, also based in St. Petersburg, the same, in fact, in which Lilienblum published his article calling for

Jewish emigration to Palestine. David Edelstadt apparently published some Russian songs when he was thirteen years old. And Aron Liberman (1845?–80) wrote for the Russian émigré press in London in the 1870s.[23] Liberman belongs only marginally to the story of Russian Jewish immigration to the United States. He came to the United States for romantic, not political reasons, shortly before the period of mass immigration, and committed suicide almost as soon as he arrived. But he was immensely influential in the Russian Jewish intellectual scene in Russia. I will speak of his contributions later.

Whether a given Jewish intellectual was actually a published author was not the only thing that mattered. What really mattered was being immersed in a culture of reading and writing in Russian. In part this is because of what this group was reading and writing, the actual ideas that its members would take with them to the new country. But it is also because reading and writing had taken on a special significance in Russian culture by the time members of this generation came of age. When Cahan, Krantz, and others entered the arena of public affairs in the 1870s and 1880s, there awaited them a model of intellectual life that emphasized the active and political nature of thought and expression, that saw reading and writing not as passive and leisurely pursuits but as forms of engaged political action. And despite any changes in philosophical outlook they may have undergone during their lives, most members of this generation of intellectuals who emigrated to America and helped found the labor movement and the Jewish press on the other shore never really abandoned the models they had learned as young men and women in Russia.

CHAPTER 2.

"In Chernyshevsky's *Kheyder*"

BEING NIHILISTS

RUSSIFIED, secularized, then politicized. This seems to be the story of the Russian Jewish intelligentsia. Not that every Jew who entered the cultural life of urban Russia in the nineteenth century immediately became a bomb-throwing terrorist, although a few did. Some remained politically moderate, and others were downright conservative in their political views. But from the 1860s on, no Russified, educated Jew could manage to be entirely divorced from politics, any more than could any educated Russian non-Jew in that most political of environments. This was the age of Dostoevsky and Nikolai Chernyshevsky, when every Russian intellectual felt a moral duty to take a stand on the burning issues of the day, whether that stand was the conservative Slavophilism of Dostoevsky or the radical utopian socialism of Chernyshevsky.

Still, it seems that most Jewish intellectuals gravitated toward the left, and for many, this gravitation seemed a completely natural outcome to the entire process of Russification they or their families had undergone. Politicization was especially natural for those who attended Russian universities or the state-sponsored Crown schools, since in the era of Alexander II, institutions of higher education were hotbeds of political activism, where students had the opportunity to participate in clandestine discussion groups, join secret revolutionary circles, read illegal literature, and eventually engage in any of a number of political activities, from spreading propaganda among the peasants to plotting the assassination of the tsar.

The Russian revolutionary movement at any given moment comprised a large variety of trends and movements, and as time went on, new trends and movements sprang into existence. Jews became involved in almost every one of these trends and movements. Over time, there were Jewish Nihilists, Populists, *narodovol'tsy* (members of the ultra-left *Narodnaia volia*, or People's Will party), terrorists, anarchists, Socialist Revolutionaries, Social Democrats, Mensheviks, and Bolsheviks. By the end of the century, there was even a distinctly Jewish political organization in Russia, a socialist labor group formed in 1897 called the Bund.

If there was one thing that was true of the Russian revolutionary movement in all of its phases, it was the centrality of the written word. The movement was dominated by books and journal articles, and its follow-ers defined themselves by what they read because their leaders defined their followers by what they, the leaders, wrote. It was a movement in which thinking, writing, and doing were practically indistinguishable. The story of the politicizing of Russia's Jewish intellectuals is, first, the story of their immersion in the written culture of the Russian revolution-ary movement. For the Jews, this means largely the written culture of the 1860s, often called the age of *Nihilism* or the age of *realism*, depending on whether the emphasis is on politics or on literature (not that the two were really separable). Though few Jewish radicals came of age earlier than the 1870s, the political principles of the 1860s would follow them through all the various political movements to which they might become attached and, if they emigrated, into their new life in the United States.

It was, second, a story of the dramatic appropriation of the written word by a people that, despite its traditional devotion to written language in the form of sacred texts, had very little history of using any vernacular language to *produce* texts designed to serve a temporal, political function. Jewish intellectuals gravitated toward the press as their primary medium of written communication, and while a legal Russian Jewish press devel-oped in Russia, beginning in the 1860s, Russian Jews made their boldest political contributions either illicitly or in exile.

And finally, for those who were politically involved in Russia, it is a story of enacting political theories, from those that Russian radical intel-lectuals preached in the 1860s under the broad, popular name *Nihilism*, to later theories elaborated by Jewish and non-Jewish radicals. Dominant among later theories were those grouped under the label *Populism*, under whose banner Russian Jews, together with their Gentile comrades, agi-tated among the peasantry, organized self-education circles for workers, worked side by side with those same workers in factories, and partici-pated in a host of other forms of political action. Nihilism and Populism were, broadly speaking, the dominant political trends in which Russian Jewish intellectuals were involved. They were also the trends most easily discerned in the activities of those who immigrated to the United States and became politically active after they arrived.

The young Russian Jew who came from a traditional religious home and who sampled the delights of Russian literature for the first time, espe-cially literature that was outright illegal, found reading now to be an entirely different experience from what it had been in a Jewish religious education. This is partly because of the nature of the new material. Some of it is fiction, like the novels of Turgenev. And much of it is criticism, both artistic and social. In fact, almost all of it, whether it is fiction or criticism, has to do with social life, and it all seems to be life-defining. The fiction seems "real," and the characters are so very much alive that the readers can refer to those characters as though they were actual people.

The characters are alive not necessarily because they are portrayed with extraordinary artistic skill, but because they confront the same social issues as do the readers. And the criticism is "real," because the critics confront these issues, too. Reading books and reading criticism about those books is a mode of social-political engagement.

The Nihilist era did not make reading and writing into forms of political engagement. That had happened about a generation earlier. The story is worth telling briefly, since it helps explain the culture of the era when a significant number of Russia's Jews first became politically active.

THE MARRIAGE OF POLITICS AND CULTURE IN RUSSIA

Vissarion Belinsky

The traditional story of the birth of a politicized culture in Russia assigns paternity to Vissarion Belinsky (1811–1848), the "father of Russian criticism." Belinsky was the one who defined for subsequent generations of Russian artists and intellectuals the relation between culture and politics, between intellectual activity and social activity, between art and life, between literature and literary criticism, between thought and action. It was Belinsky who established the peculiarly Russian notion of *critic*, a notion that blurs the distinction between *literary critic* and *social critic*.

Belinsky's views changed over his short career, but the ones that left a lasting legacy were the ones he held for the final eight or nine years of his relatively short life. From his early days as a conservative Hegelian, when he had accepted the naive view that reality was the result of a rational and lawful process and could therefore not be tampered with, he had developed a fanatical cult of reality that was to remain with him permanently. *Reality* (*deistvitel'nost'* in Russian) became a catchword for his and subsequent generations of Russian radicals. "Reality," as he exclaimed at one point, "that is the motto and the last word of the contemporary world!"[1]

So when it came to art and criticism, reality was, predictably, a dominant category for Belinsky. In his earlier days he had stressed the duty of a writer *to show* (*pokazat'*) reality and refrain from judging it or *proving* (*dokazat'*) something about it (since reality was rational, had a kind of necessity about it, and therefore brooked no judgment). But all it took to transform this view into the activist view of art that he would leave for future generations was an encounter with the reality of urban misery in St. Petersburg in 1839. As Belinsky abandoned his faith in the rationality and necessity of reality, he redefined the obligation of artists and critics, calling now for a subjective response to the injustice of one's surroundings.

This subjective response is an expression of *criticism*, which now comes to be the central activity of both artist and critic. As Belinsky describes it, "Reason destroys the phenomenon in order to revive it for itself in a new beauty and a new life, if it finds itself in the phenomenon. From the process by which reason decomposes phenomena, only those phenomena disappear in which reason finds nothing of itself. Reason proclaims such phenomena to be not real but merely empirically existing. This process is called 'criticism.'"[2]

Criticism (or critique—*kritika* in Russian means both), in other words, is a process by which the subject decomposes, analyzes phenomena, but also reads a subjective element into them. This extremely broad definition of the word *kritika* will now be used as the basis for an equally broad understanding of literature and art in which the subjective element plays the central role. Because *kritika* can mean anything from the writing of book reviews to a thoroughgoing speculative analysis of a philosophical concept or system (like Kant's *Critiques*), Belinsky is able to use the term in such a way that it embraces a vast array of meanings and blurs a great many traditional distinctions. "Historical criticism without aesthetic criticism," he says, "or the reverse, aesthetic without historical, would be one-sided and, consequently, false."[3]

The real point, we soon discover, is that the different senses of *kritika* as well as the objects to which it applies, chiefly literature and art, are at bottom all the same thing. "To cast one's glance historically over the progress and development of Russian criticism means to cast one's glance, in general terms, over the history of Russian literature, since . . . the content of criticism, as a judgment, is the very same as the content of literature, as the thing judged; the entire difference is in the form."[4]

And this leads to another feature of Belinsky's theory, namely his insistence that art and criticism are inextricably tied to their historical era. The modern age has recognized this in a way that preceding ages have not, he believes. "Now," he says, "a new task falls to criticism—reconciling freedom of creation with serving the historical spirit of one's time, with serving the truth."[5]

And so Belinsky formulated the fundamental principles that would guide Russian criticism for the entire heroic period of its revolutionary movement in the nineteenth century. By saying that literature and criticism spring from the same spirit, he has eliminated the distinction between them. By saying that both contain a subjective, critical reaction to their historical moment, he has effectively eliminated the distinction between thought and action, between culture and politics, between life and art.

What Is to Be Done?

If Belinsky was the father of Russian criticism, Nikolai Gavrilovich Chernyshevsky (1828–89) was the godfather. It is difficult to express just

how powerful and influential this man was. Chernyshevsky's contemporaries and successors would always acknowledge the role Belinsky played
in establishing a style of criticism and intellectual life, but they didn't
worship him. They worshiped Chernyshevsky. It is probably no exaggeration to say—and it has been said before—that he had a more profound
impact on the future of his country than any other writer, perhaps more
than any other individual apart from the country's rulers.[6] To judge from
contemporary accounts—among them, as we will see, many by newly
Russified Jewish intellectuals—thousands of young people changed their
lives in accordance with principles they learned in Chernyshevsky's writings. His utopian novel *What Is to Be Done? From Tales of New People*
(1863) became the gospel for generations of secularized Russian revolutionaries. One could plausibly claim that Russia's founding Marxist theoreticians, Georgy Plekhanov and Lenin, owed more to Chernyshevsky
than to Marx or Engels. And it is safe to say that Chernyshevsky and his
contemporaries in Russia had more to do with the elaboration of socialist
realism, the officially mandated style of fiction writing in the Soviet period, than did Marx or Engels. In fact, the union of culture and politics in
Russia is more Chernyshevsky's responsibility than anyone else's, not because he came up with the idea, but because he spread the word.

Most educated Russians knew Chernyshevsky through his written
works. For anyone outside this context, anyone, that is, not living in the
nineteenth century and, above all, anyone who is not Russian, it is very
difficult to understand how these works could ever have taken hold in the
way they did. The novel *What Is to Be Done?* is written in the clumsiest,
most heavy-handed style imaginable, it presents characters that are
wooden and one-dimensional, and it lacks the most rudimentary elements of a good story to support the author's openly avowed intention of
using fiction as a vehicle for instructing his readers. The philosophy is
hopelessly simplistic, forbiddingly doctrinaire, and beset with inconsis-
tencies and contradictions of the most elementary sort.

All this was part of the worldview that dominated what commonly
came to be called Nihilism after Turgenev popularized the term in *Fathers
and Sons* (1862). In Turgenev's novel, *Nihilism* describes an outlook that
has three characteristics. It is rigidly materialistic in its denial of free will
and any spiritual dimension to human life. It is strictly scientific in its
reduction of human existence to biological, evolutionist categories (Herbert Spencer was popular, and Darwin, whose *Origin of Species* came out
in 1859, enjoyed fleeting fame among the Nihilists in the early 1860s).
And it is egoistic in its rejection of any kind of a priori moral obligation.
The logic of using the term *Nihilism* stemmed from its proponents' reduction of all "prejudicial," non-empirical notions to nothing (*nihil*).

But *Nihilism* eventually came to embrace not only a wider political
program than anything hinted at in *Fathers and Sons* (whose hero, Ba-

zarov, is sufficiently Nihilist to show complete contempt even for politics) but also an entire style of life. Both the program and the style of life came primarily from Chernyshevsky. Chernyshevsky, the son of a priest, was one of a growing subgroup of the intelligentsia whose members were not from the upper classes. It became fashionable for members of this group to flout the social conventions of the gentry, so at its more frivolous level, Nihilism meant a social attitude composed of ostentatious awkwardness, a studied indifference to attire and grooming, and a taste for shocking living arrangements (all of which many newly Russified Jewish intellectuals eagerly adopted). It is easy to see why such an attitude would appeal to educated young Jews aspiring to join the ranks of the Russian intelligentsia, since they too were members of an excluded group that lacked the social refinement of Russia's propertied classes.

There was, however, a serious theoretical foundation to Chernyshevsky's political and artistic views (and to the intimate connection between them). Chernyshevsky had become famous for an aesthetic theory that defied all traditional, idealist conceptions and militantly identified beauty with life—and reality. "The true, loftiest beauty," he said, "is precisely the beauty encountered by man in the world of reality, and not the beauty created by art."[7] Like Belinsky before him, Chernyshevsky placed *reality* at the center of his theory, but at the same time, like the later Belinsky, he believed that the artist had an obligation to approach reality normatively, to decompose and judge it. "That being is beautiful in which we see life *as it ought to be* according to our conceptions," he says.[8]

Chernyshevsky followed Belinsky, too, in the belief that the life of the intellect—and such products of the intellect as art and criticism—can be understood only in its historical context. In fact, Chernyshevsky thinks one can say this of all phenomena, artistic or not: "But where reality is concerned," he says in an essay on Gogol and Belinsky, "everything depends on the circumstances, on the conditions of place and time. . . . Every object, every phenomenon has its own significance, and we may judge it only by considering the circumstances in which it exists."[9]

Elsewhere Chernyshevsky approvingly cites passages from a Belinsky essay in which Belinsky describes the impact a given historical era has on its literature and then asserts the interdependence of art and social issues in Russian society.[10] This sort of reasoning will lead Chernyshevsky to make his own observation, namely that two dominant tendencies in Russian literature make up the "life and glory" of his own era: "humaneness" and a "concern for improving human life."[11] Art is thus inescapably engaged in history, and the artist expresses this engagement by using art as an active, moral force for change.

But of course the greatest testimony to the belief that art and life, intellectual life and history, are intertwined was Chernyshevsky's *What Is to*

Be Done?, because this gospel of the Nihilist generation not only proposed such an intertwining but accomplished it too. Of all the Russian books that Jewish radicals mention in the second half of the nineteenth century (or later in their memoirs), this one is cited most frequently. Though many, if not most, writers did not see the need to specify what it was about Chernyshevsky's novel that had such a profound impact on their lives, those who did specify generally referred to three elements.

The first is the idealized vision of socialism that Chernyshevsky presents in the dreams of his heroine, Vera Pavlovna. Modern, non-Russian readers are likely to know something of the content of the dreams without realizing it, since the dreams serve as the object of satire for the bilious narrator of Dostoevsky's *Notes from Underground*. The grand vision of the social commune, the shimmering beauty of its natural setting, the happy images of its residents as they work, dine, and dance together, the spirit of enlightened self-interest, or "rational egoism," that reigns in the commune, the figure of the Crystal Palace—all this became the stuff of a radical folk mythology that young Jewish intellectuals fostered every bit as much as did their non-Jewish companions in the various Russian revolutionary movements.

The second element was the radical view of the place of women and the relations between the sexes that Chernyshevsky espoused. Few thinkers in the world were as progressive on this point as were Chernyshevsky and his Russian followers. In *What Is to Be Done?*, as in real life for Chernyshevsky and many contemporaries, marriage was a sort of reasoned business agreement between a man and woman that was ideally kept free of sexual activity. The model arrangement in the novel is one in which a man offers marriage to a young woman, not because he is in love with her in the traditional sense or because he wishes to raise a family with her, but because he wishes to offer her an avenue of escape from her own family. Once liberated from the bonds of her family, the young woman, with the sponsorship of her "husband," is free to pursue her personal and professional ambitions. Should she feel the need of sexual fulfillment—and Chernyshevsky had come to think that sexual abstinence was medically harmful to women, but not to men—she has the right to take lovers, and her husband, out of the respect on which their relationship is founded, will not protest.[12]

The third element was the character Rakhmetov, the "extraordinary man" who is often referred to as the novel's hero, even though he makes only a brief appearance in the story. This absurdly idealized revolutionary, who disciplines himself physically to acquire the strength of the hardiest barge hauler, educates himself by reading for up to eighty-two hours at a stretch, and sleeps on nails in order to toughen himself for the hardships of a life dedicated to the revolutionary cause, became the model for several generations of radicals. Many Jewish immigrants tell of attempts to imitate Rakhmetov, whose name they invoke as though he were a living person.

The age of Nihilism presents numerous examples of people, usually students, who radically changed their lives in response to ideas they had learned in Chernyshevsky.[13] To a Nihilist, this made sense. The blurring of the line separating life and fiction was the expression of a deep conviction that the artist had a duty to influence history, that art was a form of social action.

Dobroliubov and Pisarev

When Russian Jewish revolutionaries mention the Russian writers that inspired them, they usually list three names together: Chernyshevsky, Dobroliubov, and Pisarev. Any serious study of Russia's "civic critics" would call attention to the differences between the three most influential writers of the 1860s generation, but since it is clear that their contemporaries, Jewish and non-Jewish, generally regarded all three as contributing to the same spirit of political-intellectual activism, "Nihilism," and overlooked the narrower issues on which they diverged, it is largely a question of how extreme and remarkable the positions of Chernyshevsky's lesser emanations were or how they publicized positions that were already current.

No one could have better replicated the life and career of Chernyshevsky than Nikolai Dobroliubov (1836–61). He too was the son of a priest, and he too was a critic with activist views on the relation between culture and politics. Like Chernyshevsky, he blurs the boundaries between life and art and between intellectual action and political action. And like Chernyshevsky, Dobroliubov tried hard to sustain the view that the literary artist must show fidelity to reality, while recognizing the capacity of literature to serve an active purpose. When it does, he says, it becomes a force "whose significance consists in propaganda and whose merit is determined by what and how it propagandizes." In the history of literature, he continues, there have been several "acting" authors (*deiateli*, those who act or do) "who have attained such heights in their propaganda that neither those who act in a practical way for the good of mankind nor men of pure science have surpassed them."[14] Though the critic, like the author, is ideally meant to be free from tendentiousness, the ultimate object of literary criticism is not literature, but life. The critic's task is "to interpret the phenomena of life itself on the basis of a literary work."[15]

Dmitri Pisarev (1840–68) is probably best remembered as the critic who challenged the reputation of Pushkin and called for the destruction of aesthetics. In the period of his career for which he is best known, he was a rigid materialist and utilitarian whose works appear to represent nothing more than an effort to take Chernyshevsky's theories and purge them of the very few idealizing impurities they contain. He celebrates the guiding principles of his age, namely that "art must not be an end in itself" and that "life is higher than art."[16] His reviews of fictional works treat characters as though they were real people and find fault with the author when the characters behave in defiance of logic. In Pisarev's view, beauty has no autonomous meaning, and since all aesthetic systems are founded on a notion of beauty, the only responsible solution is "to destroy aesthetics completely, to send it the way of alchemy and astrology."[17]

Realism: A Style of Writing and a Style of Living

By the mid-1860s, the theory of art and literature that I have been describing had come to be called *realism* (*realizm* in Russian). The term *realism* had apparently first come into use in Russian letters in 1847, which is earlier than in almost any European country except France.[18] But it had not become common until the 1860s, when Pisarev gave it currency by putting it together with a theory that was already in existence. A cornerstone of the reigning progressive view of literature in Russia, after all, was the focus on *reality* (*deistvitel'nost'* in Russian), and so it was natural that Russians should adopt as a label the word *realizm*, their version of *réalisme*, which had been used as a literary term in France since as early as 1826.[19]

Naturally, the meaning of the term was as different in Russia from what it was in France (to the extent, that is, to which it had a uniform meaning in either place) as the meaning of literature itself was different in those two countries. In a setting where the educated but politically disenfranchised turned to art and the intellectual life as a realm of civic engagement in history, where novels—and essays about those novels—were meant not only to inspire revolutionary acts but to *be* revolutionary acts, it was no surprise that the meaning of *realism* quickly expanded to include matters that writers in France and elsewhere would be likely to consider entirely extraneous to literature.

The place where Pisarev comes closest to elaborating a realist theory of literature is an essay, published in 1864, called "Realists," where he goes out of his way to sound scientific, utilitarian, and political. Hence, statements like these: "A thoroughly consistent tendency toward utility is called 'realism. . . .' The realist constantly aspires to utility and constantly rejects in himself and others any activity that brings no useful results."[20] "The realist is a thinking worker, lovingly occupying himself with labor."[21] The effort is to broaden the literary term *realism* to a point where it appears to signify an entire attitude toward life, lest the reader think that Pisarev was talking about an autonomous sphere of activity called "art."

It is easy to see why subsequent generations will understand *realism*, first, as a term describing the dominant mode of literary composition in nineteenth-century Russia and, second, as a misleading term always requiring an explanatory footnote. Realism is not simply a style characterized by its attention to truthfulness and authenticity, by the choice of a setting that could pass for a *real* historical setting, by a style of narration that mimics the style of historical discourse and thus makes the story *realistic*; it is a style that combines all of these qualities with a didactic, moral, political intent. As the author of an essay in the standard collection of Soviet scholarship on the subject puts it, realism is born both from the link that Chernyshevsky established in aesthetic perception between "the objective existence of beauty and the 'subjective outlook' on it," or, to put it differently, from "the internal unity of the two formulae: 'the beautiful is life,' and 'that being is beautiful in which we see life as it ought to be according to our conceptions.'"[22] In other words, realism comes from the intention to represent reality objectively but with the subjective tint of the writer's moral (political) will.

Realism is thus a vehicle for propelling the literary work and its author from the world of artistic endeavor into the world of historical-political reality and then leveling the wall between the two worlds. The objective component requires heroes and settings that are indistinguishable from real heroes and real settings. The subjective component requires an engagement by the author in the historical world of real heroes and real settings; indeed it requires the author to *become* a real hero in a real, historical setting. Owing to the destruction of barriers that it demands (between life and art, and so on), realism easily becomes a manner of living—politically, historically engaged living, to be specific—instead of just a manner of writing fiction.[23]

Realism had already become a slogan for many Russian Jewish intellectuals when they immigrated to the United States at the end of the nineteenth century. The guiding principles were the ones they had learned in Russia from the great realists of the 1860s and 1870s, who had learned their lessons from Belinsky, who in turn had spawned his ideas out of an internal struggle with Hegel. For many of the émigré intellectuals, realism will come to define not only a narrow theory of literature (and a significant number will choose to write about realism in the press), but also an entire mode of life for the intellectual, one that engages the intellectual in social history, that integrates political action with activities traditionally considered separate from the arena of civic affairs. When Jewish immigrants devote lengthy articles in their Yiddish journals to Russian literature, to the great Russian critics of the nineteenth century, to the subject of literary realism, not only is it because, as elsewhere, they are attempting to keep their relatively uneducated readers aware of important cultural happenings in Europe and Russia; it is because they are justifying a style of life that they learned in Russia, brought to the United States, and will fulfil for generations to come.

IN CHERNYSHEVSKY'S *KHEYDER*

"Once she learned to read Russian, one could not tear her away from a book. She read everything—from trashy novels to the Russian classics. Books made a different person of Beti—she went from being a lively, cheerful, carefree girl to being serious, pensive, absorbed in herself." This is how Leo Deutsch describes a critical moment in the childhood of Beti Kaminskaia, Russia's "first Jewish woman student and propagandist." Kaminskaia's early friendships and her books, Deutsch tells us, caused the future propagandist quite early to confront the painful question "how one can help not just this or that poor woman, but all poor and unfortunate people."[24] Kaminskaia's concern over this problem induced her as a young woman to join the struggle for workers' rights in Russia. Before that, however, she had taken a bold step that a few hundred other Russian women, including many Jews, had taken. At a time when Russian universities did not admit women, she had gone to Zurich to study at the university, and there she had followed what Deutsch described as a typical itinerary for Russian women students. After becoming acquainted with a number of Russian émigré intellectuals living in exile, she and her fellow women students quickly abandoned their university studies to devote themselves to political causes.

Many young Russian Jewish intellectuals in the age of Nihilism and later responded to their reading in exactly the same way as their non-Jewish peers. Leo Deutsch felt that Nihilism as a whole brought about a much more profound transformation in Jewish students (or, as he puts it, "played a more salubrious role" among Jewish students) than in Gentile students.[25] This is easy to believe, if we consider that so many young Jews were still fighting the pull of orthodox life, which was far more removed from Nihilism than was the life of middle- and upper-class Russians. As for reading, the young Russified Jews surrendered themselves to the new writers and the new ideas with a passion at least equal to that of their non-Jewish comrades. In an age when, as we have seen, writers, particularly progressive ones, and their ideas wielded enormous power over readers, when a book like *What Is to Be Done?* was able to change the lives of so many people in measurable ways, quite a few young Jewish intellectuals, coming from a culture that for thousands of years had fostered reverence for the written word, committed themselves with near fanaticism to a small group of writers—prophets, almost—who were felt to hold the Truth. "Russian literature had made us Russians," exclaimed Chaim Zhitlovsky in his memoirs.[26] No clearer, simpler statement of the character of that generation was ever spoken.

Chernyshevsky, Dobroliubov, and Pisarev. These are the names that occur most frequently in the memoirs of Jewish revolutionaries. In many cases, the three writers are listed together, with no mention of what they wrote, since everyone knew what they wrote. Elias Tcherikower, who participated in Russian Jewish radical politics (to be sure, well after the age of Nihilism) and also became the leading scholarly authority of his generation on the subject, describes the requisite indoctrination for yeshiva boys and graduates of the state rabbinical schools (Crown schools). It took them a while to learn about the important issues of the day, such as peasant rebellion, village uprisings, and the "religion" of the Russian Populists, he says, but they knew where to start: with Chernyshevsky, Dobroliubov, and Pisarev (he also mentions the anarchist Mikhail Bakunin).[27]

Leo Deutsch's writings are full of references to the three apostles of Nihilism. In an article on Lazar Goldenberg, the man he considers to be the "first Jewish revolutionary," Deutsch relates the extent of Goldenberg's commitment to the political fashions of the 1860s by saying that he read Chernyshevsky, Dobroliubov, and Pisarev, and that he dressed like a Nihilist.[28] In a general article on Jews in the Russian revolutionary movement, an article that encompasses his own personal experiences in politics, Deutsch speaks of the heady era of reforms under Alexander II, when Chernyshevsky, Dobroliubov, and Pisarev introduced their readers to progressive, Western European ideas and stirred their interest in helping the oppressed masses.[29] In his book-length study of Jews in the Russian revolutionary movement he reproduces much of this same passage, this time identifying Chernyshevsky, Dobroliubov, and Pisarev as "the critics and publicists of *Sovremennik* and *Russkoe Slovo*" (The Contemporary, the journal for which Chernyshevsky and Dobroliubov both wrote; and The Russian word, the journal for which Pisarev served as the leading literary critic from 1860 to 1865).[30] Several pages earlier, in a brief footnote, he had identified the three writers as those that most eloquently "propagandized" Nihilism.[31] And later in the same book he quotes a letter to himself from his former fellow activist Iosif Aptekman. Aptekman speaks of his years as a gymnasium student, when his "teachers" were Chernyshevsky, Dobroliubov, and Pisarev.[32]

Abe Cahan talks in his memoirs about the education in Russian literature he gave himself when he was a boy. After he discovered the public library in Vilna, he would spend four or five hours a day in the reading room working through the classics of Russian literature: Turgenev's complete works, Ostrovsky, Dobroliubov's critique of Ostrovsky, and Pisarev, including a critique of Chernyshevsky's *What Is to Be Done?*[33] In 1896, fourteen years after he had moved to the United States, Cahan wrote a study of Yiddish masterpieces for the recently founded Yiddish monthly *Di Tsukunft* (The Future), preceded by a brief study of literary criticism in general. In the study of criticism in general he tells his readers that a good work of criticism should be a social as well as a literary study. Only the Russians have truly understood this, he says, and in Russia the best known critics have consequently also been known as commentators on the great social questions facing their countries. Cahan lists them: Chernyshevsky, Dobroliubov, and Pisarev.[34]

Later in the century, when the Jewish radical movement in Russia increasingly became a labor movement, libraries were set up and reading groups organized in many cities as part of a campaign to educate members of the fledgling Jewish proletariat. Over and over again one finds the names of Russia's Nihilist writers mentioned in lists of books. In an article on the character of the workers' movement in Vilna in the 1890s, for example, one writer describes the libraries that were set up for the purpose of "satisfying the intellectual needs of the workers." The libraries contained titles in Yiddish and Russian. Among the Russian authors listed are Chernyshevsky, Pisarev, and Dobroliubov, with a parenthetical note that *What Is to Be Done?* was requested especially often.[35]

John Mill (1870–1952), who was to become a prominent Bund activist, included *What Is to Be Done?* on a list of readings he and fellow members of a political circle in Ponevezh (today Panevežys, Lithuania) drew up as part of a self-instruction course. In his memoirs, the political circle and the reading list appear as part of the backdrop to Mill's own participation in the Populist movement.[36] Mill, incidentally, as a young man was denied admission to the technological institutes in St. Petersburg and Riga, apparently because of a school essay he had written that contained references to Pisarev and Dobroliubov.[37]

Morris Winchevsky, in his memoirs, describes the process by which he became a socialist. It began with "Chernyshevsky's *Chto delat'?* [*What Is to Be Done?*] and other such writings," he says, and ended with the reading of a manifesto by Aron Liberman. The result: "In short, I was a doubly fanatical, anti-religious, anti-hypocritical sentimental socialist."[38]

Emma Goldman became a young convert to Nihilism partly through her reading of *What Is to Be Done?* In her autobiography she tells how her sister obtained copies of this and similar works, which she lent to Emma. Though her mother spoke of the Russian Nihilists with utter hatred, Emma felt an instinctive sympathy for them, especially for those who assassinated Alexander II in 1881 and were later hanged for their

1. Emma Goldman in 1892.

crime. Sometime after that fateful year, she read Chernyshevsky's novel, and it had the effect of strengthening her earlier feelings of sympathy for Nihilism as a movement and for the Nihilists who had killed the tsar.[39] Two of the most vivid and personal accounts of the cult of Chernyshevsky come from Chaim Zhitlovsky and Abraham Cahan. What is curious about the testimony of these two writers is that it employs specifically Jewish cultural and religious terms—at times with a touch of humor—in order to convey the strength of the Jewish radicals' devotion to Chernyshevsky, thus providing a perfect stylistic sign of the position in which the young Jewish radicals found themselves: between the culture of their birth and their new, adopted culture.

Zhitlovsky tells about Chernyshevsky in two chapters of his memoirs, one called "The 'new' world vs. the 'old,'" the other called "In Chernyshevsky's *kheyder*." Writing a half-century after the experiences he is describing, Zhitlovsky tells of an era when Chernyshevsky was "the central sun of Russian radical thought, the truly greatest scholar and deepest theoretician." He continues: "When we became acquainted with his most famous work, the novel *What Is to Be Done?*, Chernyshevskii became for us, as for earlier generations, the beloved hero around whose life a garland of legends had been wreathed. He became in the literal sense of the word our *rebbe*, our leader, our '*er zol lebn*' ["long may he live"], and we, his ardent *Hassidim*" (a *rebbe* is a Hassidic rabbi, and *Hassidim* here can mean either "members of a Hassidic sect" or simply "devotees," "followers").[40]

It is hardly surprising that Chernyshevsky should have been treated with the same reverence that Hassidic Jews show their *rebbe*, given the standing of Chernyshevsky's work. "There is perhaps no work in *world* literature—I mean non-religious literature—that has been able to attract the interest of several generations in succession as Chernyshevsky's novel *Chto delat'?* did," Zhitlovsky says. "To judge by the way young people approached it, the way they studied it, the way they hearkened to its language, this work could almost be added to the ranks of the sacred scriptures of mankind: the Bible, the Gospels, the Koran."[41] In those days, he says, "people approached *What Is to Be Done?* as they would the Zohar [the holiest book of Kabalah], because they expected to discover in it the *sisre-toyre* [mysteries of the Torah]."[42]

Not, of course, that the subject of *What Is to Be Done?* was religious. On the contrary, Zhitlovsky reminds us, it addressed such earthly issues as private property, the family, and division of labor. The future we see in *What Is to Be Done?* is not a messianic future, but a socialist one, one that is based on the sublime dream of a Fourierist society. *What Is to Be Done?*, Zhitlovsky says, "is the first and the most important purely socialist work in Russian, not because it was written by a socialist in a socialist spirit, but because it speaks directly about the socialist future."[43]

And so the ardent *Hassidim* studied at the feet of their *rebbe*. Or their *melamed*, as the teacher of young children in a *kheyder* was called. Zhitlovsky and the members of his generation were pupils "In Chernyshevsky's *kheyder*," as the title of his chapter suggests. The lessons they learned there? In addition to reading about the future socialist order, they learned about the essential nature of man. "Man is by nature an egoist." "The wider [man's] spiritual horizon becomes and the more developed his reason becomes, the nobler and richer his pleasures become." "With the abolition of the moral standard and of morality in general, it makes no sense to apply our judgment to men, their actions, or the way they conduct their lives." Moral judgments are "a human invention that does not have the least foundation in nature or reason." "Once human reason has freed itself from the old, false thoughts and discovered the correct ones, nothing will be able to halt their triumph for long."[44]

In a passage that is unusually rich in Hebrew phrases and expressions,

Zhitlovsky goes to some length to point out that reading Chernyshevsky's novel was not like reading any other book. The value of both the Holy Scriptures and *What Is to Be Done?*, Zhitlovsky concedes, has been exaggerated, but Chernyshevsky's novel cannot really be placed on the same level as the Scriptures. Nonetheless, he says, "it was read and its contents were thought about with no less seriousness and, if you will, with no less sanctity than when the Holy Scriptures were read and reflected upon by members of the pious Jewish communities from which we had come."[45]

Abe Cahan is just as emphatic about the reverence his generation showed Chernyshevsky, though he speaks about it with a little more ironic distance than Zhitlovsky. Writing in the 1920s about his youth in Russia, Cahan says this about Chernyshevsky and his novel: "In later years I came to realize that the novel *What Is to Be Done?* had no literary merit. In those days, however, in 1880, the person of its author and every word he wrote were sacred. To say an unfavorable word about any one of his works would have been a *khilel hashem* [blasphemy or, literally, profanation of the name]. He was the great martyr, the highly respected and beloved teacher of all thinking men. So the radical critics (and there was no other kind in Russia) saw only great virtues in *What Is to Be Done?*" In his day, Chernyshevsky had been thought of as "the greatest critic and, after that, the greatest economist, thinker, and leader of the progressive young generation."[46]

If *What Is to Be Done?* was the Torah of this generation, then *Sovremennik*, the journal that Chernyshevsky helped edit, in which he first published *What Is to Be Done?*, and to which Dobroliubov contributed literary criticism for several years, was its Talmud. The statement that one read *Sovremennik* was like the statement that one read Chernyshevsky and Dobroliubov, not only because reading *Sovremennik* actually meant reading writers like these, but because, from around 1856 until the journal was closed down in 1866, its political positions were sufficiently clear and consistent that its devoted readers could easily be said to fit a certain political profile.

Leo Deutsch reports that Lazar Goldenberg and his fellow students at the university organized a self-education program whose primary activity was reading *Sovremennik* and *Russkoe Slovo*.[47] Iosef Getsov, a comrade of Deutsch, wrote in the 1920s about the political activities in which he had been engaged in the 1870s. He, too, had set up a self-education program with some of his comrades. Among the few works that made up the reading list for his group were *What Is to Be Done?* and Chernyshevsky's other contributions to *Sovremennik*.[48] Cahan tells in his memoirs how in 1881, by a stroke of fortune, he had acquired two years' worth of issues of *Sovremennik* and how these were among his most valued possessions. The issues he acquired included the ones containing Chernyshevsky's translation of John Stuart Mill's *Principles of Political Economy* (which dates them in 1860).[49] Apparently the police knew the significance of owning and reading this subversive periodical, because when they raided Cahan's apartment a few months later, they immediately seized the precious collection.[50]

Chernyshevsky, Dobroliubov, other authors published in *Sovremennik*, and Pisarev were not the only ones the Jewish revolutionaries read in the 1860s and 1870s. There were others: Belinsky, of course, Herzen, Bakunin, the Populist theoretician and critic Nikolai Mikhailovsky, the champion of "anarchist-communism" Petr Kropotkin, to name only a few. Nor was Cahan the only Jewish radical to read Russian fiction. Like their Russian counterparts in the progressive intelligentsia, young educated Jews were fond of Russian novelists, above all those whose works confronted contemporary social issues (whether from a progressive or from a conservative perspective). Turgenev is probably mentioned more than any other novelist, but there are references to Gogol and Dostoevsky as well. Another writer whose name appears frequently in memoirs and on the reading lists of radical study groups is Mikhail Saltykov-Shchedrin, an independent-minded critic, satirist, and publicist who feuded publicly with both the very radical Pisarev and the conservative Dostoevsky. Jewish intellectuals also read many of the Western thinkers who had served as an inspiration to Russian writers: John Stuart Mill, Herbert Spencer, Jeremy Bentham, Darwin, Proudhon, and others.[51]

Some Jewish intellectuals were even reading Marx, though Marxism did not really catch on as a movement in Russia until the early 1880s. In the 1870s, Mark Natanson, a revolutionary who had participated in the student uprisings of 1869, became involved in political circles whose purpose was to promote the study of Marx and Marx's disciple Ferdinand Lassalle.[52] Aron Liberman wrote about Marx in the European-based Russian revolutionary journal *Vpered!* (Forward!) in the mid-1870s.[53] Abraham Cahan obtained a copy of *Kapital* in Russian translation in 1881 and "sat for entire evenings reading it and penetrating the profundities of its contents."[54] And Leo Deutsch claims that the Populist movement in the 1870s, in which he and many other Jewish radicals played a role, was in part Marxist.[55]

We must not forget, of course, that the Jewish émigrés who imbibed Russian literature did not present a uniform political front either before they emigrated or after they arrived in the United States. Cahan and Zhitlovsky, to take only the two whose vivid descriptions of a Chernyshevskian past I have cited at length, ended up about as far apart politically as two people can be while still being on the left, Cahan with his popularized and cosmopolitan social democracy and Zhitlovsky with his eventual devotion to Yiddishism and territorialism (a theory that Jews should occupy their own territory and that this territory need not be Palestine).

Nonetheless, all shared an intellectual legacy, and the dominant figures in that legacy, to judge from the accounts of the Jewish radicals themselves, were the Russian socially engaged critics (and, of course, the Western writers who had contributed to the intellectual formation of those same Russian critics). The model of political life the émigrés learned from their reading was one in which there was an easy and natural passage from reading to action, whether that action eventually took the form of union organizing or whether it eventually took the form of promoting Yiddish as the mother tongue of the Jews.

NIHILISM IN PRACTICE: STYLE, DRESS, AND MANNERS

Not all action, of course, was political in the strict sense. Nihilism brought with it certain rules for social comportment that would probably strike a later age as relatively silly. There was, for example, a code governing attire and grooming. Just as the members of the sixties generation in the United States (the 1960s, that is) elevated selected forms of sartorial indifference to a kind of orthodoxy, the sixties generation in Russia (1860s) knew how to make an ideological statement in this sphere of social life. When Jewish members of this generation, especially those who themselves had made the break with orthodox life, adopted the styles of their non-Jewish radical comrades, they were necessarily thumbing their noses at two groups: at traditional Jews by wearing "goyish" clothes (thus being Russian) and at refined, Gentile society by wearing shabby clothes (thus being radical).

One Jewish intellectual who embraced the new manners was Lazar Goldenberg, Deutsch's "first Jewish revolutionary in Russia." Using an autobiographical letter that Goldenberg had written to him, Deutsch shows how both books and clothes made the man in the days of Nihilism: "Goldenberg was considered a good student and an excellent comrade, one who was ready to help anyone with all the means available to him. At the same time, he had read much of the radical literature of Chernyshevsky, Dobroliubov, Pisarev, and, as he himself tells it, 'I was, in my views, my clothes, and my manners, a true nihilist.'"[56]

In a general article on Jews in the Russian revolutionary movement, Deutsch paints an amusing picture of the style the new generation of Russified Jewish students cultivated, giving at the same time a glimpse of the involvement of women in the radical movement. The description could almost have been lifted from the pages of *Fathers and Sons*. The Nihilists distinguished themselves from everyone else, Deutsch says, above all in their outward appearance: in their clothes and their demeanor. And Nihilism found its followers among Jewish students, so that "new opinions, habits, and manners developed in us. [Nihilism] had freed us from many specifically Jewish traits and characteristics and had made different people of us." He continues:

> Thus I remember how in the first half of the 1860s, in Kiev, there was an entire large group of Jewish students, women and men, who adhered to the opinions and habits of the Nihilists. One would frequently encounter on the streets of the city a Jewish [male] student dressed in a coarse plaid cloak, wearing his hair long and holding a thick walking stick in his hand. The girls, on the other hand, went about with close-cropped hair and hats made of simple oilcloth. This strange appearance provoked laughter in some and indignation in others, but it had a beneficial effect, namely that the youth learned not to care about clothes and not to waste time or money on that sort of thing.[57]

A few years later, as we will see, on the streets of New York, journalist Hutchins Hapgood would observe the same styles in the "Russians" (that is, Russian Jewish immigrants) who frequented intellectual gathering places on the Lower East Side.[58]

The Jewish intellectual youth was just as much swept up in the social-political movement inspired by Chernyshevsky as was the rest of the student population. One of the cornerstones of the movement in Russia, for Jews and Gentiles alike, was the emphasis on *activity*. Irina Paperno has shown in her study of Chernyshevsky that the notions of reality and activity, the terms for which are almost homonymous in Russian (*deistvitel'nost'*, *deiatel'nost'*), were intimately connected in the age of Nihilism.[59] A commitment to reality logically and ideologically implied political activity designed to rectify social reality's flaws (just as for Belinsky a writer's commitment to reality implied a critical attitude toward that reality and an active effort to change it). When Zhitlovsky tells about the education he received in "Chernyshevsky's *kheyder*" he reveals that his lessons had a practical component and were not merely abstract theories about egoism and the abolition of morality.

One of the chief doctrines of the age was that the true path to socialism lay in a form of agitation (not the term Zhitlovsky uses), in the active dissemination, that is, of Chernyshevsky's writings and ideas.[60] Abe Cahan, in a humorous account of the activity in which he and his friends engaged at the height of their Chernyshevskian fervor, tells how they would stay up late discussing politics and then go to sleep on the bare floor. What might appear to be an uncanny anticipation of the floor-bound counter-culture of American college life in the late 1960s and early 1970s has a specific explanation. Rakhmetov, the hero of *What Is to Be*

2. Morris Winchevsky, from the 1880s.   3. Abe Cahan in 1885.

Done?, sleeps on nails in order to toughen himself. "Even if [the members of my generation] were not in the habit of sleeping on nails," Cahan says, "the least they could do was to sleep on the bare floor."[61]

In spite of its apparently superficial character, much of this behavior had a special political meaning for the fledgling Jewish radical intelligentsia. When we look at a picture of the young Morris Winchevsky and see a clean-shaven face and a necktie (he apparently did not always dress like Deutsch's Nihilists), we must remember what we are *not* seeing: the full beard, the sidelocks, the covered head, and the traditional clothing of an observant Ashkenazic Jew. When we read about Lilienblum and his smoking on the Sabbath, we must remember what even Winchevsky tells him, namely that he will be practically taking his life in his hands if any pious Jews should see him. When we read about Zhitlovsky's name change, we must remember the Jewish tradition he is casting out with his Hebrew name. Like the Jewish anarchists in London and like those in the United States a generation later who, in an intentional and almost unsurpassable act of blasphemy, organized dances on Yom Kippur, these Jewish intellectuals equated the practice of non-Jewish habits not only with cultural assimilation, but with political emancipation of the most general sort.[62] Freedom from Jewish tradition went hand in hand with freedom from capitalist or tsarist exploitation.

CHAPTER 3

"Critically Thinking Individuals"

GOING TO THE PEOPLE

THE PHASE of the Russian revolutionary movement in which Jewish intellectuals in Western Europe were involved in the 1870s is broadly called Populism (*narodnichestvo* in Russian, from *narod*, "people"). On the surface, Russian Populism was a movement dedicated to improving the lot of the "people," the Russian peasant serfs, who were officially emancipated in 1861. But Populism was more than just a movement to help the peasants. Its importance lay also in the way it defined the relationship between the writer-intellectuals who led the movement and those in society to whose welfare the programs of the writer-intellectuals were dedicated. Once this relationship was defined, the members of society to whom the intellectuals devoted their efforts could easily change.

And they did. The basic principles of what started as a movement committed to improving the lives of the recently emancipated peasants and organizing peasant support for a revolution were easily integrated before long into a movement whose focus had changed from the peasants to industrial workers. Put simply, if you take Russian Populist doctrine from the 1870s, substitute "worker" for "peasant," substitute "proletariat" for "people" (*narod*), and add some rudimentary terms from Marxism, you will have the basic ingredients of Jewish labor politics both in Russia and in emigration. And those basic ingredients include the role of the writer-intellectual who uses the press as a forum from which to lead the movement. The Populist movement was thus decisive in determining the peculiar character of Russian Jewish radicalism both in Russia and, after emigration, in the United States.

The term *Populism* presents a host of problems. As with so many terms that designate a political trend or movement, its usage has been at least partly determined by observers who have their own political bias and who are in many cases separated by a number of years from the people and events they are observing. Andrzej Walicki has given perhaps the most careful and nuanced reading of the term, in a book on the Russian Populists. He distinguishes between Populism in the narrow sense as a relatively short-lived, organized political movement in the 1870s and Populism as an ideology, "a broad current of thought" comprising many different theories, movements, and individual thinkers. In the first, narrow sense, Populism is a program that promised a social and political revolution from which the peasant masses would gain power over the intellectual classes. In the second, broader sense, it represents a range of thinking whose emphasis was the relation between the intellectual classes and the *narod*.[1] What the two senses of Populism have in common is an ideology that focuses on the people, that is concerned with the relationship between the people and the intelligentsia, and that offers a prominent place to the interests of the people in any proposal for a political solution to Russia's social problems.

A PARTLY JEWISH VOICE IN EXILE: *VPERED!*

Petr Lavrov and Russian Populism

But the essential thing for the *legacy* of Populism is the relationship between the people (or workers) and the intelligentsia, and the thinker who helped define this relationship both for the Jewish intelligentsia and for later Russian radicals (like Lenin, for example) was Petr Lavrovich Lávrov (1823–1900). Lavrov proposed an approach to history and to contemporary reality that gave the individual (pictured always as a member of the intellectual elite) wide power to effect positive change in society. History for him was an arena in which the thinking individual, acting on the basis of a subjective critique (as in Belinsky), could exert force on events and bring about positive change. So, in a left-Hegelian age when the term *development* (*razvitie* in Russian) was prominent in radical thought as a description of the progress of history from one stage to the next, Lavrov was using the term to refer to the personal development of the individual. In his view, this development, and not historical law, is the basis of progress.

The work that most clearly presented Lavrov's ideas about the role of the intellectual in society and the concept of development, the work that brought him fame almost comparable to what Chernyshevsky enjoyed from the publication of *What Is to Be Done?* was *Historical Letters*, a series of essays, or "letters," originally published in the periodical press in 1868 and 1869, then issued in book form in 1870. *Historical Letters* is generally considered one of the seminal documents of the Populist movement (in Walicki's second, broad sense), if not *the* seminal document. In them, Lavrov defines the position and the responsibilities of the intellectual in society and hands down to all future generations of Russian radicals, Jewish and non-Jewish, a carefully argued theory of political activism that applied specifically to the intelligentsia. If there is one figure by whom more phrases will be picked up and repeated in the Jewish press in the United States than by any other, it is no doubt Lavrov.

Populism and the leading role of the intellectual are subjects that for Lavrov are intrinsically related by human history. The intellectual elite, he says, owes its very position to the enormous sacrifices that the masses have made throughout human history. Many have toiled, suffered, and died so that a few might have the leisure to sit in their studies and ponder the problems of human existence. The intellectual elite thus owes its very position to the masses. But the intelligentsia alone is in a position to bring about positive change. The change it brings about must, then, have the people as its object, since the intelligentsia is indebted to the masses and as a consequence has a responsibility toward them.

In what does the discharge of the intelligentsia's debt to the masses consist? It consists in "the dissemination, among the majority, of the comforts of life and of intellectual and moral development, the introduction of scientific understanding and justice into social forms."[2] And how is "the introduction of scientific understanding and of justice into social forms" to be accomplished? Lavrov has a special term for the intellectual vanguard in society. It is "critically thinking individuals," since members of this group engage in a subjective critique of society and its institutions. Everything depends on the manner in which these individuals exercise their critical faculties and translate their critique into action. Among the tools they have at their disposal are literature, art, and science.[3]

Here is where the concept of development (*razvitie*) comes into play. Lavrov puts it like this: "*The development of the individual physically, intellectually, and morally. The embodiment of truth and justice in social forms*—here is a brief formula embracing everything, it seems to me, that can be considered progress."[4] Though individual development has come at a price that the common people have paid, Lavrov still prizes it as the hope for future salvation, since it lies at the heart of the individual's virtue. This is Lavrov's rule for living, as he expresses it in the letter called "The Price of Progress": "Live in conformity with the ideal you have set for yourself as the ideal of a *developed* person!"[5]

The essential thing is *thought*. "Thought is the sole agent that imparts *humane* dignity to social culture. The history of thought determined by culture, in connection with the history of culture, and as culture changes under the influence of thought—this is the entire history of civilization." And when Lavrov speaks of thought, he speaks of *individual* thought. It is the critically thinking individual confronting social institutions who is the true agent of change.[6]

But the solitary individual does not bring about massive change on his own. Solitary individuals need to become a *force*. This they do by organizing themselves into a party—and Lavrov devotes an entire letter (one that anticipates the theories of Lenin) to a description of the structure and functions of the "party." The party is a type of living organism whose parts must be subordinated to the whole. This means that it should tolerate no significant disagreements among its members.[7] True change can ultimately be accomplished only through collective force, and this means the critically thinking individuals must bend their efforts toward a common purpose and carry on the struggle as a group.[8]

In 1870, Lavrov, who had been arrested in 1865 and had spent the intervening time in internal exile, escaped to Western Europe, settling first in Paris and then, two years later, in Zurich. It is here that his story intersects that of the Jewish intelligentsia, because it is here that he managed to establish himself as the central figure in a loosely defined political circle that counted a significant number of Russian Jewish intellectuals among its members. The activity that gave coherence to this group was the writing, publication, and dissemination of a journal that Lavrov helped found in 1873. It was called *Vpered!* (Forward!—the exclamation point is part of the title). It was relatively short-lived, lasting only until 1877, but since it was published beyond the reach of Russian censorship, it became during its brief existence one of the boldest and most influential revolutionary publications in Russian. The *Vpered!* organization issued many revolutionary publications in addition to *Vpered!* itself.

By the time he began working on *Vpered!* Lavrov's views had undergone some slight modifications. For one thing, he had begun to take account of Marxism and to see the industrial proletariat as a target of revolutionary activity, and, for another, he had increasingly come to assert that the intellectual elite must play only a preparatory role in the revolution. The true responsibility for the revolution would fall on those it would most benefit, namely the *narod*, understood as the peasants, or the workers. "We assign a primary position to the tenet that the rebuilding [*perestroika*] of Russian society must be accomplished not only with the *goal* in mind of the good of the people, not only *for* the people, but also *by means of* the people," he said in the programmatic article he wrote for the first issue of *Vpered!*[9]

Preparation is the new concept. In his *Vpered!* articles, Lavrov speaks over and over of the minority's obligation to *prepare* both themselves and the peasants, emphasizing that the minority can and should do no more. "Only by explaining to the people their needs and preparing them for independence and conscious activity toward the attainment of goals that they clearly understand," he says in the first issue of *Vpered!*, "can a participant in the contemporary preparation for an optimal future for Russia consider himself truly useful."[10]

Three years later, Lavrov reiterated his preparationist view and brought in some old-fashioned principles of Russian Populism, but this time with a quasi-Marxist slant. The revolution, he said,

> must be produced not by the intellectual class, but by the people [*narod*], resting on the tradition of communal and collective solidarity that already

exists among them; the intellectual class, in the guise of convinced socialists, can be for the revolution nothing more than an initiator, inducing in the people, by means of propaganda and agitation, a feeling of the solidarity of the entire working class of the Russian land and a consciousness of the necessity of preventing the return of the old social calamities, having established the principle of *workers' socialism* as the basis for the construction of a new society.[11]

All this may well sound like an acknowledgment of the impotence of the intelligentsia and a major concession to a Marxian economic determinism. But when all is said and done, Lavrov's programmatic article for *Vpered!* and his other articles published in *Vpered!* show that the activity of the "civilized minority" is a *sine qua non* of the Russian revolution. The masses must produce the revolution and they must do so in order to fulfil their needs, but they can never know what those needs are until the intelligentsia, through propaganda, tells them. And they can never know how to produce a revolution until the intelligentsia, through agitation, shows them.

Propaganda and agitation, in fact, are cardinal concepts of Russian intellectual activism, and they are mentioned abundantly in the pages of *Vpered!* But propaganda largely means *writing*, and by advocating it Lavrov is supporting the activist role that Russian revolutionary politics had assigned the intellectual since at least as far back as Belinsky. His Jewish associates will follow his example and use the power of the word to address not only the general political problems of Russia but also the specific problems of Russian Jews.

Aron Liberman and the Jewish Vperedovtsy

Though the number of Russian Jews involved in the revolutionary movement in the 1870s was small and included few of the future emigrants to the United States, there were a number of Jews among the *vperedovtsy*, as those associated with *Vpered!* were called. In part this was because Lavrov provided a hospitable climate for Jews in his movement, something that was relatively uncommon at a time when the Russian revolutionary movement was often either silent on the "Jewish question" or openly hostile toward Jews. *Vpered!* avoided expressions of anti-Semitism, something that required courage since it meant refusing to publish a certain number of politically significant submissions that contained anti-Semitic remarks.[12] Lavrov took an active interest in the Jewish question, especially after the era of *Vpered!* In 1886 he made a speech to the Jewish Workers Association in Paris, in which he praised the Jewish people for the determination they had shown throughout their history and called attention to the lessons of endurance and patience that all socialists could learn from Jewish history. He made many of the same points in a letter of 1892 to the editor of *Der Veker* (The awakener), the Yiddish-language organ of the London Socialist Workers Association. The Paris speech was published as a brochure in Yiddish translation and had the distinction, according to Elias Tcherikower, of being one of the earliest Yiddish socialist brochures ever published. The letter to the editor of *Der Veker* was published in Yiddish translation. Both writings have become important texts in the history of Jewish socialism.[13]

Lavrov's writings on the revolutionary movement are filled with references to Jewish activists.[14] But during the *Vpered!* years, before Lavrov had made any memorable statements on the Jewish question, some of the most influential Jewish intellectuals to take part in the Russian revolutionary movement were closely involved in Lavrov's activities, especially in the publication and distribution of *Vpered!*

By far the most important Jewish writer among the *vperedovtsy* was Aron Liberman.[15] Liberman was a *maskil* born in Grodno and educated at the Rabbinical Seminary (one of the Crown schools) in Vilna. He distinguished himself by his application of Russian revolutionary principles to a specifically Jewish political problem. While Lavrov and many of his other colleagues were busy redefining Populism by substituting *working masses in general*, or, in certain cases, *industrial proletariat* for *narod*, Liberman was redefining Populism by substituting *Jewish masses* for *narod*.

He was clearly conversant with the dominant theories of the age. He was not a card-carrying Lavrovist, and yet it seems clear he was already familiar with Lavrovism before his involvement with *Vpered!*.[16] Like everyone else in the movement, he knew his Chernyshevsky. His published correspondence with Lavrov's associate Valerian Smirnov, much of it, to be sure, from a later period in Liberman's life, is sprinkled with references to the author of *What Is to Be Done?*[17] In fact, if Liberman was difficult to classify politically, it appears to be less because of any deficits in his political education than because of the degree to which his own ideology joined specifically Jewish concerns with Russian revolutionary doctrine.

Liberman arrived in London in 1875, after the police began looking into political activities at the Vilna Seminary, and started his association with Lavrov and *Vpered!* soon after. His contributions fall into three categories. There was a series of articles, based on recent memories or on information obtained from friends, titled "From Vilna" and "From Belostok."[18] There was a set of governing statutes he wrote for the Jewish socialist organization he founded in London, with the Hebrew name *Agudat ha-sotsialistim ha-ivrim* (Hebrew Socialist Union). The statutes were issued in Hebrew and Yiddish versions before appearing in *Vpered!*. And there was a manifesto he had written earlier.

The ideology that comes through in these writings clearly bears the marks of the author's cultural and intellectual biography. They are the work of a man with a solid Jewish upbringing who adopted the Nihilism of Russia's civic critics, committed himself to a form of Populism, then superimposed on the entire worldview some rudimentary concepts from Marx—all without losing his commitment to his own people.

In fact, in his first publication in *Vpered!*, Liberman shows that there is an intrinsic connection between all these different components of his ideology and that Judaism is what provides this connection. After briefly discussing the plight of the Jews in Russia, he asserts that the only possible salvation for the people (*narod*) lies in social revolution. He then makes one of the points for which he was best known, namely that socialism is a natural course for the Jews because it has always been present in Jewish history. He enumerates all the features of socialism, as a Russian Populist would understand it, and shows how they bear a close connection with the Jewish people. "Socialism is not foreign to us," he says.

> The *obshchina* [Russian peasant commune] is our very existence; revolution is our tradition; the commune is the basis of our system of law. . . . Our ancient social order is anarchy; the current bond between us over the entire surface of the globe is the International [established by Marx in London, 1864]. The great prophets of the current age, Marx, Lassalle, and others, were nurtured and ripened in the spirit of our people.[19]

All the articles titled "From Vilna" and "From Belostok" are distinguished by their sharp, often sarcastic attacks on the Russian regime (to which Liberman refers, for example, as the "prison-gendarme state") and by their placement of the Jews at the center of the pressing social and political issues of the day. The political views represent a broad swath of contemporary Russian radical thought. Liberman describes, for example, an attempt by Vilna's revolutionaries to educate the students of their city in the latest political theories. The students had been treated to a diatribe by a local church official against all the current radical ideas, among them *propaganda*, *socialism*, and *communes*. In an effort to educate the students and steer them clear of such reactionary biases as those of the church official, the revolutionaries sought to explain these terms to the students in their politically proper senses and to introduce other terms as well. The list reads like a basic lexicon of Russian radical ideology with a recent accretion of Marxist terminology: in addition to *propaganda*, *socialism*, and *communes*, there is *proletariat*, *exploitation*, *bourgeoisie*, *International*, *solidarity*, *agitation*, and *social revolution*.[20]

For Liberman, a concern specifically for the Jews is unquestionably a *national* matter (the Jews being regarded as a nation or nationality within the larger nation of Russia), and the question is how to work specifically for them without violating a fundamental principle of socialism. Liberman provides a solution to this problem that is Lavrovian to the core. Lavrov, we have seen, had devoted much energy to encouraging the intelligentsia to engage in preparatory work for the revolution, feeling that a violent revolution was premature and also that it was not the place of the intelligentsia itself to make a revolution. Liberman, in acknowledging the cosmopolitan nature of the socialist movement, insists that preparatory work must be done and that this preparatory work consists in working with the various nationalities *separately*. Hence the propriety of waging a socialist campaign among the Jews.

And this leads to the central, Lavrovian question of the relation between the intelligentsia and the masses, which for Liberman means the question of the relation between the *Jewish* intelligentsia and the *Jewish* masses. The problem concerns the youngest members of this class, those who are students. These, he complains, are entirely out of touch with the Jewish masses, or, to be more accurate, have *lost* touch with the masses, through the process of assimilation. "For this reason," he explains, members of the Jewish student intelligentsia "cannot conduct Populist activities among their coreligionists. They belong entirely to the broad intellectual class that has been called upon to carry out the preliminary work, to bring social-revolutionary thought to the minds of those who are closest to the people and then—to recede into the background once a sufficient amount of revolutionary strength has been developed among the people themselves."[21] The task for propagandists, by which Liberman presumably means older propagandists like himself, is to show these students the way, since it is from this group, as well as from the Jewish working class, that the fighters for socialism will be drawn. "I am confident that, once it has begun to engage in socialist activity, the [Jewish] youth will give us the most ardent champions in this matter and will then also spread the socialist faith among other popular elements to which they are close."[22]

The statutes for the Hebrew Socialist Union and the manifesto, both of which were published in *Vpered!* in the summer of 1876, can be seen as Liberman's answer to his own call, since both seek to enlist the Jewish intellectual youth in the socialist cause.[23] The statutes point to the evils of capitalism, call for the abolition of private property, and find humankind's sole salvation in a fundamental social, political, and economic revolution. The immediate goal of the union will be "to spread socialist ideas among the Jews, wherever they live, and among individuals of other nationalities." The ultimate goal is to replace the current order with "the reign of labor, justice, freedom, and the brotherhood of all humankind."[24] The ultimate order will thus transcend nationalities.

The manifesto to the Jewish intellectual youth shows even more clearly Liberman's Populist orientation, since the entire project outlined there is conceived as the resolution of a conflict between the masses and the intelligentsia. Those seeking to bring change, Liberman says, invariably end up in league with the enemies of the people (*narod*). The people in general are just beginning to understand this, he says, and now even the Jewish people are beginning to understand. In fact, the Jewish intelligentsia has become so assimilated to the ways of the exploiters that it has itself become the central problem. "And we," he writes, "the children of our people; we, the friends of all the suffering masses, say to the face of the entire world: we repudiate these destroyers of the working people!"[25] Liberman invites the Jewish youth to join him in doing what the assimilated intelligentsia has failed to do, namely to become "fighters for the good of the masses, for the good of all humankind!"[26] The new intelligentsia will then play the role that Lavrov had outlined in his writings.

The entire manifesto is a curious blend of classical Populist ideology (the word *narod* occurs in practically every sentence) and the Marxism that was gradually attaching itself to Populism. Nowhere is this clearer than in the two calls to action Liberman issues in the final paragraphs. "Go to the aid of the proletariat, youth!" he says first, and then, "Go to the people."[27] This second admonition is the cry of the "going to the people" campaign of the previous two years, a campaign in which several thousand young Russians, including some Jews, went into the countryside and lived among the peasants, for the purpose of spreading socialist doctrine (that is, engaging in propaganda) and inciting rebellion (that is, engaging in agitation).

What shines through in all of this is the dominant ideology of *Vpered!* The emphasis on the *narod* is here, as is the basic Populist tenet that political revolutions have something essential to do with the relationship between the people and the intelligentsia. We find the same attitude toward this educated minority as in the writings of Lavrov, an attitude that strangely combines profound mistrust for the intellectual classes—or at least for their ability unilaterally to promote change—with the belief that nothing can ever be accomplished without them. Liberman, after all, is simply proposing to replace an obsolete intelligentsia with a younger, invigorated one (under the guidance of people like him).

Liberman's career did not end with his participation in the Lavrov circle. In the few years of life that remained to him, he founded the short-lived Hebrew monthly *Ha-emet* (The truth) in Vienna in 1877, involved himself from abroad with revolutionaries in the south of Russia, and spent some time under arrest and in prison in both Germany and Austria. Finally, he fell in love with Morris Winchevsky's cousin Rachel, a married woman who did not love him in return, and pursued her to the

United States in 1880. One day in November of that year, when he was thirty-five years old, he came to her house in Syracuse, New York, and shot himself to death.

Liberman did little in the way of political activity in the United States. But no historian of the Jewish radical movement in Russia or, for that matter, of the Jewish radical movement in the United States would dispute the claim that Liberman played a role so vital in the formation of Jewish radical ideology that without him neither movement would have been the same. Tcherikower puts it quite simply: "Liberman and his comrades first prepared the soil, something without which the further development [of the movement] would perhaps have been impossible."[28]

Even Jonathan Frankel, who takes a much dimmer view of Liberman's impact on the movement, sees him in at least two important ways as a first: one of the two first Jewish socialists, the other being Moses Hess, a German, and the first (again, with Hess) to show "the type of inner tension that was to constitute a basic characteristic of Jewish socialism." Both Hess and Liberman were "unusually clear examples of men thinking a generation ahead of their time," he says.[29] That, too, is why no history of Jewish revolutionary politics can overlook them.

Two pieces of evidence will show the impact that Liberman had on Jewish labor politics in the United States. Both have to do with men who would play a powerful role in Jewish culture and politics here. In his memoirs, Abe Cahan describes the period of his own political awakening, during his student days. He and some friends in Vilna had rented a room in which they held secret meetings and read secular literature. One day a young boy came to the room carrying a leaflet, which he said a certain Jewish man had asked him to deliver. Cahan, writing more than forty years later, remembers clearly that the leaflet was printed in two languages: Yiddish on one side and either Hebrew or Russian on the other. He remembers that it was by Liberman, remembers that he didn't quite understand it, and, in a footnote, relates a circumstance or two from Liberman's later years. There is no doubt that the leaflet he read was either Liberman's statutes for the Hebrew Socialist Union, which were originally printed in Yiddish and Hebrew, or the manifesto to the Jewish intellectual youth, which was printed in Russian and Hebrew (in this case Cahan's memory would have deceived him slightly) and widely distributed among Jewish students in Russia. Cahan says the leaflet was the first underground writing he had ever seen and then immediately goes on to say that soon afterwards he and his friends all read Chernyshevsky's *What Is to Be Done?*[30]

The other piece of evidence is Morris Winchevsky's claim in his memoirs, published in *Di Tsukunft*, that the process by which he himself became a socialist had begun with Chernyshevsky's *What Is to Be Done?* and ended with Liberman's manifesto to the Jewish intellectual youth.[31]

In the previous issue of *Di Tsukunft*, Winchevsky, referring to a moment in 1875 when he had adopted Russian ways and taken a "goyish" name in place of his real name, explains by saying, "We were *narodniks* [Populists], our natural brothers were the peasants."[32]

Liberman's brochures and articles were all part of what Lavrov referred to in his reminiscences of the Populist movement as "cultural activity," that is, the use of written material to spread the word and ultimately to elevate the intellectual level of the masses.[33] Though Liberman was attempting to reach not the masses themselves but the social class that was itself meant to reach the masses, this, too, was an essential phase of the propaganda campaign, and Cahan's and Winchevsky's anecdotes show that to a measurable extent it was successful.

GOING TO THE (RUSSIAN) PEOPLE

In the annals of Russian political theory, two of the most frequently encountered terms are *propaganda* and *agitation*. If propaganda was a form of political action that consisted largely in writing, agitation was a form of action that consisted, though it sounds redundant, in doing. Some Russian revolutionaries, including a small number of Jews, had seen the distinction and *acted* on it as early as the mid-1870s, that is, at a time when the *Vpered!* group was just beginning its activities. If ever there was an instance of agitation, of translating theory into action, in the earlier stages of Russian revolutionary history, it was the movement that inspired Liberman's call, in his manifesto to the Jewish intellectual youth, to "go to the people."

Much of the movement up until this point was admittedly consumed with sterile academic speculation or with such trivial matters as dress and demeanor, but the "going to the people" campaign showed that the radical youth could truly act on its principles. The high point came in the summer of 1874, when a few thousand students went into the countryside hoping to find an embittered peasantry that would be fully prepared to start an armed rebellion, overthrow the tsar, and build a new society modeled on their own communal way of life. The whole affair ended, of course, disastrously. The peasants were anything but rebellious, at least in the way the students wanted them to be, and huge numbers of the young *narodniki* were arrested and sent to jail, frequently because the peasants had turned them in.

Among the Populists who "went to the people" was Leo Deutsch. In 1900, he wrote about his adventures in a booklet titled *How We Went to the People* (published in 1910). For Deutsch and his immediate circle, the target "people" were not typical Russian peasants but a group of zealous religious sectarians called *molokane*. The feeling was that sectarians, persecuted and oppressed as they were, would be naturally inclined to rebel against an order that had always been hostile to them. And so the young activists set out, "carrying, together with an unshakable faith in a successful outcome, the advocacy of the new teaching, which was made up of an astonishing melange of utopian socialists' views, the anarchism of Bakunin, and Marxism."[34]

Posing as a common laborer, Deutsch succeeded in taking up residence in a family of *molokane*, where he soon discovered that he was as wrong about sectarians as the other *narodniki* were about the peasants in general. He was lucky enough not to be arrested, and he fled just as his hosts were beginning to suspect that he was a Jew and not the person he claimed to be. But the true reason for the failure of his mission, as he himself explains, was not that he almost blew his cover. It was simply that the *molokane* did not behave as his theories had predicted. "Neither the life circumstances of the followers of this sect nor their personal characteristics and qualities made them in any way more receptive to socialist teachings than were the Russian Orthodox peasants."[35]

Though Deutsch's experiences in this campaign were perhaps typical for Russian student Populists, they were hardly typical for Jewish youth. Of Russia's newly radicalized Jews, few participated, besides Deutsch, and the Jewish participants accounted for only a small proportion of those who "went to the people." Deutsch's view, in fact, is that the Jewish contribution to the Populist movement as a whole was secondary.[36] While others dispute this claim, one thing remains true, and that is that Jewish involvement in the "going to the people" campaign itself was important less for the impact it had on the Russian Populist movement in the 1870s than for the impact it had on Jewish politics after the pogroms of 1881. The "going to the people" campaign ultimately provided the Jewish labor movement, both in Russia and in the United States, with a model of political action, one whose basic inspiration may be found in Lavrov's *Historical Letters* and whose applications may be found in the unsuccessful campaign of 1874. What it would take for "going to the people" to work for Jewish radicals was for the "people" to be Jews, not Russian peasants.

CHAPTER 4.

"A Crisis of Identity"

THE POGROMS AND AFTER

EVERYTHING changed for all Russian Jews, assimilated or not, active in politics or not, in April of 1881, when the first of a series of anti-Jewish pogroms broke out in Elizavetgrad, in the south of Russia (Ukraine today). On March 1, Alexander II had been assassinated by members of the radical *Narodnaia volia* (People's will) group. Russian Jews responded to this event in at least two different ways. Many, including quite a few who were assimilated and educated, but not involved in radical politics, had regarded Alexander as a savior of their people. Emma Goldman writes in her autobiography of her mother's response to stories of earlier plots to assassinate the tsar. "The good, gracious Tsar—Mother had said—the first to give more freedom to the Jews; he had stopped the pogroms and he was planning to set the peasants free. And him the Nihilists meant to kill!"[1] Some of Russia's most cultivated and Russified Jews shared this sentiment, at least for a few weeks after the assassination. The Russian Jewish newspaper *Razsvet* (The dawn), which was published from 1879 to 1883 in St. Petersburg and which initially represented the highest reaches of the cultural elite—but a politically moderate elite—among Russian Jews, responded with what appeared to be heartfelt sympathy for the late tsar. "Even for us, the Russian Jews," their editorial ran in the first issue after the tsar's death, "His Majesty Alexander II, who now reposes in God, was the magnanimous Liberator, and at the time when with His loving soul He was granting rights to those without rights, He did not forget even us [Jews]."[2]

Others had a different response. Abe Cahan is a good example, and he shows that he was not the only one. To believe the account that he gives in his memoirs, young Jewish socialists in general, even those, like himself, who were not members of terrorist organizations, practically danced in the streets the day they got the news of the assassination. One of Cahan's friends had burst into the room where Cahan himself was waiting to break the good news to another friend. "Ubili—nakonets! (They've killed him, at last!)," the friend had screamed in Russian.[3] And this emotion endured among the young Jewish radicals who emigrated: Yiddish socialist newspapers in America would create a pantheon of Jewish heroes and heroines of the assassination conspiracy and for years, long after the events in question, would run worshipful articles about those great men and women.[4]

But after it became clear that anti-Jewish violence would not be confined to the single incident in Elizavetgrad, but would be repeated many times in many cities during the next few months, all Russian Jews were obliged to reevaluate their position. Those who had eulogized the tsar for his efforts to help the Jews were reminded forcefully that the politically moderate dream of "equal rights for the Jews" could not come true in light of the unspeakable atrocities that common Russian people were committing against the Jews and that, many believed, the succeeding regime was encouraging. Those who had rejoiced at the success of the revolutionary movement's most radical wing soon came to see that their non-Jewish fellow revolutionaries had betrayed them by lending their support to the anti-Jewish rioters. "Not only Jewish members of the intelligentsia in general," as Leo Deutsch describes it, "but even some Jewish revolutionaries who earlier had not felt the slightest tie to their nationality, because they had assimilated completely with Christians, suddenly came to recognize that they were obliged to devote their forces and abilities to their unjustly persecuted coreligionists."[5] He might have put it more strongly: in circumstances like these, every Jew had to come to terms with the fact of being Jewish.

BEING JEWISH AGAIN: THE POGROMS AND AFTER

Even the initially moderate *maskilim* writing for *Razsvet* changed their thinking dramatically in the few short months after the first pogrom. As the violence against the Jews continued and spread, *Razsvet*, which, had always been dedicated to specifically Jewish problems, became increasingly bold in asserting the rights of the Russian Jews and in implicating the government in the violence against them. By July of 1881, the paper had begun to call for various forms of action, in particular, emigration. One writer who made an early plea for this option, in a candid and strongly worded article, was the young Jacob Rombro, better known later under his pen name Philip Krantz. Declaring the current situation of the Jews hopeless, Rombro says that the only solution to the immediate problem is *"correctly and well organized emigration*, primarily to America."[6]

Another eloquent and far more powerful plea for emigration appeared in October of 1881. It was "The General Jewish Question and Palestine" by Moses Leib Lilienblum.[7] Here the Pisarevist and Populist-turned-Palestinophile played the role of a critically thinking individual leading his Jewish *narod* to salvation in the Holy Land. Since Jews are doomed to be foreigners in any land other than their very own, he said, "we need to have our corner, we need Palestine." He finished with ringing words: "And we are capable of this. To work!"[8]

The penitent Jewish university students in Kiev were responding to precisely the same circumstances as Krantz and Lilienblum, and in precisely the same way. In all three cases, the pogroms had inspired both a call for emigration and a reassertion of Jewish identity. As it happens, Cahan published several versions of this story. In the one I quoted at the beginning of the book, the one Cahan gave in his article for the *Atlantic Monthly*, the spokesman finished his speech with the cry, "To America, brethren! To America!"[9] He gave a slightly different version in his memoirs. There he leaves out the final cry, blandly substituting for it his own statement that these students came to be known as the "Americans," presumably because of their desire to emigrate to America. At the same time, he attributed to the speaker an equally emphatic, though slightly different affirmation of Jewishness. "We are your brothers," he has the group's leader say. "We are Jews, just like you. We are sorry that up till now we have thought of ourselves as Russians and not as Jews. . . . Yes, we are Jews." Cahan then supplies a detail that he had not included in the English version, describing how some Jewish radicals even started speaking Yiddish instead of Russian and changed back from their adopted Russian names to their original, Jewish ones. "Iakob, for example, started calling himself Yankel; Natasha would not answer until she was addressed as Etel [a Yiddish form of Esther]," he writes.[10] Cahan also gave a fictionalized version of this story in *The White Terror and the Red*, his novel about the Russian revolutionary movement. There the speaker who addresses the congregation abandons the Russian his listeners are accustomed to hearing from him and speaks Yiddish instead.[11]

Cahan goes on to say that Jewish revolutionaries who responded to the pogroms by becoming "nationalists," like the students in the synagogue, were small in number, and he tells of those who cheered the violence, believing that it signaled the beginning of a larger social and political revolution. Nonetheless, rediscovering one's Jewishness, whether or not this meant becoming a *bal tshuve* (penitent who returns to Judaism) and a nationalist, became the order of the day. With Jews under attack or under threat of attack in Russia, virtually every major figure in the Russian Jewish intelligentsia was drawn back to some sense of solidarity with the Jewish people. Chaim Zhitlovsky, who in his youth had been convinced that *"we were not Jews,"* now embarked on a spiritual journey that would ultimately lead him to repudiate his earlier assimilationism and formulate a theory combining socialism with the notion of Jewish national redemption. Morris Winchevsky, who in his youth had gnashed his teeth in anger every time he passed a *bes medresh*, went to London and began his career as a Yiddish journalist, helping to found the world's first radical Yiddish journal, *Der Poylisher Yidl* (The Polish Jew). Winchevsky now began to treat Jewish politics as a specifically Jewish, national problem.

Even the future Menshevik, Pavel Akselrod (1849 or 1850–1928), a

Jewish activist who more than most was to remain committed to a cosmopolitan ideal (that is, one unrestricted to a single national group) of Marxist social democracy, engaged in some serious soul-searching in 1881 and
1882. He wrote a pamphlet in which he offered one of the most sensitive
and penetrating accounts by any contemporary Jewish intellectual of the
position in which the pogroms had placed his people.[12]

After describing how Jewish intellectuals, who had been raised on Russian literature and had adopted a cosmopolitan political stance, cast aside
all concern for the Jewish masses, Akselrod tells how the pogroms opened
their eyes to the mistake they had made. The pogroms showed conclu-
sively that Jews were indeed a separate nation because all Russia treated
them that way. The Russian Jewish intelligentsia thus realized that in Russia, cosmopolitanism was out of place—the non-Jewish Russian masses,
after all, had just demonstrated that they were about as far from cosmopolitanism and class solidarity as one could be—and its members could properly dedicate themselves to their own people. This, he says, is the conclusion to which a significant part, if not the great majority, of the Jewish
intellectual youth had come.[13]

Jews who had been involved in the revolutionary movement, even members of *Narodnaia volia*, found an especially compelling reason to reevaluate their ethnic origins. On September 1, 1881, a proclamation was issued
in Ukraine, in the name of the Executive Committee of *Narodnaia volia*.
It was written in Ukrainian and was addressed to "the Ukrainian people."
In it the author congratulated the "people" for their recent acts of violence
against the Jews, saying that the Jews were indeed their oppressors. He
urged the people to continue their struggle against the Jews but also to
expand it to include as targets all landowners, both Jewish and non-Jewish, and the tsar himself.[14]

Narodnaia volia had counted a number of Jews among its members,
and Jewish men and women were involved in the assassination. It is easy
to understand the sense of betrayal this proclamation aroused among Jewish radicals, and even though it was later shown to be the work of a rogue
anti-Semite acting outside the authority of the Executive Committee, many
Jews who had dedicated their lives to what they saw as a broadly Russian,
or even cosmopolitan, revolutionary struggle understandably felt that
their non-Jewish comrades-in-arms had thrown in their lot with the forces
of medieval darkness and national hatred.

GOING TO THE (JEWISH) PEOPLE: IN RUSSIA

After the pogroms of 1881, those Jews who cared to do something about
their plight essentially had two options: to emigrate or to stay behind and
participate in a political movement that was going to be increasingly

worker-oriented and increasingly Jewish-oriented. Those who chose to emigrate can be classified according to their destination. A few chose to go to Western Europe, although Western Europe often turned out to be merely a way-station on a journey that ended either in America or, sometimes, back in Russia. Otherwise the choice was between America and Palestine. For those who were not leaving simply out of poverty and desperation, the choice usually represented a political attitude: America was for socialists, and Palestine was generally, but not always, for those who had strong feelings about the Jewish ancestral homeland. What was common to both groups was the sense that they were engaged in a "going to the people" and that the "people" in question were specifically the Jews.

In fact, "going to the people" was a feature of virtually all progressive Russian Jewish intellectual life after the pogroms, including the leadership of the labor movement, and this is why, as we will see later, the Jewish labor movement in the United States in so many of its phases was to adopt a Populist character in imitation of the Russian model. Again and again we find Jewish intellectuals referring to their own activities or to the activities of others in the movement in the same terms that were used for the Russian campaigns in 1874. In his pamphlet on the pogroms, Akselrod speaks twice of going to the people. In the first instance he refers to a seldom-mentioned "going to the *Jewish* people" movement, centered in St. Petersburg, that apparently was in the works even as the pogroms broke out. In the second instance, he calls upon Christian workers to conduct "agitation among the people" as a means of countering the anti-Semitic nature of the pogroms.[15]

Another case worth mentioning is the movement called *Am Olam* (the eternal people—in Yiddish pronunciation, *Am Oylem*). This movement urged emigration to Western lands where Jews would engage in a pursuit that had long been denied them, namely agriculture. Members of this movement actually established settlements in such unlikely places as South Dakota and Oregon. They also set up communes in New York City. Abe Cahan, in fact, came to the United States as part of an *Am Olam* group. The first organized groups in the *Am Olam* movement sprang up in Russia in the wake of the pogroms, and the ideology as well as the theoretical origins were thoroughly Populist. The idea was to take the Jewish people back to the soil, to make of them what the intended beneficiaries of the Russian Populist movement had always been: farmers, people of the earth.[16]

There are many more examples of the new Jewish Populist ideology as it expressed itself in the aftermath of the pogroms. More than one writer referred to the visits Jewish students paid to synagogues as "goings to the people."[17] "Going to the people" characterized a range of political ideologies, from emigrationism of the *Am Olam* sort, to Palestinophilism, to labor socialism both in the United States and in Russia.[18] What unites all these outlooks is the Lavrovian belief that the Jewish intelligentsia has a duty to lead its own common people in a political struggle for rights and economic well-being.

There is thus no doubt that 1881 represented a great divide for Russia's Jews. In an era when the Jewish intelligentsia could no longer afford to make theoretical work a central form of activity, when activity in its traditional sense for the intelligentsia as well as for the Jewish masses had truly become a matter of survival, Jewish politics swung sharply from the intellectual pole toward the practical pole. Being political meant doing Populist work and, once again, being Jewish.

Even such relatively intellectual work as propaganda in this era reflected the shift to being Jewish, as activists began to write for the first time in Yiddish, instead of Russian. The first illegal Socialist Revolutionary newspaper to be published in Yiddish appeared in Russia early in 1881. Like the extremely influential American Yiddish newspaper that appeared about a decade later in New York, it was called *Arbeter Tsaytung* (Workers' paper). Abraham Menes, a historian of the Jewish labor movement, wrote that the change in tactics in the Russian Jewish revolutionary movement from propaganda to agitation parallels the change from the use of Russian to the use of Yiddish, as an entire revolutionary culture in Yiddish was created.[19]

Certainly nothing in the history of Jewish radicalism in Russia more clearly represents a turn to practical work than the Jewish labor movement, whose activities eventually came to be concentrated in the organization known as the Bund (Yiddish for "alliance"), founded in 1897 in Vilna. The labor movement was Populism at its very best—though with industrial workers, not peasants, as the "people"—because it was truly a mass movement: at the height of its influence in Russia, in 1906, the Bund had some 40,000 members, according to one estimate.[20] The history of this movement shows that, like other Russian radical movements, it evolved from an intellectual, reading culture to a culture of action.

The principal modern historian of the Russian Bund, Henry J. Tobias, describes how the Bund and the movement leading up to it grew out of a system of reading circles in the mid-1880s. He shows that the Bund's pioneers were at first primarily teachers and students, who turned to practical work fairly late in their careers. And though the Bund was to adopt a heavily Marxist ideology, much of what these pioneers taught and studied was the literary and the intellectual culture associated with Nihilism and Populism.[21]

As always in the story of the Russian and the Russian Jewish revolutionary intelligentsia, propaganda and agitation were never entirely distinct. The Bund, with its successful campaigns to organize and mobilize Jewish labor, with its efforts to improve working conditions through strikes and other forms of direct action, with its general focus on agitation over propaganda, was deeply committed to true action. But this meant it was also committed to an active intellectual shaping of its followers. Ezra Mendelsohn has described how the Bund set out to make its members over as people, changing their personal habits, offering them a new secular religion in place of the Judaism they had grown up with, in short, making of them a Jewish version of what Chernyshevsky idealistically promised in the subtitle of *What Is to Be Done?*: they would be "new people." All this was the result of agitation—and propaganda. Agitation stemmed from theoretical training, which meant reading, which meant propaganda. As Mendelsohn shows, the true leaders in the messianic movement toward newness participated in political circles and agitated too, that is, they were readers, teachers, and doers, all with a view to establishing a new sort of Jewish being.[22]

The Bund did not provide the Jewish radical movement in America with its initial leadership; it came too late for that. By the time the Bund came into existence, the American Jewish radical movement was well under way. But Bund members came to the United States. Since the peak period of Jewish immigration to the United States was the decade immediately preceding World War I and since this decade included the time when Bund membership was at its highest, many Jewish workers who came from Russia after the turn of the century were likely to have been involved in Bundist politics. And while the ideological spirit of the Jewish labor movement in America owed far more to such figures as Abe Cahan, people, that is, who had been schooled in the earlier, pre-Marxist phase of the Russian revolutionary movement, the Bundists still served the function of strengthening theoretical elements—Marxism, for example—that many of the original founders had begun to develop only after arriving in their new homeland. They also contributed to the spirit of activism that the first generation of immigrants had developed.

Going to the other shore was itself, of course, a significant form of action, and, for many besides the desperate, an expression of Populist ideology. Once they arrived, Jewish intellectuals had a considerable amount of practical work cut out for them: there was, at the most basic level, a living to be made, but there was also a movement (or several movements) to be built. And when it came time to build a movement, the intellectuals showed their Russian roots by mingling the professions of writer-publicist and organizer-activist, not only in the sense that many leaders of the new movement engaged in both forms of activity, but also in the sense that, as in Russia, the two forms of activity, propaganda and agitation, were not always clearly distinguished.

Contributing to and editing a mass-circulation workers' newspaper in Yiddish was itself a form of action, just as writing *What Is to Be Done?* had been a form of action. To be sure, publishing a workers' newspaper in Yiddish was no more a form of action than publishing one in some other language, and political writing of this sort is always designed to have a practical effect. But the Jewish immigrant intellectuals, when they wrote and published, were conscious of following the Nihilist model of political action (where intellectual work is a form of action), in this case for the practical purpose of building a labor movement. In addition, they imported that model as an intellectual, cultural concept and disseminated it, together with enormous amounts of general information about Russian politics and culture, in their new homeland. This is one of the most significant ways in which Russian politics and culture came to the other shore.

PART TWO

CHAPTER 5

Coming to Shore

THE FEW THOUSAND Jews who left the Russian Empire for the United States in the first few years after the pogroms of 1881 undoubtedly knew that there was already a Jewish community in America. They may not all have known that there were already Russians. Abe Cahan and Michael Zametkin, for example, who both arrived in 1882, found a number of non-Jewish Russian intellectuals who would shortly become their collaborators in the political-intellectual arena. William Frey, born Vladimir Konstantinovich Geins, a highly visible non-Jewish figure in the early years of Jewish political activity in New York, had come to the United States in 1868 and had spent some time trying to set up communal colonies in Kansas. Vladimir Stoleshnikov, a former follower of Russian radical Petr Tkachev, had come in the late 1870s. And Sergei Schevitsch, a multilingual Russian nobleman whose incalculable influence on the movement Cahan described in his memoirs, had immigrated in the 1870s and had become an editor for the German-language socialist paper *Die New Yorker Volkszeitung*.[1] Frey and Schevitsch, in fact, had been involved in the agrarian *Am Olam* movement, though they were not Jews.

A progressive political movement, even a socialist movement, was already well under way in America by the early 1880s. The non-Jewish Russians themselves had found their way into various forms of activity that smacked of both the mid-nineteenth century in Russia—one scholar of the era refers to this group as *shestidesiatniki*, "men of the sixties," that is, men like Chernyshevsky—and various European trends.[2] Frey, for example, declared himself a positivist in the spirit of Auguste Comte, much like Russians of the Nihilist generation, and fulfilled a Russian Populist dream in the 1870s by joining an agricultural commune in Kansas and becoming a crusader for vegetarianism. Other Russian émigrés joined Frey in his communal venture in Kansas.

In the 1870s, though, the American radical movement was dominated by German immigrants, many of them political refugees from the failed European revolutions of 1848, and Schevitsch's collaboration on the *Volkszeitung* shows how he and his fellow *shestidesiatniki* had linked up with that movement. German immigrants were instrumental in establishing affiliates of the Marxist International in America, and it was Germans who in 1869 founded the first important American political organization to have a Marxist program. Morris Hillquit, in his history of socialism in

4. Michael Zametkin in 1890.

the United States, acknowledges his own debt to the Germans by saying
that the true history of the socialist movement in America can be dated
from the foundation of this organization.[3]

The *Volkszeitung*, one of the major forces in American socialism, had
begun publication in 1878. Its inaugural issue contained a quotation
from Marx over its editorial statement of purpose, which pledged the
paper's resources to the struggle against class rivalry, wage slavery, and
the unequal distribution of property.[4] This newspaper would play a central role in the political and intellectual future of the newly arrived Russian Jewish intellectuals, especially Cahan, who claims that many immi-

5. Morris Hillquit in 1901.

grants learned German before they learned English, just so they could read the *Volkszeitung*.[5]

So when intellectuals like Cahan and Zametkin arrived, the closest thing to an organized and ideologically coherent group they found was the one surrounding the publication of the *Volkszeitung*. And what gave this group its ideological coherence was its Marxism, something that was relatively new to many of the men and women who had been schooled "in Chernyshevsky's *kheyder*." In addition to (and in some cases collaborating with) the German Marxists were the sixties- and seventies-types from Russia whose ideology one could not describe more succinctly than to say it sounded like Russian Nihilism or Russian Populism—or a little of both. In this jumble of worldviews Cahan had a spiritual-political crisis in 1887 that led him to abandon the anarchism he had officially embraced during his first years in the United States and to take up the banner of Marxism instead. As he put it in his memoirs, at this moment a fog lifted from his brain and he felt he had "come to shore."[6]

The subsequent history of the Russian Jewish émigré intelligentsia will certainly show that Cahan was not the only one whose passage to shore was obscured by fog. Conditions in the United States forced all immigrant intellectuals to reevaluate entrenched political views that they had acquired in Russia. But the confusion went even deeper than political outlook. It went to one's national and ethnic identity, too. For, despite the crisis of identity that the pogroms and their aftermath had so recently brought upon these immigrants (a crisis that in many cases was responsible for their *being* immigrants), despite the recent memory of having been forced to confront anew the fact of their Jewishness, many Jewish intellectuals arrived in America with the idea that they would now be free to pursue their old political dream from before the pogroms, that is, to be Russians, cosmopolitans, intellectuals, socialists, any such thing they chose, but not (or not primarily) Jews.

Considered in the context of the entire period of mass immigration, this phase would not last very long. Before too long, the intellectuals would have to recognize and affirm their Jewishness, if only for the pragmatic purpose of gaining a political audience among their fellow Jews. But even after this, most intellectuals did not for a minute cease thinking of themselves as Russians. And one of the clearest signs of this fact is the very nature of the material that constitutes the bulk of evidence in the story I am telling. The press, in addition to lectures and meetings, is where the political and cultural drama of the Russian Jewish immigrants is played. The Russian Jewish intellectuals never stopped being civic critics, like Chernyshevsky, Dobroliubov, and Pisarev. Nor did they ever stop regarding the life of letters—in the press or, more rarely, in books and pamphlets—as a life of action.

CHAPTER 6

"We Are Russian Workers and Besides in America"

WRITING IN RUSSIAN

No ONE expressed the position of the Russian Jewish *intelligent* in America and the problems of national and linguistic identity better than Abe Cahan, in a passage in his memoirs. He is describing his early years in America. His friends at the time fit into three categories: those who spoke Russian (and in most cases Yiddish too, but preferred Russian), those who spoke Yiddish but no Russian, and those who spoke English. His Russian-speaking friends were intellectuals, and they included a man named Nicholas Aleinikoff and his family. These were the people with whom Cahan ran political meetings and spent time after those meetings. Even with the friends who helped him organize socialist meetings for Yiddish-speaking workers, Cahan says, he would speak only Russian when they were by themselves. He explains this, at the same time showing the mass of conflicting emotions the linguistic problem aroused in him. In the society of his Russian speaking friends, he says,

> I felt completely different from the way I felt among my Yiddish-speaking friends. During the last few years I spent in Russia I had spoken very little Yiddish. Russian was the language of my intellectual [*inteligent*] self. I thought in Russian.
>
> I always spoke Yiddish, however, the way all Jews do, and I always loved the language—"the way Mama speaks"—and often fought for it. Some of my friends from the south of Russia would treat it with contempt, and I would get into heated debates with them, show them how succulent [*zaftig*] and powerful our *mame-loshn* is and how one can express the most beautiful and most delicate thoughts in it.
>
> Among my Russian-speaking friends, I felt more at home [*heymish*], and yet Yiddish had a strong pull on me, much stronger than it had in Russia. When I would run into a *landsman* from the old country I would throw myself upon him and take great pleasure in the Yiddish I spoke with him.[1]

Other Russian Jewish intellectuals, however, appear to have felt the conflict a little less strongly in the early years of mass immigration. "We are Russian workers and besides in America." So wrote the editors of *Znamia* (The Banner), the first Russian-language newspaper to appear in America in the period of mass immigration. In the beginning, there is no doubt the intellectuals viewed themselves as Russians first and Jews second, or, in some cases, Russians first and Jews not at all. And, despite the humble tone of their claim to be "workers," there is also no doubt the *Znamia* editors were following the Russian, Lavrovian model of top-down organization. They were the "critically thinking individuals" leading the masses, except that, for a number of years, they seem to have forgotten entirely who those masses were and how to lead them.

The first political organizations the immigrants formed were Russian in name and used the Russian language as the primary medium of communication. And the first newspapers the immigrants published were Russian in name, were written in Russian, and made few overt references to the fact that almost all the editors, contributors, and advertisers—with such obviously Jewish names as Gurvich, Kagan (Cahan), and Margolies—were Jewish.

Consider the names of the early political associations. In early 1884, a group of Jewish immigrants organized the Russian Workingmen's Union (*Russkii rabochii soiuz*), whose purpose was to sift through the baffling array of different ideologies in circulation and find a coherent position. The name was clearly disingenuous on two counts: the organizers were Jewish in addition to being Russian, and they were not really workingmen but intellectuals. When the Union split later the same year, a new, competing organization was formed by Abe Cahan and some others. It was called the Russian Labor Lyceum, and it, too, conducted its business almost exclusively in Russian.

Most of the organizations formed in those early years were short-lived and ineffectual. Their importance lies in the contributions they made to the political and philosophical development of the intellectuals who would later assume positions of true leadership. The Russian Workingmen's Union did not do much to advance the interests of Russian workingmen, and the Labor Lyceum had little impact on labor. Still, in the welter of clubs and circles that came and went in the 1880s, two have a symbolic importance in the history of Russian Jewish immigration. The Russian-Jewish Workingmen's Association (*Rusisher-idisher arbayter farayn*), formed in January 1885 from a group that had started out calling itself the Russian Workingmen's *Party*, was the first political group of its sort to include the word "Jewish," or any reference to Jews, in its name. As Cahan describes the organization in his memoirs, it was designed to steer newly arrived Jewish workers away from anarchism, and though Cahan consented to give speeches at their meetings, this was before his moment of coming "to shore," and his loyalty to the anarchist cause prevented him from joining.

The second organization absorbed the first and called itself simply the Jewish Workingmen's Association (*Idisher arbayter farayn*). The dropping of the word "Russian" from the name is significant, because it repre-

sents an early effort to abandon the elitist Russian model of political leadership and reach out to the working masses of immigrant Jews. So is the
change of language used for the name. The new organization largely
switched over from Russian to Yiddish, allocated funds for the establishment of a Yiddish newspaper, and devoted itself to bridging the gap between intelligentsia and workers.[2] It thus shows an early step in a process
that would lead the intelligentsia to recognize the necessity of using Yiddish and eventually to adopt that language in order to communicate with
the working masses.[3]

But the insight that led to the introduction of the word "Jewish" into
the names of political organizations does not appear to have carried over
to the Russian-language press quite so soon. In fact, the Russian-language
press first came into existence only after the political groups had begun
reaching out to the Yiddish-speaking workers, and, oddly, though it was
produced by the very same people who had been involved in the political
groups, it largely ignored Jewish issues.

The Russian-language press in America can be divided into two phases
during the era of mass immigration. With only a few exceptions, Russian
newspapers were published either between 1889 and 1894 or after 1910.
The earlier phase is the one that is associated with the period when the
intelligentsia was struggling with its national identity.[4]

THE FIRST PHASE

In fact, national identity is one of two pressing concerns that emerge in
the early Russian newspapers. At issue is not only whether the Russian
intellectuals consider themselves to be Jews, but even whether the ultimate target of their revolutionary activity is the workers in America or the
Russian *narod* that they were forced to abandon when they emigrated.
The second concern is the role the intelligentsia is to play in the revolutionary movement that still lies ahead. Are the intellectuals to continue in
the role of "critically thinking individuals," as so much of Russian Populist theory, and especially Lavrov in his Populist period, had urged, or are
they to step aside and allow the natural, dialectical (not a word they used)
process of history to take its course, that is, allow the workers spontane-
ously to revolt without the benefit of their theoretical goad, as some followers of Marx would urge?

Znamia (1889–90) is a perfect illustration of the conflicts the Russian
Jewish community faced.[5] The nameplate of the newspaper appears over
a banner (*znamia* means "banner") bearing the closing words of the
Communist Manifesto. The programmatic statement of the inaugural
issue, a salad of left-Hegelian and Marxist phrases, loudly proclaims the
paper's adherence to the new gospel that had lifted the fog for Abe

Cahan. But everything else about the paper is Russian. It was launched by Lev Bandes, who had been a comrade of Abe Cahan in Vilna and who died of tuberculosis only two months into the *Znamia* venture. Bandes's younger brother Louis, who had adopted the last name Miller on coming to America and who would remain one of the most influential members of the immigrant Jewish intelligentsia, took over after him. Schevitsch was involved in the activities that led to the founding of *Znamia*, and Stoleshnikov participated in editing the journal, in addition to contributing two poems.[6] Also contributing to the paper were men who would soon become the most influential members of the Russian Jewish intellectual vanguard in America: Philip Krantz, who had authored the impassioned plea for emigration that appeared in *Razsvet* in August of 1881; Michael Zametkin, a frequent contributor to both the Russian and, later, the Yiddish press; Morris Hillquit (signing himself "M. Gil'kovich," the Russified version of his original name), one of the most visible immigrant Jewish intellectuals of the era, a founder of the Socialist Party in 1901, a mayoral candidate in New York City in 1917, and the author of a respected history of socialism in the United States; and David Edelstadt, who would soon become famous as a Yiddish-language poet.

But these were only the "American" contributors. The contents of many issues of *Znamia* make the publication look like a Russian revolutionary organ pure and simple. There are contributions by Pavel Akselrod, Petr Lavrov, and Vera Zasulich, renowned in revolutionary circles for her attempt in 1878 to assassinate the governor of St. Petersburg. *Znamia* serialized a novel by Chernyshevsky and published an article on Chernyshevsky by Lavrov. The primary focus of the paper is always Russia and the movement in Russia, so, in addition to reading about the pantheon of Russian revolutionary heroes and heroines, we read about such events as a gathering in Cooper Union whose purpose is to "curse the Tsar."[7]

Still, the driving force behind the paper is clearly the intellectuals for whom *Znamia* was an initial foray into the arena of "civic criticism," with little fear of government reprisal. And, with the exception of Schevitsch and Stoleshnikov, these intellectuals were Jews. That is why there is something very odd about an editorial policy that is clearly designed to conceal this fact.

Again and again the reader of *Znamia* is reminded that the ultimate goal of radical activity in the United States is the political advancement of the Russian *narod*. This is partly because the paper printed so much material by writers who were living in Russia or Western Europe and devoting their lives to the Russian struggle. Pavel Akselrod's article on "The relation of the revolutionary intelligentsia in Russia to the struggle for political freedom" is, not surprisingly, about the Russian movement and not the American. Yet it is addressed to Akselrod's American comrades and to readers who may have a variety of specialized interests, as Akselrod himself says. Akselrod is confident that an article about Russian life is bound to be instructive for these readers.[8]

A contribution by Lavrov is even clearer on this point. It is called "Our tasks. A letter to comrades in America," and, in it, the author unequivocally addresses his American fellow fighters but never loses sight of what he regards as their ultimate purpose, namely to further the cause of the Russian movement.[9] Nothing could be less ambiguous than this statement: "There lies before the vast majority of Russian socialists both in America and in other countries outside the homeland, in the name of their socialist convictions and in the name of the means by which they can develop individually, one difficult task: to prepare themselves for the struggle in their distant homeland, the struggle for the future of the Russian people under social conditions very distinct from those under which this struggle has originated."[10] Or this: "The possibility of a victory for the socialists in New York or Chicago is an extra chance for the future victory of socialism in Russia, too."[11]

Even when Philip Krantz comes to express his views, the story is much the same. In a letter to the editor called "The present field of activity," published in February of 1890, Krantz discusses the labor movement in America and in particular the Jewish labor movement.[12] This, incidentally, is the place where he says that he had taught himself Yiddish as an adult.[13] Despite this, and even though he calls for more writing in Yiddish and announces the imminent inauguration of his own Yiddish newspaper, *Di Arbayter Tsaytung* (The workers' paper), he never so much as intimates that he himself is a Jew. His proud announcement that he had taught himself Yiddish could easily have been written by a Gentile.

Throughout his article Krantz has adopted the identity of a Russian, not a Jewish, intellectual living abroad, and at the end he addresses the needs of his class. Native Russian intellectuals, he says, in the expectation of better times at home, when they can better wage a struggle for their own people, can lend support, at least of a "literary" sort, to the Jewish labor movement in particular and to the American movement in general. In short, they can support *Znamia*.[14] And, to give his plea additional moral authority, he quotes a passage from Lavrov's "Our tasks," printed three weeks earlier, in which the great Populist leader had said that "the Russian socialist in America may and must participate in all the peripeties of the struggle between labor and capital that are occurring around him, until he is in a position to take part directly in the struggle in his homeland."[15] If this is the line that *Znamia* was still taking in the second year of its existence, then it should come as no surprise that the obituary of its first editor, Lev Bandes, a year earlier, praised the late revolutionary's work for the "humiliated and insulted" (as in the title of Dostoevsky's novel) in America as a sign of his "burning love for his homeland."[16]

Znamia was also wrestling with the issue of political identity. The article by Akselrod I mentioned is largely devoted to a critique of the traditional role that the intelligentsia has played in the Russian revolutionary movement. Akselrod is eager to abandon Lavrov's earlier notion of a class of "critically thinking individuals" in favor of an intelligentsia that belongs to the workers.[17] And yet a half-year after Akselrod's article appeared, Lavrov, who himself had presumably tempered his enthusiasm for an all-powerful intelligentsia, is writing in the pages of *Znamia* about socialism as the movement "in which all the most advanced [*peredovye*] Russian minds hope to find the salvation of our homeland."[18] "Advanced minds" are not those of the workers or peasants; they are those of the intelligentsia, which even in this stage of Lavrov's thinking is entrusted with the responsibility of preparing the masses for revolution.

And Krantz, as he surveys the impressive series of recent successes in the American labor movement, is careful to toe the editorial line *Znamia* had established from the first, giving credit not to "great and renowned thinkers, writers, or orators," but to the "natural movement of the class struggle as it flows from the very conditions of the capitalist order."[19] Yet no sooner has he pronounced this bit of social democratic piety than he reverts to the Lavrovian model he was never able to abandon. If only we could garner the support of more Russian Jewish *intellectuals*, especially those who might reach out to the masses by writing in Yiddish, he muses, the number of unions and "conscious socialists" would increase threefold. After belittling the role of thinkers, writers, and orators, he complains that "so few truly capable and developed journalists and orators" are participating in the workers' movement.[20] Krantz's use of the originally Hegelian term *developed* (*razvityi*) as a qualifier for an individual is reminiscent of Lavrov's theory of individual development and his identification of it as the source of human progress.[21]

Progress (1891–94), a somewhat brainier journal than *Znamia*, appears to have picked up where *Znamia* left off, and it shows essentially the same tendencies as its predecessor. The dominant figure in this journal was Isaac Hourwich, who was known in Russian circles as I. A. Gurvich. Hourwich was an exact contemporary of Cahan and was, like Cahan, born in Vilna. Like many others of his generation he had come to the United States because he was having political troubles at home, and like many others he had spent some time in prison. A secular intellectual from top to bottom, he was just finishing a doctoral dissertation at Columbia called "The Economics of the Russian Village" at the time he began publishing *Progress*.[22]

Progress betrays the identity of its intended readership on its advertising pages. Not only are almost all the advertisers Jewish (there is a Katz, a Goldstein, a Bresler, a Sachs Brothers), but many are important figures from the Russian Jewish progressive movement. We find, for example, an ad for the services of Nikolai Aleinikov (spelled in Cyrillic characters), identified as a member of the law firm Wakeman and Cambell. Nicholas Aleinikoff (as he came to spell his name in America) was the leader of the Am Olam group in Kiev. One member of Aleinikoff's Am Olam group was a young intellectual named Anna Bronshteyn, who had become Abe Cahan's wife in 1885. A reader who looks carefully will find an ad for a teacher of English named Anna Kagan—the Russian form of Anna Cahan. Also advertising his legal services is E. (Eliezer) S. Mashbir (printed in roman letters in an ad whose text is half-English and half-Russian), a member of the Am Olam group that had brought Cahan himself to America.[23]

The editorial statements in *Progress* show the hesitation between Russian and Jewish identity, between Lavrovism and Marxism that characterized *Znamia*. The opening statement in the first issue, "A Russian newspaper on American soil," announces clearly that the political struggle in Russia is the primary interest of the editors, who see themselves as participating in the international effort to attract public opinion in the West that will be favorable to the Russian "nihilists" (the editors themselves put this word in quotation marks).[24] So the big question is this: "What can these Americans do for Russia?" And in the one phrase that mentions the Jewish identity of the Russian immigrants to whom this newspaper is addressed, the unnamed writer says that "class interests and spiritual solidarity link the local Russian Jewish population with the oppressed masses in Russia."[25]

Like Krantz, the editors of *Progress* are eager to move away from the early Lavrov's faith in "critically thinking individuals," but like Krantz their entire conceptual apparatus is dominated by Lavrov. The very first column of the first issue contains the phrase "highly developed individuals," though it appears as part of a claim that the sympathies of such individuals in America are not sufficient for waging a struggle in the name of a foreign (that is, the Russian) people. The editorial statement that opens the second issue takes the orthodox social-democrat tack of locating the source of revolutionary force in the "naturally historical movement of the development of capitalist industry" (here using *development* in the sense in which it was used by Marx and Engels, who borrowed it from Hegel), rather than in the "propaganda of socialist ideas," but it ends with stirring words that show the hybrid of Marxism and Lavrovism that was typical of this era: "We know that our ideas constitute the scientific expression of an historical process that is being accomplished, that the truthful and objective exposition of the facts of real life must lead every critically thinking individual into the camp of the socialists."[26] If the allusion was not sufficiently obvious, the reader could find Lavrov's own words in the pages of *Progress*, once in the first issue and once a few months later in a brief letter to the editor.[27]

Progress never had a circulation of more than 1,500.[28] But it attracted attention even outside the Russian-speaking community. The editorial statement I just mentioned is titled "Concerning our program." The editors did not trouble to print their program, because, as they point out at the beginning of the article, that program had already been published in Philip Krantz's *Arbayter Tsaytung* (in *Russian*, for the intellectual reader of that Yiddish-language paper), in the *New Yorker Volkszeitung* (in German), and in the socialist *The People* (in English).

But without some prior knowledge of the organization behind *Progress*, the Russian-speaking reader of *Arbayter Tsaytung*, the German-speaking reader of the *Volkszeitung*, and the English-speaking reader of *The People* would not have guessed that the new socialist newspaper was aimed specifically at Jews. The notice in *The People* describes the intended readers of the new paper as simply "the Russian colony of America." The programmatic statement begins with a reference to "the terrible despotism of the Czars," continues with a Marxist analysis of a society "based upon the exploitation of the non-possessors by the possessors," and then lists the chief purposes of *Progress*: "To maintain the moral kinship between the thousands of Russian-Americans and Russia herself, to wake up and strengthen the sympathies for the Russian revolutionary movement, in a word, to serve to the best of our abilities the cause of Russian freedom." And, while the authors of the "program" promise to discuss American affairs, the bulk of the material concerns purely Russian matters.[29]

What was true of *Znamia* and *Progress* was true for almost all the Russian-language periodicals published in New York for the remainder of the nineteenth century. Almost all were minor and short-lived; almost all announced themselves as Russian but were in reality published by and written for Russian-speaking Jewish intellectuals; all were the affair of an educated elite. *Russkii Listok* (Russian leaflet), which appeared for a short time in 1892, billed itself as simply an information sheet for what it estimated to be 200,000 Russian immigrants in New York. *Russkie Novosti* (Russian news), which appeared in 1893, dedicated itself to "the interests of truth, humanity, and freedom" without party or national affiliation. The publisher of both was George M. Price, himself an educated Russian Jew who had come to the United States in 1882 and who in 1892 was completing a series of articles in Russian on the experiences of his fellow immigrants. These articles were published in St. Petersburg in the Jewish newspaper *Voskhod* (Sunrise), then collected and brought out as *The Russian Jews in America*, also in St. Petersburg.[30]

To judge from the description he gives of himself, Price was the very picture of a Russian Nihilist, complete with long hair, a pince-nez, and his Russian school uniform, when he first arrived in America, and he felt obliged right away to part with a substantial portion of his pocket money in order to get a haircut and some new clothes.[31] Price quickly became a sort of professional supplier of Russian culture to the émigré community in the United States, as one can tell from the advertising pages of numerous periodicals, where G. M. Price & Co. offered Russian books for sale. Despite the Anglicized name he adopted in America ("Price" for the Russian Jewish "Prais," from the Yiddish word for "Prussian"), on the one hand, and his involvement in what appeared to be purely Russian cultural activities, on the other, Price was a Jewish intellectual, and his newspapers show it despite themselves. The advertising pages reveal the standard array of names (Aleinikoff, Mashbir, Hourwich, Louis Miller, and so on), and the interests are clearly those of the Jewish immigrant community.

From time to time, these interests appear explicitly. In the midst of news from Europe and Russia, *Russkii Listok* prints notices about Jewish mutual aid organizations, Baron de Hirsch's Colonization Association, and other Jewish philanthropic organizations in New York.[32] *Russkie Novosti*, alongside news from Russia, prints a "Letter from a Jew to Alexander III," a notice for a celebration in honor of *Arbayter Tsaytung* at which one Ab. Kagan (Abe Cahan) will be a featured speaker, and many other references to such prominent Jewish intellectuals as Cahan and Hourwich.[33] The editor of this paper was Jacob Gordin, who had arrived in America only two years earlier and begun writing his plays for the Yiddish stage. In 1893, Gordin, who would soon be recognized as the preeminent Yiddish playwright in the country, if not in the world, was still writing articles in Russian.

Other Russian-language newspapers are the same. "Do we need a Russian newspaper in America?" asks an editorial in *Russko-Amerikanskii Vestnik* (Russian-American herald) in 1893. The author, Grigorii Dolinskii, proclaims members of his immigrant community to be full-fledged Russian-Americans and uses his article to address the needs of the Russian intelligentsia. But one of the primary concerns he raises is the "Russian Jewish question" and the need to "convince Russian society of the injustice and impracticality of persecuting the Jews." This paper and its predecessor, *Spravochnyi Listok* (Information leaflet), which appeared in 1892 and 1893, were edited by an I. Rozental' and by Mitia Gretsch, presumably the Gretsch who was a friend of Cahan and a founder of the Jewish Workingmen's Association.[34]

But in some cases, Jewish concerns were almost entirely absent. Perhaps the most clearly "Russian" of all Russian American journals in this phase of the Russian American press was the last one to be published in the nineteenth century, called *Ezhegodnik* (Annual). It appeared once, in 1899, and was the official organ of the Russian Social Democratic Society. This organization was founded by Dr. Sergei Ingerman and served as a sort of American outpost for the theories of Akselrod. The journal was even more directly focused on Russian issues than the other Russian-language journals of the period, containing virtually nothing related to the Jewish question, and yet, with one exception, every contributor was Jewish.[35]

THE SECOND PHASE

After the turn of the century, the Russian-language press in America offers a considerably more complicated picture than in its earlier phase. In the 1880s and 1890s, every Russian-language periodical in America was essentially an organ of the Jewish intelligentsia. It was here that the fledgling Jewish progressive movement, presenting itself as Russian, had given the news and political theory that would serve as guidance to a group of activists who were almost exclusively Jewish and intellectual. When the next phase of the Russian-language press in America opens, at the end of the first decade of the twentieth century, there are more Russian-language publications than ever before, including many whose editors and writers are not Jewish and many that are not politically progressive in orientation. But even among those that are, circumstances have changed considerably.

To begin with, Russia itself has entered a new political era, with the reforms that followed the unsuccessful 1905 Revolution. Among Russian émigrés, then, Jewish or not, there is a new sense of urgency in the need for political action that directly affects Russia. In addition, the revolutionary movement in Russia has been divided into several discrete factions, each with its own distinct political ideology and each generally hostile to the others. Earlier, to be sure, there had been Nihilists, Populists, anarchists, and eventually Marxists, and there had certainly been plenty of friction between these groups. But now a collection of political parties has sprung up that is far more influential and, above all, far more internationally visible than such conspiratorial societies as *Narodnaia volia* had ever been. Now the immediate future of Russia looks very different to a Bolshevik, a Menshevik, and a Socialist Revolutionary. Finally, since the 1890s, the Yiddish-language press in America has taken over as a forum for political discussion directly affecting the Jewish community. As a result, a Russian Jewish intellectual who decides to write an article in a Russian publication will generally use this forum to examine Russia specifically, to treat socialism broadly and internationally, or to discuss issues in the American political scene that are not specifically Jewish.

Nonetheless, Jewish intellectuals, many of whom were concurrently writing for the Yiddish press, continued to find reasons to publish in Russian, and the politically progressive Russian press in this new phase would certainly have been different without them. A dominant figure in one of the earliest publications of this phase, *Russko-Amerikanskii Rabo-*

chii (The Russian-American worker), was M. Baranov (pseudonym of Moyshe Gormidor, 1864–1924). Baranov's profile is very much like that of such other formidably talented émigrés as Hourwich and Krantz. Like Hourwich, he came from a family that had moved toward modern, enlightened thinking, and like Krantz, with whom he worked in London, he was not initially at home in Yiddish—in fact, the articles he wrote for Krantz's Yiddish-language newspaper in London in the late 1880s had to be translated from Russian into Yiddish. He had come to America in 1895, after a series of arrests and imprisonments in Russia and periods of exile in Europe, and by 1908, when *Russko-Amerikanskii Rabochii* appeared, he was already a well-known and prolific contributor to the *Forward* and other Yiddish publications.[36]

Baranov's persona in the Yiddish press had hesitated between that of a Russian intellectual and that of a Russian Jewish intellectual. The bulk of his contributions concerned Russian politics, history, and literature and the array of Western European interests that had enlivened Russian intellectual life in the mid-nineteenth century. But he also wrote an occasional article that recognized his own and his readers' Jewishness, like the reviews of Yiddish theatre he wrote for *Arbayter Tsaytung*.

But in the Russian press, Baranov was strictly a Russian intellectual surveying both the American and the Russian scene, his eye sometimes ultimately on Russia but never on the Jews. In an article on a workers' demonstration in New York, for example, he turns to the topic of terror as a revolutionary tactic and sees fit to conclude with a lengthy discussion of the advisability of using this tactic in Russia.[37] His article on the success of American socialism is a quasi-Marxist analysis of the contemporary political scene in America, again without reference to the Jews.[38] And a letter to the editor is devoted entirely to an ideological dispute with a rival Russian-language newspaper.[39] *Russko-Amerikanskii Rabochii* was published by the Russian-American Social-Democratic League and thus in a sense continues the work of Ingerman's *Ezhegodnik*, so it is no surprise that it subordinates Jewish concerns to larger political concerns.

This is how it went with the most influential Russian-language papers of the teens. One could characterize this era fairly accurately by referring to the presence of Leo Deutsch in the United States from 1911 to 1916. During this time, Deutsch was contributing numerous articles in Yiddish to *Di Tsukunft*, but even though many of these were about Jews, the topic in such instances was always the role of Jews in the Russian revolutionary movement. Deutsch had always been hostile to the idea of a Jewish movement distinct from the Russian movement, and his activities in the United States showed that he was generally indifferent not only to the needs of the Jews as a separate group but also, perhaps because of the relatively short time he spent in America, to the American labor movement as distinguished from the Russian revolutionary movement.

6. The cover of the first issue of *Di Tsukunft*. The words on the tablets are "Workers of all countries, unite!"

The two Russian-language journals with which Deutsch was associated show different levels of interest in the American movement, but they appear to be equally disengaged from the particular needs of the Jewish community, though both were clearly dominated by Jewish immigrants. *Novyi Mir* (New world, 1911–38) was one of the most influential Russian-language journals in America, reportedly with a circulation of over fourteen thousand in 1914.[40] Deutsch was the founding editor, but it was edited at various times by Baranov, Ingerman, and another Russian Jewish intellectual who resided briefly in the United States—Leon Trotsky. The other journal was the monthly *Svobodnoe slovo* (The free word, 1915–16), which was sponsored by the Russian Social Democratic Party and which served as a forum for some of the elite theoreticians of the social democratic movement in America.

Deutsch, together with Georgy Plekhanov (the "father of Russian Marxism") and Pavel Akselrod, had organized *Gruppa osvobozhdeniia truda* (Group for the liberation of labor), the first Russian Marxist group outside of Russia, in 1883, and the interests of that group are clearly visible in both of Deutsch's Russian-language publishing ventures. The names of Deutsch's comrades appear frequently in the pages of *Novyi Mir* and *Svobodnoe Slovo*, but in addition to this, both journals are devoted to the advancement of the social democratic program in Russia, as the reader of *Novyi Mir* is reminded in the regular feature "What's happening in the homeland?" The second issue of *Svobodnoe Slovo* begins with an article by Deutsch on a conference of social democrats and socialist revolutionaries in Geneva that had issued an appeal to the "conscious working population of Russia," a phrase that, with its emphasis on the role that workers with a developed consciousness can play in the face of impersonal, historical forces, betrays the peculiar Marxist slant of its authors. The signatories to the appeal include, in addition to the entire editorial board of *Svobodnoe Slovo*, Plekhanov and Akselrod.[41]

Svobodnoe Slovo enjoyed the collaboration of another extraordinary Russian Jewish immigrant, Louis Boudin (signing himself Budin in Russian and either Budyanov or Budin-Budyanov in Yiddish), who had come to the United States in 1891, at the age of seventeen. Boudin (1874–1952) had completed an American university education and law school by seven years later, contributed extensively over the years to the Yiddish and English-language press, elaborated what may well be the first sustained Marxist theory of literary criticism to appear in America, and published, in English, a widely respected book on Marxism.[42]

Like so many others of his intellectual class, Boudin had written material in Yiddish that had acknowledged the fact of Jewish identity in America. But when he wrote for *Svobodnoe Slovo*, he was a pure Russian intellectual, a cosmopolitan. In fact, on one occasion he appears to go out of his way to thumb his nose at the Yiddish-speaking socialists. In an article on the war in Europe (he is writing in 1915) and the American socialists, he says that he wishes to speak of only those socialists who can be called American and who speak English. He makes an exception, however, for the group that writes for the *New Yorker Volkszeitung* since the members of this group (unlike the Jews, he seems to hint) are "completely free of any nationalistic inclinations and prejudices whatsoever."[43]

There is another document that shows the detachment of this group from specifically Jewish affairs. Boudin apparently wrote to Deutsch sometime in 1912 requesting his participation in a journal. Deutsch's reply survives in Boudin's collected correspondence. It is in Russian, the language in which Deutsch was most at ease as a writer and correspondent, and it in turn contains an invitation to Boudin. Deutsch says he is working on the first issue of a journal to be titled "Golos pravdy" (The voice of truth). He lists the titles of the articles he has planned: there is a programmatic statement, a general piece on openness (*glasnost'*) and truth, an essay on the electoral campaign in Russia, but nothing that has to do with the Jews, in either Russia or America. Apparently nothing ever came of this project, but the description Deutsch gives of it makes it sound similar to his other journalistic enterprises in America.[44]

There were other Russian-language newspapers and journals to which Jewish immigrants contributed heavily. Most were quite short-lived and undoubtedly without any broad impact. For example, a group calling itself the American Delegation of the Socialist Revolutionary Party put out a paper called *Volia* (Freedom), which bore ads for Jewish businesses and services. Its contributors included Leo Deutsch and Isaac Hourwich, writing about the war and immigration. The editors even saw fit to mention the Jewish question in one instance.[45]

Despite this, *Volia*, like the other papers to which Deutsch contributed, was a Russian publication. Its name, which means both "freedom" and "will" in Russian, was reminiscent of *Narodnaia volia*, the name of the organization that had assassinated Alexander II and the name of that organization's periodical publication. Thirty-four years after that assassination and two years before the revolution that would change things for good, Russian Jewish intellectuals still had their eyes on their homeland.

CHAPTER 7

"We Are Jews"—At Least, *You* Are

WRITING IN YIDDISH

IN ALL the versions of the story he told about the penitent Jewish students, Abe Cahan included a common element: the affirmation of Jewishness. The version in the memoirs and the fictionalized version in *The White Terror and the Red* both show a rejection of the Russian language for Yiddish. In only one of these versions does Cahan name the speaker. It is in the memoirs, and the speaker is identified as Nicholas Aleinikoff, the head of the Kiev Am Olam group and fellow activist of Cahan in the early Russian radical émigré circles in New York. The fictional version has the speaker, a doctor, abandon the "Russian or Germanised Yiddish which he habitually affected with uneducated Jews" in favor of "the plain, unembellished vernacular of the Ghetto," a "fluent, robust Yiddish." The *Atlantic Monthly* version does not indicate the language of the speaker. But the memoir version tells the truth: Aleinikoff addressed the congregation in Russian.[1]

There is considerable irony in the circumstance that Aleinikoff, who would soon resume his political activities on foreign shores but in the gentile idiom of his native country, is the lead actor in a drama whose touching conclusion is a rededication to Jewish ways of life. But Aleinikoff was hardly an isolated case. Though the Jewish intellectual immigrants recognized the need to reach out to their compatriots by means of the "unembellished vernacular of the Ghetto," this recognition, and its fulfillment in the rise of the Yiddish press, hardly represented a perfect culmination of the noble dreams of the Jewish students in the synagogue, who purportedly abandoned their Russian names for their original Jewish ones and, in a show of solidarity with their fellow Jews, spoke Yiddish from that moment on.

No one will dispute that the Yiddish press made Jewishness a central factor in immigrant culture. But the Yiddish press was created and run by an elite vanguard of intellectuals whose political stance continued to be defined by Russian models they had learned before emigrating. Whatever the official ideology of a particular publication—Marxist, anarchist, socialist in a broad sense—the editors always seemed to be following those Russian models, providing their readers with a steady diet of Russian culture, history, and politics, or simply retaining the stance of the Lavro-vian critically thinking individual.

THE YIDDISH PRESS

The Yiddish press in America did not start after the brief era of Russian-language political organizations. There had been Yiddish papers since as far back as 1870. Most of the early ones did not last long. Abe Cahan and other "Russians" had made a few attempts, starting in the mid-1880s, to launch radical Yiddish newspapers, but none of these had lasted long, either. Kasriel Sarasohn, a newspaper editor the later Yiddish socialist press was fond of reviling, founded a Yiddish paper in the mid-1870s that lasted over ten years on its own and almost another forty as the supplement to the same editor's successful *Yidishe Tageblat* (Jewish daily). The *Tageblat*, which enjoyed a respectable circulation for many of its more than forty years of publication (1885–1928), was religiously and politically conservative from the outset and thus was not destined to serve the interests of intellectuals like Abe Cahan. By the early 1890s, it was the only serious competitor for anyone hoping to establish a progressive Yiddish periodical.

The 1890s is when our story truly begins. In 1890, Philip Krantz, Abe Cahan, Morris Hillquit, and Louis Miller founded *Di Arbayter Tsaytung* (*The Workman's Paper*, as it was officially called in English), a weekly that lasted until 1902. In the same year, a group of anarchists founded a rival weekly, *Di Fraye Arbayter Shtimme* (*The Free Voice of Labor*), which was published, with a few interruptions, until 1977. In 1892, the same group that had founded the *Arbayter Tsaytung* began publishing a literary monthly journal called *Di Tsukunft* (The future), which celebrated its centennial in 1992 and still comes out, in Yiddish, today. In 1894, Philip Krantz started the *Abend Blatt* (Evening paper) as a daily counterpart to the *Arbayter Tsaytung*, which became the *Abend Blatt*'s weekly Sunday supplement. Like the *Arbayter Tsaytung*, the *Abend Blatt* folded in 1902. And in 1897, Cahan and Louis Miller founded *Forverts* (*The Jewish Daily Forward*), which is still published today in both an English and a Yiddish edition (but no longer as a daily in either edition). All these publications were run by Jewish intellectuals who had learned their politics in the Russian revolutionary movement. These were the publications that would dominate politically progressive intellectual life in the Yiddish-speaking world for the next two generations.[2]

It would be a gross exaggeration to say that none of the publications I have mentioned had any other purpose than to serve as forums for nineteenth-century Russian radical ideologies. Officially and publicly, Yiddish publications had purposes that were grounded quite firmly in the needs of the Jewish immigrant workers, and so they differed significantly from the Russian-language publications in their new emphasis on those needs.

The *Fraye Arbayter Shtimme*, for example, offered a weekly podium to Russian anarchist Prince Petr Kropotkin and provided other Russian cultural matter in its early years, but it also included news about anarchism in America. The *Arbayter Tsaytung* was affiliated with the United Hebrew Trades, a federation whose purpose was to provide a central administrative structure for Jewish unions. The United Hebrew Trades had been organized in 1888 by the Yiddish-speaking and Russian-speaking sections of the Socialist Labor Party, which was the guiding force in immigrant socialism in the United States from the time it was founded, in 1877, until the end of the century. The *Arbayter Tsaytung* and the companion *Abend Blatt* were, in effect, organs of the Socialist Labor Party, and the Socialist Labor Party as a whole was not a Russian or even a Jewish organization. Its leading figure during the period of the Jewish labor movement's early flourishing in the 1890s was Daniel De Leon, and though De Leon was Jewish, he hailed from Curaçao and culturally had almost nothing in common with the immigrants from Russia.

The *Forward* is another example. It, too, came into existence in significant measure because there were compelling reasons that had to do with the Jewish labor movement and socialist politics—and not only because its founders took it into their heads to provide themselves with an American *Sovremennik* or to provide the Yiddish-speaking masses with a Russian education. Abe Cahan and Louis Miller had quit the Socialist Labor Party in 1897 because of conflicts with the leadership, and the *Forward* was their effort to provide the Jewish masses with an alternative to the *Abend Blatt*.

The immediate motivation for publishing Yiddish papers was thus clearly something other than the desire of their editors to follow in the path of Chernyshevsky and Lavrov (though that desire was present, as we will see). This is one respect in which the Yiddish papers set themselves apart from the Russian ones. Another is that the official programs of the Yiddish publications overtly revealed little about the Russian cultural identities of their editors. In the first issue of the *Arbayter Tsaytung*, the editors spoke of their dedication to a social order based on principles of liberty, fraternity, and equality, identifying themselves as socialists, revolutionaries, internationalists, democrats, and "progressivists or evolutionists." Their language was vaguely Hegelian, suggesting an attempt to give their readers a diluted form of Marxism.[3] The *Forward* went to great lengths to show its loyalty to social democracy by routinely printing editorial political analysis whose purpose was transparently to educate its working class readers in the terms and concepts of Marxism.

Di Tsukunft, in its opening statement, identified its editors as social

democrats and spoke of Marx's theory of surplus value.[4] The statement
is full of standard Hegelian-Marxist vocabulary, including the all-impor-
tant *development* (*entviklung* in Yiddish) as applied to history and its
stages. Strengthening the impression that the Yiddish press represented a
marriage of Jewish culture and the new ideology of social democracy (but
without reference to Russia) was the picture on the cover of the early
issues of *Di Tsukunft*: a woman wearing antique garb, surrounded by
various articles symbolic of Western science and art, and supporting two
stone tablets with an inscription in Hebrew letters. What appears at first
glance to be the Mosaic code is really the work of a more recent prophet:
it is the concluding exhortation, in Yiddish translation (hence the Hebrew
letters), of the *Communist Manifesto*.

It is true that many of the leaders of the Jewish labor movement first
learned their Marxism either in Russia or from Russians, as a glance at
their memoirs will show. Cahan, for example, had first studied Marx in
Russia, and during the crisis of the "fog," when it came time to review
Marxism, he read not only Engels but a work by the founder of Russian
Marxism, Georgy Plekhanov.[5] According to Morris Hillquit, Plekhanov,
who sought a strict application of Marx's theory of history to Russia, was
a common topic of discussion among the young Jewish immigrant intellectuals with whom Hillquit associated in his early years in the United
States.[6] But the presence of Plekhanov would hardly have been evident to
the casual reader of a Yiddish newspaper or journal. On the surface, then,
the Yiddish press was a spontaneous response to the need for giving the
Jewish masses propaganda (in the affirmative sense in which the Russian
radicals had used the word) and news that was relevant to their needs.

But there was more to it than this. Once you looked a little more
closely, you could see how intimately connected the interests of the editors remained with those of the movement in their homeland. It helped,
too, to know some of the terms and concepts the editors' Russian mentors
had used. But a good, dedicated reader would soon learn these, since the
editors made a special effort to school the masses in the ideologies in
which the Jewish intelligentsia in Russia had been indoctrinated.

FROM MERELY "YIDDISH-SPEAKING" TO JEWISH

Nevertheless, it must be said that the Yiddish publications openly acknowledged the obvious fact that their readers were Jewish and were
likely to be interested in matters affecting the lives of Jews. This, in fact,
was the most important respect in which they differed from the Russian-
language publications. Not, of course, that these publications were like
the modern-day *Forward*, which publishes mostly stories with a Jewish
angle. Back then, the editors of newspapers had the responsibility of giv-

ing their readers general news, not just "Jewish" news, and the editors of a literary journal like *Di Tsukunft* had the responsibility of giving their readers a general education. Nor were these publications interested in Judaism as a religion. The progressive periodicals without exception offered a notion of secular, cultural Jewishness, instead of "tribal," religious Judaism. Religion rarely entered the scene, except as an object of scientific curiosity.

But the secular, cultural Jewish element was noticeable. The socialist newspapers kept their readers regularly informed of events affecting the Jews in their original homeland, for example. This was certainly true at the time of dramatic events like the anti-Jewish pogroms of Kishinev in 1903 or the tsar's approval of a plan that gave local authorities in Russia the right to flog Jews.[7] And it was true at other times as well. The *Arbayter Tsaytung* and the *Forward* routinely ran articles of a general nature on the life of Jews in Russia, seizing every opportunity to remind their immigrant readers how bad things were in their homeland. Both papers took a continuing interest in the Jewish labor movement in Russia.

Di Tsukunft, too, maintained an interest in Jewish affairs in the motherland. Jacob Milch, who contributed frequently to the journal and then edited it briefly in 1907, wrote an impassioned article in the wake of the Kishinev pogroms (under the Chernyshevskian title "What is to be done?"), attacking Zionism as a coward's way out and ending with a stirring appeal to Russia's Jews to struggle.[8] In an article on the Jewish movement in the United States, however, that combines the Russian intellectuals' earlier focus on Russian revolutionary politics with the new interest in the Jews as a group, Milch says that the immigrant Jews are in America in body only; in their hearts they are far away, in Russia.[9]

Di Tsukunft, as it happens, shows in an especially striking way the transition from cosmopolitanism to an assertion of Jewish identity. The clearest sign of this is the manner in which the journal listed its party affiliation over the first two years of its existence. The change turns on the two meanings of the word *yidish* (or, in this case, *idish*, as it was generally written in the early years of the Yiddish press): "Yiddish" (the language) and "Jewish." From 1892 to late in 1894, *Di Tsukunft* identified itself as a monthly journal published by the "Yiddish [*idish*]-speaking sections of the SLP [Socialist Labor Party]"; beginning in September 1894, however, it became a monthly journal published by the "Jewish [*idish*] sections of the SLP." Thus the distinguishing factor in the targeted readers of the magazine went from their being Yiddish-speaking (in theory, anyone could speak Yiddish) to their being Jewish. The reason for the change was undoubtedly Abe Cahan's takeover of the editorship from Philip Krantz in February of 1894. But, as a later contributor to *Di Tsukunft* pointed out in a history of the magazine, even Krantz, a die-hard cosmopolitan and antinationalist, during the slightly more than two years of his first stint as editor (he would edit *Di Tsukunft* again in 1904 and 1905), did much to promote specifically Yiddish culture.[10]

Since the socialist periodicals were aimed at the Jewish working people, it is no surprise that they consistently provided news about the Jewish labor movement in the United States. There is no need to enumerate the articles that fall into this category; what is surprising is that the same writers and editors had devoted so little attention to this movement during their earlier involvement with the Russian-language press.

But the permission the intellectuals gave themselves to recognize their own coreligionists led them to notice aspects of Jewish life besides labor and the labor movement. An aspect of Jewish life that always received a tremendous amount of attention was the Yiddish theatre, which was enjoying a surge in respect in the 1890s. The press looked at other aspects of Jewish life, too. From time to time, one could find an article on the history of Jewish immigrants in New York, an article on the status of the Yiddish language and the proper way to write it, a review of the work of a Yiddish poet. Above all, there were hundreds of original literary works, many of them in their first published form, by such famous Yiddish writers as Sholem Aleichem and Isaac Leib Peretz.[11] Even the *Fraye Arbayter Shtimme*, which concerned itself relatively little with Jewish matters, printed an occasional article on Yiddish theatre or literature.

"FOR US, RUSSIANS"

Still, when it came right down to it, few Jewish intellectuals were willing to forget that they were "Russian." We saw how Abe Cahan in his first few years in the United States felt most comfortable with Jews who spoke Russian as their language of preference. He tells another story in his memoirs that illustrates the enduring force of this sense of national identity. In 1901, that is, at a moment when he had worked in the Yiddish press for over a decade, he went with a group of American journalists to interview Petr Kropotkin, who was visiting the United States. The journalists clearly had no understanding of what sort of creature a Russian anarchist might be, and one of them was silly enough to ask Kropotkin how to make a bomb. Cahan was a Russian and understood these things, so he huffily put his fellow journalist in his place, telling him his question was senseless. The "Russian colony" in New York later threw a party for Kropotkin.

Cahan's perception of himself is the key element in this story. Being Russian allowed Cahan to understand what a Russian anarchist was, it overcame the personal differences that might have arisen between an anarchist like Kropotkin and the social democrats who made up the Russian colony, and, above all, it gave Cahan and his fellow intellectuals an appreciation of Kropotkin's stature. "For us, Russians," Cahan remembers, "Kropotkin was above all the famous hero of the struggle against tsarist despotism."[12]

Cahan remained a Russian in another sense, too. The idea of an intelligentsia in America and the role it was to play in educating the Jewish masses was always on his mind, and it is clear that his conception of these matters was the one he had brought from the enlightened milieu he left behind in 1882 (but rediscovered in a new form in New York). As late as 1910, when the *Forward* was already well underway and Jewish mass immigration was well into its second generation, Cahan wrote about the Jewish intelligentsia in an article for *Di Tsukunft*.[13] With pride, he describes the Jewish immigrants' predisposition to form an intelligentsia. Many, he points out, through study of Talmud have been well equipped to read and learn, and others have schooled themselves by attempting to read serious books in English. The Jews, after all, are the "people of the book" (*am haseyfer*). But even those who have some education are often ignorant in matters of secular, Western learning, and here Cahan shows his Lavrovian colors by saying we can be grateful to the socialist movement since it "is leading the masses from the Jewish emigration into *development*, into intellectual growth."[14] He celebrates popularization as a means of spreading enlightenment among the masses. The model for such an idea? "Pisarev the critic preached popularization and himself fulfilled what he preached," he says (without, incidentally, thinking it necessary to identify Pisarev).[15]

For Cahan, popularization was a guiding idea from the outset. His memoirs include a characteristically self-congratulatory passage on his assumption of the editorship of *Di Tsukunft* in 1894. Cahan managed to get an issue out every month, unlike his predecessor—and on time, to boot. But most of all, he used the journal to fulfill his plan for his less-educated fellow immigrants. "I required every writer of an article to bear in mind our masses. I was convinced that to issue popularizations of science and articles written in a very popular vein on political and social questions was our most important duty, that in this lay the most important part of our work."[16]

Cahan gives an almost indignant tone to his reminiscence about the years when he edited *Di Tsukunft*, as if he had been the only one to see the journal's purpose in this way. But, despite some ideological and professional differences from one editor to another, what Cahan describes was a consistent characteristic of *Di Tsukunft* throughout the era of mass immigration, and that is why *Di Tsukunft* is so important in the history of the Jewish immigrant intelligentsia. It is also why *Di Tsukunft* is probably more important for the light it sheds on the attitudes of the intelligentsia than it is for the "light" of secular learning it may have shed on a few Jewish workers.

More than any other publication in this period, *Di Tsukunft* was dedicated to the "development" of the masses. Despite any parochial political purposes the magazine may have served (stemming from its party affiliation, for instance), the idea was to create a publication that would cultivate its own readership to the point where, one day, it could be a Yiddish-language *Sovremennik*, or, to take an American analogy, a Yiddish-language *Atlantic Monthly*, a journal, in short, that would be written for an enlightened, progressive, intellectual readership and that would provide literature, literary criticism, and learned articles on a host of widely varied subjects. Pisarev had sought to popularize, as Cahan says. But Pisarev had written for *Russkoe Slovo*, a necessarily elite journal that published the very best that Russia's mid-nineteenth-century intelligentsia had to offer and offered it to other members of the intelligentsia. Cahan's idea seems to have been to use his magazine to create a larger intellectual elite among the Jews—like the relatively large educated portion of the American population that could read the *Atlantic*—but to insist that they help edify the masses.

It would be stretching things to say that *Di Tsukunft* succeeded in this grand mission. It might well have helped to edify a small number of immigrant Jews and speed their progress toward the status of educated readers like the native-born Americans they envied, but it never created a sufficiently large readership of this sort to turn itself into a wide-circulation, Yiddish *Atlantic*. Jews who wanted to be the sort of people who read the *Atlantic* became that sort of people by learning English. Then they could read the *Atlantic* and not a pale imitation written in the language of the ghetto.

Still, *Di Tsukunft* intrepidly tried at once to edify and to look like an elite journal. In a market where the prestige of a periodical stood in inverse proportion to the frequency of its publication and in direct proportion to its price, *Di Tsukunft* was proud to be a monthly, not a weekly or daily, it was produced in a relatively luxurious format, and, at a time when *Arbayter Tsaytung* was three cents an issue (already high, considering that a decade later the *Forward* would sell for a penny an issue), it fetched the hefty price of ten cents. It offered breadth by printing articles on many subjects, including science, but, as Cahan said in his article on the intelligentsia, it unapologetically informed the less sophisticated reader what the North Pole was.[17] It treated its readers to theoretical discussions of Marxian economics, but used a simplified vocabulary that assumed little prior knowledge on the part of those readers.

Di Tsukunft was not the only publication that attempted to carry out this mission. *Arbayter Tsaytung* and the *Forward* filled their pages with instructive articles of a general nature in addition to news and instructive articles of a political nature. Often this was owing to the presence of Cahan. A glance through a series of issues of any publication with which

Cahan was affiliated will show a large number of articles on such subjects as "The wild Indians that Columbus found in America," "The pyramids of Egypt," or "The crocodile."[18] This was not unique to Cahan. Every editor of a Yiddish publication who wanted to stay in business recognized the absolute necessity of adopting the role of the "advanced (*peredovye*) minds," as Lavrov put it in *Znamia*, teaching, leading, elevating the masses.

"WHAT'S HAPPENING IN THE HOMELAND?"

To the working-class, Yiddish-speaking reader of a left-wing Yiddish periodical published in the three decades or so after 1890, one thing must have seemed very strange. Almost every such periodical regularly featured the works of some of Europe's best known and best loved Yiddish writers, most of whom wrote not about America or Western Europe, not about the world of non-Jewish Russian intellectuals in Russia, but about ordinary Jewish life in Russia, with its special customs, life cycle, and language. Many of these writers, in fact, made their worldwide reputations in the American Yiddish press. But just as writers like Sholem Aleichem were creating and presenting to American immigrant readers a literature built on the old life, a literature that at once drew attention to the peculiarities of that life and presupposed an intimate knowledge of it, the editors, while implicitly and explicitly recognizing their readers' Jewishness and consistently dealing with specifically Jewish concerns in America, were serving up, alongside the fiction of Sholem Aleichem, a menu of reading matter that was as devoid as possible of any references to traditional, old-world Jewish life. This contrast was most glaring in the treatment of the old country. Sholem Aleichem was giving American immigrant readers the Russia of *yontev* (Jewish holiday) life, complete with the foods, the ceremonies, the prayers, the joys and sorrows that are particular to Russian Jewry—all presented in a language rich with Hebrew words and expressions that are natural only in a world where liturgical and ordinary language are inextricably intertwined. Abe Cahan and his fellow intellectuals, however, were giving the same readers a Russia whose center was always Gentile life, where the Jewish world existed only insofar as it came into confrontation with non-Jewish politics.

So whether they liked it or not, Jewish newspaper readers were kept informed of happenings in the mother country. Not all happenings, of course—the editors were careful to select those they thought most likely to arouse interest among the Russian Jewish proletariat, which really meant those likely to arouse interest among themselves, the intellectuals. Anything showing the brutal excesses of tsarist tyranny was generally a safe bet. A front-page feature in *Arbayter Tsaytung*, in May of 1891, is typical. The content can hardly be described as "news," but the title appears as a banner headline, reading "Alexander the Third and his victim." A drawing that occupies much of the page is a riot of savage details. The dark, forbidding figure of Alexander is in the center. Behind him lurks the spectral figure of Death. In front of him, kneeling, his clothes in tatters, is one of his subjects, the "victim." To the left, in a swirling cloud of smoke are the instruments and symbols of tsarist oppression: the knout, a ball and chain, a suit of armor with a cross on the breastplate. To the right, in another cloud of smoke, are the instruments and symbols of civilization upon which the tsarist regime has trampled, together with the names of some of the tsar's most prominent victims. Behind the tsar one sees the rising sun of freedom and socialism. The accompanying text, by Abe Cahan, contains a stirring cry for the victory of socialism.[19]

Socialist Yiddish periodicals frequently ran general articles on such subjects as censorship in Russia, the Romanov family (especially the more lurid moments in its history), and life in Siberia. They also ran articles on the hardships of economic life in Russia, to show how the systemic failings of autocracy had led to great suffering for the Russian people. The famine of the early 1890s attracted particular attention in the Yiddish press. A scandalous extradition treaty that the United States signed with Russia in 1893 was the occasion for numerous impassioned indictments of both signatories, since, even though the treaty exempted perpetrators of political crimes, in practical terms it still threatened to lead to the repatriation of Russian political refugees.[20] The press brought out the best in its arsenal of *Yidishkayt* to assail the agreement, speaking of it sarcastically as the *shidekh* (arranged engagement) or the *ksube* (Jewish marriage contract) between the two nations.[21]

Even better than stories detailing tsarist brutality in general were those detailing tsarist brutality against its political victims, the revolutionaries. One of the most sensational stories to appear in the *Arbayter Tsaytung* was called "Buried Alive. The terrible torments of the Nihilists exiled in Siberia."[22] It is based on the eye-witness reports of the American adventurer George Kennan (1845–1924). Kennan, an ancestor of twentieth-century diplomat and ambassador George F. Kennan, had gone to Siberia in 1865 as part of an expedition to set up telegraph communication with the United States and then returned there in 1885 to study the Siberian prison system. He published his findings first in a series of articles that appeared in *Century* magazine from 1888 to 1891 and then in book form, with the title *Siberia and the Exile System*, in 1891. The *Arbayter Tsaytung* article provides, in sickening detail, an account of the tortures inflicted upon the tsar's political prisoners, complete with a drawing of a woman revolutionary named Sigida (Madam Hope Sigida in Kennan's report) as she is flogged to death under the impassive gaze of what ap-

7. Abraham Liessin in 1897.

pears to be the prison commandant. Another drawing shows a prisoner named Kohn Bernshteyn (Kohan-Bernstein in Kennan's report) as he is hoisted out of bed with a noose around his neck, to be hanged. The author concludes with an appeal to avenge the deaths of a long list of revolutionary heroes.[23]

Yiddish publications were particularly conscientious about teaching their readers the history of the Russian revolutionary movement and keeping them apprised of its progress. This was especially true beginning in the mid-1890s, when the growth of the workers' movement in Russia, both Jewish and non-Jewish, gave American Jewish editors plenty to report. In February of 1896, for example, the *Arbayter Tsaytung* ran an article on the "new" workers' movement in Russia and that summer printed a number of additional articles on the same subject. As increasing political turmoil in Russia brought strikes and other acts of protest, the Yiddish press in America followed closely, often with on-the-scene reports.

In 1897, when an émigré named Abraham Liessin (Avrom Lyesin in Yiddish) arrived in America, the New York editors suddenly found themselves with a contributor who could write regularly but who had been close to happenings in the motherland only a short time before. Liessin (1872–1938) was a dazzling yeshiva boy-turned-socialist, like many others in the American movement. He had been sending poetry to the Yiddish press by mail from Russia since 1894 (*Lyesin*, in fact, was a pseudonym that Cahan invented to protect the writer's identity in Russia), and when political trouble forced him to leave his native Minsk for New York, he plunged immediately into the political and literary life of the immigrant Jewish intelligentsia.[24] He would be best remembered in the Jewish community as the man who edited *Di Tsukunft* for a quarter-century, from 1913 to 1938. Cahan tapped him for literary and political contributions to the *Forward*, and in 1899, Liessin drew upon his own recent experience to write a series of articles on economic policy, censorship, literature, the intelligentsia, and student unrest in Russia.[25] Liessin clearly had no trouble fitting in when it came to Yiddish journalism in America. The articles on Russia deal almost exclusively with non-Jewish Russian life, analyzing the various dimensions of that life in slightly simplified Marxist terms.

Di Tsukunft, always eager to provide the most thoughtful coverage, printed numerous articles, often in series, about the Russian revolutionary movement. V. Zhuk, who had coedited the Russian-language *Progress* with Hourwich, wrote an article on the early stages of the Russian revolutionary movement.[26] There were many other general discussions of the movement. The number of articles on Russia dramatically increased later, in 1917, when observers had two actual revolutions to write about. A glance through the contents of *Di Tsukunft* for that year and the following year shows dozens of articles on the Russian revolutionary movement, the two revolutions, Bolshevism, Trotsky, and Lenin.

IN PRAISE OF CRITICALLY THINKING RUSSIAN INDIVIDUALS

Doers

Actually, many heroes of the Russian revolutionary movement were not just critically *thinking* individuals; in the proper spirit of the Russian intelligentsia, they were critically *doing* individuals, and the Yiddish press in America celebrated their exploits the way older American history books celebrate the exploits of Samuel Adams and Paul Revere. The most celebrated of all were undoubtedly the *Narodnaia volia* members who had participated in the various plots to assassinate Alexander II, especially those who carried out the successful plot of March 1881, and were martyred for their actions afterwards. Jewish intellectual émigrés raised this event, and all the unsuccessful plots before it, to legendary status.

So it is not surprising to read in *Arbayter Tsaytung* "A Nihilist's job in the Russian Tsar's palace," an article about Stepan Khalturin. Khalturin was a worker who found employment in the Winter Palace in 1879 (the article wrongly gives the year as 1880), smuggled dynamite into the basement, and finally detonated the explosives under the dining room in an unsuccessful attempt to kill the tsar.[27] This article appeared in May of 1890, two months after *Arbayter Tsaytung* began publication.

Beginning in the July 4 issue of the same year, next to an editorial about the meaning of the American Independence Day, the paper ran a series of articles on Ignatii Ioakimovich Grinevitskii, "the hero of March 1, 1881."[28] Grinevitskii was one of four "throwers" positioned with bombs along various routes the tsar was considered likely to take on what turned out to be his final outing. If a cache of dynamite buried in a tunnel underneath one of these routes failed to kill him, the nearest thrower was to do the job by hand. Two had a chance, and Grinevitskii was the lucky one whose bomb blew the tsar's legs off and killed him (Grinevitskii himself died from wounds he sustained in the blast). The writers for the Yiddish press, even at something of a remove in space and time from the assassination, show unalloyed sympathy for the perpetrators. As he is portrayed here, Grinevitskii is no steel-nerved killer who performed a necessary but repugnant deed; he is a generous man who loved humanity and cared for the poor. Philip Krantz contributed a personal reminiscence of Grinevitskii in which he describes the warmth, simplicity, and sincerity of the assassin.[29]

The following fall, *Arbayter Tsaytung* ran a series of articles on another heroic figure in Russian revolutionary annals, Vera Zasulich, whose most noteworthy deed was her attempt to kill the governor of St. Petersburg by walking into his office one day in 1878 and shooting him at point-blank range with a revolver. General Trepov, the governor, was guilty of flogging another revolutionary in prison, and Zasulich had personally undertaken to punish him. She was immediately arrested, but the state was unable to obtain a conviction in her trial, which ended in her acquittal. In 1890, Zasulich was ill with consumption, and *Arbayter Tsaytung* used the occasion both to launch a fund-raising drive for her (organized, it informed its readers, by a committee of "Russian emigrants" meeting in the editorial offices) and to inform the public about her. The articles speak lovingly and admiringly of her accomplishments, calling attention also to the hardships she endured despite her acquittal.[30]

In April of 1891, ten years after the conspirators in the assassination of

Alexander had been executed, the reader of *Arbayter Tsaytung* was treated to a front-page spread on some of the less known heroes of the Russian movement. The theme was actions that had been committed in the month of April. Aleksandr Konstantinovich Solov'ev, for example, had fired a revolver at the tsar in April 1879, but missed. Andrei Ivanovich Zheliabov was a key member of *Narodnaia volia*, involved in the continuing plans for the assassination of the tsar. Though he was arrested before the tsar was killed, he was hanged in April 1881 for his participation in the plot. Aleksandr Aleksandrovich Kviatkovskii and N. E. Sukhanov were both *Narodnaia volia* conspirators involved in assassination plots. Abe Cahan, writing under the name "Socius," contributed the brief text that accompanies a drawing of the revolutionaries, under the headline "Four Russian Heroes. In Commemoration of the Month of April."[31] In subsequent years, in March, *Arbayter Tsaytung* would often run commemorative articles on the heroes of March, 1881.

Di Tsukunft, too, in its early years, featured articles on the heroic "doers" of the Russian terrorist movement. Sofiia Perovskaia, one of the best known figures in the assassination conspiracy, the participant who had handed the bombs to the throwers and had been hanged for her efforts, was the subject of an adoring biography during Cahan's editorship.[32] And Cahan himself wrote a biography of Hesia Helfman, a Jewish conspirator with a particularly touching story: pregnant at the time of her trial for her role in the assassination, she had her sentence suspended, but her child was taken from her, and she died in prison.[33]

In the text he wrote to accompany the drawings of the "four heroes," Cahan expressed regret at not having a picture of another conspirator, Presniakov, since "it would be most interesting for the socialists who read *Arbayter Tsaytung* to become acquainted with the face of Presniakov."[34] Still, he says, he is glad to know that his readers will be able to see a picture of Presniakov's friend, Kviatkovskii. Cahan knew what other editors and writers knew, namely, that they could not expect all their readers, or even most of them, to know the names or faces of all the revolutionary heroes. He knew that too many of his readers had come to the United States not because they had engaged in the same activities as Perovskaia or Zheliabov and then been forced to flee, but simply because life had become too difficult in Russia. This, in his eyes, was clearly a shortcoming, and he used the Yiddish press to school his less educated fellow immigrants in the lore of the movement that had shaped him and his fellow intellectuals.

But there were other heroes, too, heroes who were given much more extensive treatment in the Yiddish press because they were known above all for their thought: the thinkers and writers in whose names many of the "doers" *did*. Not that thinkers and writers never acted; as we have seen, many of them did, and as we have seen, it was an essential characteristic of the Russian movement that the boundary separating thought and action was consistently blurred. But men and women like Zheliabov and Perovskaia did not leave behind the same written patrimony as did such figures as Chernyshevsky and Lavrov. The Yiddish editors saw the need to provide their readers with thoughts in addition to deeds, and so they launched a campaign, one that lasted the entire period of mass immigration, to give their readers a solid theoretical foundation in Russian revolutionary politics, in addition to the watered-down Marxism these readers were routinely given in the press.

Thinkers

Someone could do a revealing sociological study of the Yiddish press and its readership by looking at only the commercial products promoted in the advertising pages. The same makers of patent medicines made their fraudulent claims here as in English-language publications of the era, and a host of firms, offering anything from clothing to cigarettes to real estate appealed to the class ambitions of the Jewish immigrants by dangling in front of them images of upper-crust elegance and respectability. But apparently the turn-of-the-century equivalents of our modern-day market research experts believed they had uncovered the Yiddish-speaking readers' cultural interests, too, and if their market research was accurate, we can safely infer that Tolstoy was a widely recognized hero among the immigrant masses. In the early years of the new century, one can see ads for "Tolstoi Cigarettes" in the newspapers, and a little later a manufacturer of artificial hair coloring advertises its product, with unintended comic effect, by showing the severe and venerable face of Tolstoy *before* (white hair and beard) and *after* (youthful, dark hair—and beard).

Tolstoy was certainly not a member of the Russian radical pantheon that included such figures as Chernyshevsky, Bakunin, and Kropotkin, yet interest in him was clearly strong among the Jewish immigrants. From the late 1890s on, almost no detail of his life escaped notice: Tolstoy's message to the tsar, Tolstoy's views on America, Tolstoy weak from illness, Tolstoy excommunicated. The Yiddish press printed serialized translations of many of his works and advertised editions of his collected works in Yiddish translation. At times, commentators expressed exasperation with his moral views. Louis Miller, for example, reviewed *The Kreutzer Sonata* for *Di Tsukunft* (which had just run a serialization of the novella in a translation by Abe Cahan) and likened Tolstoy's Christian philosophy, appearing as it does in the midst of such glorious literary artistry, to a pig running free in a wondrous garden.[35] Still, the austere critic of the hereditary class system and proponent of patriarchal peasant morals was the object of endless fascination. After he died, in November of 1910, there was at least one article about him in every issue of the *Forward* for months.

The prominence of Tolstoy in the Yiddish press, however, is not by itself evidence of intense interest in Russia on the part of the editors. Almost every English-language publication at the turn of the century, regardless of its political sympathies, ran articles on Tolstoy and published English translations of his works. To some radicals, Jewish or not, Tolstoy was a hero both because of what they perceived as either anarchist or socialist views in his writings and because of his undying commitment to the welfare of the Russian peasants; to others, he was a false prophet; to political moderates and conservatives, he was an object of curiosity as the head of a growing international movement; to all, he was a powerful symbol of resistance. In any case, his presence in the Yiddish press is evidence that the editors' attention remained turned toward their motherland.

Further evidence of Russophilia comes in the numbers of Russian writers besides Tolstoy whose names appeared in the Yiddish press. Most of these were more clearly associated with progressive politics and the revolutionary movement than was Tolstoy. They were also less likely to be known, at first, to any but former members of the Russian intelligentsia. They are the writers who shaped the political views of the Russian Jewish intellectuals before they emigrated from Russia.

For example, when Petr Lavrov died in early 1900, the Yiddish press ran a number of articles on his life and political career. Of these, the most penetrating and informative were those in a series contributed by David Pinski, under the name "D. Puls," as he had signed himself in stories he published in *Abend Blatt* in the mid-1890s while he was living in Berlin.[36] Pinski had come to New York in 1899 and would soon become one of the best known Yiddish writers in the world. In a preamble to his study of Lavrov, Pinski/Puls explains that he has taken his material from a biographical study of Lavrov by "Tarasov" (a pseudonym for Lavrov's associate Nikolai Sergeevich Rusanov) published in the Stuttgart-based socialist journal *Die Neue Zeit*. Despite any editing and translation the biography may have gone through (considering that it was written by a Russian for a German magazine and then translated into Yiddish), the essential thing is that it was written by a Russian revolutionary intellectual and that it provides a view of Lavrov and his movement that can come only from intimate acquaintance with both.

The focus of the article is thus on Lavrov's ideas, his "industrious scientific and literary activity." The reader of *Arbayter Tsaytung* is treated to a thorough account of the intellectual context in which Lavrov lived and wrote. We read that *Historical Letters* cannot be understood apart from Russian Nihilism. We read about Pisarev, rational egoism, and "thinking realists" (a term for adherents of Nihilism—perhaps a hy-

brid of Lavrovian and Nihilist concepts). We read about the original contribution that *Historical Letters* made to public debate, about how it su-
perseded Nihilism by replacing the Nihilist's obsessive devotion to natural science with an understanding of the historical process that has produced a minority of possessors and a majority of dispossessed. We read
about Lavrov's acquaintance with Marx and Engels and how it reshaped
his thinking. And we read about *Vpered!* and the impact it had on its
generation.

Morris Winchevsky contributed some personal reminiscences about
Lavrov to the *Forward* shortly after Lavrov's death. He departed from the
standard practice among his fellow émigrés and spoke about the Jewish
question, praising Lavrov for being a Judeophile.[37] And a few weeks later
Liessin wrote a short piece in which he spoke of Lavrov as one of the few
revolutionaries to attain the venerable, grey-haired old age that the great
writer had, in fact, attained.[38] As early as 1894, *Di Tsukunft* had featured
Lavrov as the subject of its monthly biographical sketch in February. Like
Pinski in the *Arbayter Tsaytung*, the editors of *Di Tsukunft* turned to a
German publication for their article, using a biography that had appeared
in the satirical social democratic journal *Der wahre Jakob.*[39]

Another popular hero, to judge from the coverage he received in the
Yiddish press, was Petr Kropotkin. For years, the anarchist paper *Fraye
Arbayter Shtimme* ran a selection by Kropotkin, in Yiddish translation, in
every issue and advertised Yiddish translations of books by him. One
would see his name from time to time in *Arbayter Tsaytung* and the *Forward*. At the time of his visit to New York in 1901, when Cahan inter
viewed him, the *Forward* ran a short biographical sketch on him and an
article by him on student disturbances in Russia.[40]

One of the most thorough descriptions of Kropotkin's life and political
career, though, was one that Leo Deutsch wrote for *Di Tsukunft* in 1913,
called "Petr Kropotkin as Man and Thinker."[41] Deutsch tells the notable
incidents in Kropotkin's life, including his privileged youth, his move into
radicalism, his daring escape from prison, and his life of exile in Europe.
Deutsch also sets the context for the evolution of Kropotkin's political
beliefs, and here as elsewhere in such articles in the Yiddish press, one can
read of the 1860s and the influence of such figures as Herzen, Chernyshevsky, and Dobroliubov.[42] But mostly the article is a celebration of
Kropotkin's life in politics, a celebration that Deutsch provides even
though, as he reminds us, Kropotkin was an anarchist and he, Deutsch,
was a social democrat. In Deutsch's account, based on personal acquaintance in Europe, Kropotkin was entirely dedicated to the task of freeing
the working masses, and he lived his life in a simple, modest way that was
consistent with that task.[43]

The Yiddish editors were able to include relatively frequent reports on
such eminent figures as Lavrov and Kropotkin because these men were

still alive or had only recently died during the time when the Yiddish press flourished. But what of the founding figures in the Russian revolutionary movement, the ones in whose *kheyder*s the editors themselves had studied before coming to the United States? It is true that the daily and weekly press, the press with a primary interest in *news*, did not run frequent articles devoted exclusively to Belinsky, Chernyshevsky, Dobroliubov, and Pisarev. Nonetheless, these names do appear in the daily and weekly press, usually in articles like those I have already mentioned. *Di Tsukunft*, however, the monthly with an interest in larger questions than just the events of the day and with the goal of educating the Jewish masses, gave significant coverage to these men.

In an article in the *Arbayter Tsaytung* on "The Russian Victims," Khaim Aleksandrov, an émigré from St. Petersburg and a former student at the Vilna Teachers' Training Institute, writes of the martyrs of the Russian revolution. Aleksandrov (1869–1909) was a perfect blend of the Jewish and the Russian. He was devoted to Yiddish and came to believe, along with such writers as Zhitlovsky, that Yiddish should be a national language for the Jews and that it deserved to be a respected literary language. At the same time, he enjoyed the fruits of a Russian education that dated back to his early years. As a schoolboy he had already begun writing songs in Russian and Yiddish and was a thoroughly trained Russian intellectual by the time he moved to the United States in 1898. He draws on his Russian education in this article, which he begins with a quotation from Belinsky. His theme, as usual, is the relation between "thinking Russian society," as he puts it, and Russia's despotic rulers, and he uses Belinsky's observation to frame this theme, very much in the manner of Ivan Karamazov, as a question about paying for the horrors that history has visited on its various victims—in this case, the Russian revolutionaries. He addresses the question by quoting at length from Tolstoy's *Resurrection*.[44]

In February of 1904, when Russian radical critic and activist Nikolai Mikhailovsky died, the *Forward* ran an article on his role as a critic. The author of this article appears to be Dr. Karl Fornberg, a Lithuanian Jew with a dazzlingly multilingual background and a German doctorate in political economy.[45] Fornberg (1871–1937) had had the solid upbringing of a modern, very Westernized *maskil* and, by the time he moved to the United States in 1903, had already published widely in both Russian and Yiddish. In fact, he was one of the few Russian Jews to have published not only in Russian-language Jewish papers but in the non-Jewish Russian press as well. Fornberg's study, written, of course, for readers many of whom had probably never heard of Mikhailovsky, shows that he was in a class apart even from many of his fellow Jewish intellectuals. He traces the history of social activism in Russia and its connection with literary criticism, listing Belinsky, Chernyshevsky, Dobroliubov, and Pisarev as the chief figures in this movement. He mentions a wide range of thinkers on whose work Mikhailovsky drew. He shows a thorough knowledge of Mikhailovsky's life and work, from his literary criticism to his pioneering efforts to introduce Marxism to Russia. And finally, he shows something all too rare in the Jewish intellectual community: instead of uncritically relaying to his readers the ideas of a great Russian master, he shows a sufficient degree of sophistication to hold himself at a distance from his subject, citing Mikhailovsky's weaknesses as a thinker.

The finest discussion of Belinsky, Dobroliubov, and Pisarev to appear in the Yiddish press was a series of articles in *Di Tsukunft*, under the general title "Russian Critics," by Frank Rosenblatt. Rosenblatt (1884–1927) was a *kheyder* boy from Ukraine who, like Cahan and others, had come to his Russian identity by way of a cultural conversion. He had studied to be a rabbi, experienced a revelation when he discovered the Hebrew writings of Moses Leib Lilienblum, taught himself Russian in a few months at the age of thirteen, and then immersed himself in the works of Russian novelists and critics. He came to the United States in 1903 and soon became intensely involved in the Yiddish literary scene. After receiving a doctorate from Columbia in 1910, he devoted himself to civic activities less literary in nature, but during his brief stint as a critic and commentator, he was one of the most impressive contributors to the Yiddish press, especially in matters relating to Russian culture.[46]

In 1904, Rosenblatt had written two articles for *Di Tsukunft* on Mikhailovsky. The second, "Mikhailovsky's Polemic with Marxists," had contained a review of the basic principles of Marxism as well as a defense of Mikhailovsky's belief in free will and opposition to the concept of historical law.[47] In the "Russian Critics" series, Rosenblatt provided his readers with a more complete picture of his generation's mentors than had been seen before in the Yiddish press.

In his study of Belinsky, Rosenblatt tells the traditional story of the conversion from right-Hegelian conservatism to social activism and assesses Belinsky's position in Russian intellectual history, describing him as the teacher and guide for writers who followed him.[48] His study of Dobroliubov is a celebration of that critic's life-long pursuit of an ideal he had established as a young child.[49] Dobroliubov had understood early on that "society does not conduct itself honorably" and that "we must alter the social order so as to benefit the simple people." All his subsequent activity can be understood in the light of this simple childhood idea, Rosenblatt thinks.[50]

Pisarev was Rosenblatt's favorite Russian critic, as his four-part article on the Nihilist critic shows.[51] It is a study that does not overlook the complexities and transitions in Pisarev's short life, something that many treatments of him do in an effort to portray him as a one-dimensional *enfant terrible* of nineteenth-century Russia. Among Pisarev's chief virtues was his ability to play the role of the true Russian socially engaged writer, Rosenblatt says. His articles "were able to penetrate to the broad masses, which was his chief purpose." Other writers attempted to do this, too, "to spread useful literature and instruction among the people," but no one succeeded in the way Pisarev did.[52]

One last figure deserves to be mentioned, perhaps the most important of all, and that is Chernyshevsky, whose name and reputation made an extraordinary journey in the American Jewish community, especially after his death in 1889.[53] Remarkably, Chernyshevsky had some non-Jewish champions in the United States as early as the mid-1880s. One was Benjamin Tucker, an American anarchist who published the radical bi-weekly *Liberty* from 1881 to 1908 and who had an enduring interest in Russian radicalism and Russian literature. Tucker printed his own English translation (from a French translation) of *What Is to Be Done?* (or *What's To Be Done?*, as he called it) in serialized form in *Liberty* from May of 1884 to May of 1886 and then published the entire translation in book form in 1886. Another admirer was Nathan Haskell Dole, who with the help of a certain S. S. Skidelsky, published an expurgated English translation of the same work in the same year.[54] The Tucker translation has its own minor history in the United States, since advertisements for it appear often in English-language radical publications, frequently in lists of "labor literature."[55]

By the time of his death in 1889, Chernyshevsky appears to have had something of a following in the United States. There are at least two reports of a meeting convened in New York to eulogize the late revolutionary after the cable announcing his death arrived. One report includes the information that a resolution was passed at the meeting to build a monument to Chernyshevsky in New York and that a collection was taken up for that purpose.[56]

The stage was thus already set for Chernyshevsky's role in Jewish cultural affairs. *Znamia* had published a novel by Chernyshevsky during its short existence. *What Is to Be Done?* had a life in Yiddish, too. The short-lived anarchist weekly *Der Morgenshtern* (The morning star) offered Chernyshevsky's novel as its *feuilleton* selection from its first issue in January 1890 until April of the same year, perhaps as a form of eulogy to its author. *Der Morgenshtern* folded in June, but Yiddish-speaking workers who took the paper would have had the chance to read the first few chapters of the book that had done so much to shape the Russian Jewish intelligentsia. Many years later, in 1917, a complete version of the novel came out in New York, in a Yiddish translation either by Michael and Adella Kean Zametkin or by Dr. Karl Fornberg.[57]

In its early years, *Di Tsukunft* presented the biography of a great revolutionary thinker as the first article in each of its issues, and it is a sign of the position Chernyshevsky occupied in the minds of the journal's editors that he was featured, with his picture on the frontispiece, in the third issue ever published (the first and second issues had featured Marx and Engels, respectively). The author was Simon O. Pollock, who would become known in 1908 and 1909 as an attorney in the legal case of a Lettish peasant immigrant threatened with extradition under the 1893 Russian Extradition Treaty.[58] Since Pollock is writing in a journal that has proclaimed its adherence to the tenets of social democracy, he goes to some length to show that Chernyshevsky's ideas were quite similar to those of Marx and Engels, but the primary fact about the author of *What Is to Be Done?* is his stature as a "great teacher for truth and right" in Russia.

The description of Chernyshevsky's mission as a great teacher could have been drawn from the writings of Lavrov, but Pollock takes it from Chernyshevsky himself. Members of the intellectual elite rarely shared their knowledge with the people, Pollock says in a virtual paraphrase of Lavrov, "knowledge that they had acquired precisely because the people had worked for them and thus given them the opportunity to study and learn."[59] He quotes Chernyshevsky on the duty of every writer and learned man to spread science and art among the common folk.[60] He describes the impact of *What Is to Be Done?* and, like many of his contemporaries, dwells on the great hardships Chernyshevsky suffered during his years of imprisonment and exile.

Chernyshevsky's name crops up in other places in *Di Tsukunft*, though primarily in discussions of the role of literature. Rosenblatt apparently planned an article on him in 1907, since the January issue of that year announces such an article for the February issue. He mentions Chernyshevsky frequently in his essays on the other Russian critics, for example, to point out that though Pisarev gave the term "realism" its currency in Russia, his celebrated theory of realism was ultimately derived from Chernyshevsky.[61]

Chernyshevsky appears in some nonjournalistic Yiddish publications, too. Cahan, of course, talks about him repeatedly in his memoirs, though these did not begin appearing until 1926, after the period of mass immigration. Readers of Yiddish who took an interest in Russian affairs during World War I might have seen a booklet published by Bund activist A. Litvak (Khaim Yankel Helfand) called *Revolutionary Russia*.[62] It was compiled early in 1917, after the February Revolution that swept the Provisional Government to power and Nicholas II from power, and as it was written months before the October Revolution, its purpose was to celebrate *the* Russian Revolution—understood, of course, as the one that occurred in February (March, by the Western calendar). In a section called "The Driving Forces of the Revolution" Litvak tells the story of the revolutionary movement in Russia and includes a portrait of Chernyshevsky with a caption identifying him as "the teacher of the intelligentsia in the 1860s." Litvak characterizes him as one of Russia's literary heroes who were "famous warriors of the word and often martyrs."[63]

GOING TO THE (JEWISH) PEOPLE—IN AMERICA

"So many Jewish revolutionists have sacrificed their lives by 'going to the people'—to the Russian people. It's about time some of us at least went to our own people." So says Elkin, the Jewish revolutionary hero of Abe Cahan's *The White Terror and the Red*. He is advocating emigration for the Jews. Clara, a fellow Jewish revolutionary, disagrees. "My heart is bleeding for our poor Jews, but even if it were solely a question of saving the Jews, even then one's duty would be to work for the revolution. How many Russian Jews could you transport to America and Palestine? Surely not all the five million there are. The great majority of them will stay here and be baited, and the only hope of these is a liberated Russia."[64]

Not everyone in the movement agreed with Clara that the Russian people were the people to whom the revolutionary intelligentsia must go. Chaim Zhitlovsky is one who did not. He took many turns in the intellectual and spiritual journey of his life, and one of the most significant was the turn from the sentiment that he was not a Jew (as he had been taught "in Chernyshevsky's *kheyder*") to a pronounced affirmation of his Jewishness. That was in the late 1880s. Two decades later he attended a famous conference in Czernowitz, then in the southeastern corner of the Austro-Hungarian Empire (today in Ukraine), where Jewish writers gathered in 1908 to establish Yiddish as a Jewish national language and to declare a new sense of prestige for what was still contemptuously referred to in those days as "zhargon" (jargon). Zhitlovsky was a formidable presence at the Czernowitz Conference, as it came to be called, and returned to New York determined to further its aim of raising the level of respect for Yiddish.

So he founded *Dos Naye Leben* (The new life, 1908–1913), a magazine that he dedicated to many of the same aims as those that *Di Tsukunft*'s editors had embraced a generation earlier. Most of these aims had to do with raising the cultural and educational level of his readers, but there was a difference between *Dos Naye Leben* and *Di Tsukunft*. Krantz and the cofounders of *Di Tsukunft* had never regarded Yiddish as an object of pride. They grudgingly recognized it as a stopgap, an interim medium they would be obliged to use until they had succeeded in raising their readers to a level of sophistication beyond anything to which the second-rate vernacular language of their forebears could pretend. Zhitlovsky, however, with the spirit of Czernowitz fresh in his mind, was now

8. Chaim Zhitlovsky (right) and Sholem Aleichem (left). Photo from
YIVO Institute for Jewish Research.

ready to proclaim that Yiddish was the equal of any other language and
was fully capable of expressing thoughts of the most advanced sort, in
any field of human endeavor,

The programmatic article Zhitlovsky wrote for *Dos Naye Leben*, titled
"The program and the goals of the monthly *Dos Naye Leben*," is a fasci-

nating document, because even though the author has staked out new ground in the struggle of the Jewish people, even though his focus on the Jews as Jews shows a rejection of the cosmopolitanism and internationalism that many of his peers in the press continued to advocate, his approach to his task is still that of a Lavrovian intellectual.[65]

The opening paragraphs of the article suggest that "the program and goals" of his magazine have almost entirely to do with the position of the intelligentsia. The whole problem of the Jewish people, in fact, is defined in terms of the intelligentsia, complete with the traditional Lavrovian vocabulary. What is needed, Zhitlovsky insists, is a new Jewish intelligentsia, one that will feel its duty or debt (the Hebraism he uses, *khoyv*, means both) to its *folk* and repay that debt (or discharge that duty). So, after speaking of the many political ideologies from which today's intellectual has to choose, and of the necessity for avoiding blind faith in any of them, Zhitlovsky comes to speak of the Jews and the mission of his magazine. Never a knee-jerk Zionist, Zhitlovsky cautions his readers to avoid the kind of pessimism that leads many Jews to think an ineluctable historical process has condemned them to endure a life of terrible hardships while they await the moment when an irresistible force will suddenly sweep them away to Eretz Israel. Like the Lavrov of the *Historical Letters*, Zhitlovsky has no use for what he calls an "unconscious-necessary" concept of historical process, one, that is, that leaves no room for the actions of thinking individuals. The task at hand is thus to concentrate attention on the Jewish people by giving them reading material that will bring them up to date on the latest developments in science and culture and keep them abreast of progress in the socialist movement—primarily in Russia, of course.

But he saves the big topic for last: Yiddish (Zhitlovsky consistently uses the German-sounding *yudish*, instead of *yidish*, for "Jewish" and "Yiddish"). "It is certain and clear to us," he says, "that [Yiddish] has within itself the power to express the most profound and complicated thoughts from science and philosophy; that any work of international literature, even the most difficult, can be rendered into Yiddish as into any other cultivated language. Yiddish has already grown up for an educated public."[66]

The only question is, then, how big that educated Jewish public is. And this brings us back to the central issue of the intelligentsia's duties. For too long, the intelligentsia has disdained Yiddish. The task now is to begin using Yiddish for the most advanced forms of discourse but at the same time to recognize that the public lacks the most basic higher learning necessary for an understanding of the sophisticated subjects Zhitlovsky proposes to treat. So, like the founders of the American Yiddish press a generation earlier, he proposes to fill in enough fundamental knowledge for his readers to allow them to understand what he publishes. In this way, he says, the "Yiddish [*yudish*] book" will come into being at the same time as the Jewish [*yudish*] intelligentsia.[67]

Filling in basic knowledge was to remain the job of the intelligentsia for some time to come. There is a curious subchapter to the story of the Jewish intelligentsia in America that illustrates this point in a realm of life rather far removed from the topics we have encountered so far in the Yiddish press. It is part of the surprisingly small segment of the movement devoted to women's issues—I say "surprisingly" because of the eminence of Russian feminism in the mid-nineteenth century and because of the degree to which it caught on in Jewish intellectual circles. Beginning in 1918, Adella Kean Zametkin ran a weekly column in *Der Tog* (The day) called "Fun a froy tsu froyen" (From one woman to another, or from one wife to another—*froy* means both), which she soon began to supplement with a second weekly column called "In der froyen velt" (In the world of women/wives).

The columns consisted largely of advice on household management: cooking tips, recipes, recommendations on how to wash dishes, and so on. But Zametkin, like her common-law husband Michael, was an old-time Russian radical, and even though she appears to have played an entirely traditional role in her household and dispensed advice on that role in her columns, she played the part of the Russian Jewish Populist leader with the women who read those columns. This meant that she served as a political, and not just a domestic mentor to them. It meant that her pupils were not only the wives of *working* men, but also the *Jewish* wives of working men. And finally it meant that she felt a responsibility to instruct those pupils in matters that most American women with a modicum of education would have considered elementary.

Her first column starts off with the following militant-sounding language:

> It is no news that the worker's plight in our society is hard and bitter. He carries on his shoulders an unbearable yoke. He is sold, he is oppressed, he is exploited. He is a slave. But the plight of his wife is much worse, because she is the slave of a slave. He toils away for a set number of hours in the factory and then comes home to rest. But who ever saw a worker's wife rest? Her work has no fixed hours. Her work has no end. She knows no rest.

Then, to show that her concern lies not with workers and their wives in general, but with Jewish workers and their wives, she says this:

> The worker in the shop these days has people to defend him, people who deal with the wrongs done to him: the union, his fellow workers. But the wife of a Jewish worker rarely finds anyone in her bitter condition who takes an interest in her at all. She is the center of the worker's home, and the home,

they say, is the heart of society. And yet in the Jewish American press there is no aspect of social life that has been so neglected as the life of the Jewish housewife.

So this column will have a clear purpose: "The task of the articles in 'From One Woman to Another' will consist in providing the wives of workers every week with a chance to find useful discussions about the difficulties they encounter every day."

From here she moves on to the topic of the week: "Wash the dishes but don't wipe them dry." The nature of her advice requires her to give her readers a lesson. The reason one must not wipe the dishes dry, the way our *bobes* (grandmas) did in the old country, is that wiping them spreads *microbes*. But of course the women reading *Der Tog* have never heard of microbes, so she tells what they are, explaining that microbes can't survive in hot water but can be spread with towels.[68]

Future columns will advance different components of Zametkin's program. She wages a campaign against the poisons we consume in processed food, she urges women to take time every day to get some fresh air, she gives advice on child rearing, and she contributes to the general education of her Jewish women readers, having drawn an unfavorable comparison with native-born American housewives, who seem to find time to read. "Never too late to learn," she titles the column in which she presents that comparison.[69] From time to time, she will give the working-class Jewish housewife a wholesome bit of knowledge about history, science, or noteworthy women like Florence Nightingale.

Admittedly, there is precious little documentable Nihilist or Russian Populist doctrine in Zametkin's columns, and the obligatory bits of social democratic jargon that appear from time to time could easily have been picked up in the United States by someone who had no Russian background at all. Neither is this a truly militant feminism or, for that matter, an especially militant anything. Zametkin did not lead that sort of life. We know this because her daughter, Laura Hobson, in her memoirs has given us something we have in the case of very few of the Jewish socialist leaders in America: a glimpse of the lives the Zametkins led at home. Adella Kean Zametkin, this remarkably well educated Russian intellectual, always dreaming of a calling that conflicted with what she saw as her domestic responsibilities, was never able to pursue a career that would take her away from her children. She went to dental college as an adult but gave it up after six weeks of anxiety over the well-being of her children. Hobson, in fact, places special emphasis on the traditional social roles her parents played, telling us that her mother fell in love with Michael Zametkin in a way that "might drive some latter-day feminists into a disapproving snit," because she presented herself as an "adoring inferior woman."[70] Her father, for his part, this tried and true socialist with his mid-nineteenth-century Russian ideas about social organization, was prickly and domineering at home, always enjoying the privilege of speaking with unchallenged authority.

Still, the columns in *Der Tog*, retrograde though they may appear today, with their underlying assumption that Jewish working-class women need look no farther than their homes for contentment, helped fill the gap in the Jewish press that Zametkin herself pointed out. *Di Tsukunft* had been running a series on notable women for the last few years, by a recent émigré named Esther Lurye, but, apart from that, there had in fact been relatively little notice taken of women's issues in the Yiddish press. Zametkin brought attention to some of those issues and did so in the way that had been characteristic of the Russified Jewish intelligentsia in America in its "Jewish" populist phase: addressing her readers as Jews, as members of the working class, and as cultural and social inferiors in need of intellectual leadership.

There is no doubt that the Yiddish-based movement in America was a fulfillment of the sentiment to which Elkin gave expression in *The White Terror and the Red*. After an initial phase during which the immigrant intellectuals both maintained a Russian identity and effectively ignored the needs of the Jewish "people," the Yiddish phase represents something of a "going to the people." To be sure, the relation between the Jewish intellectuals and the Jewish workers in the United States was not identical to the one between the Russian intellectuals and the Russian peasants in Russia. Jewish intellectuals in the United States, who were never more than a generation or two removed from a social and economic level just as humble as that of the Jewish workers, could hardly claim to have arrived at their status by exploiting the labor of their intellectually less exalted brethren for centuries on end. Nor, as a consequence, does it truly make sense to speak of a "debt" the intellectuals owed the workers in the same way that Lavrov felt he and others of his class owed the Russian *narod* a debt. The Jewish intellectuals, after all, together with the Jewish workers, had quite recently been very much like what the Russian intellectuals imagined the Russian peasants to be: a group oppressed by the upper classes as well as by the tsar, a group whose interests could well be served by the downfall of the tsar. For this reason, a "going to the people" in the United States could never replicate one of the most distinctive elements of the Russian "going to the people" campaign, namely the immense cultural distance that separated the "goers" (some of whom, let's not forget, were Jews) from the people.

Still, the writings of many Jewish intellectuals betray a distinctly Lavrovian attitude toward the less educated Jewish workers. The Russian Populists, of course, had not sought to win over the Russian people by arousing in them a feeling of ethnic solidarity with their saviors, the Populists. But for the Jewish "Populists," who were not members of the privileged classes even in America, it was necessary to arouse such a feeling in the *narod* they served. Different Jewish writers showed different degrees of concern for the Jewishness of their people, and many who did show concern did so not simply because it was politically expedient but because they took their own ethnic legacy quite seriously. Even for these, though, "going to the people" did not mean a total identification with the Jewish workers. Socialism, union organizing, "going to the people"—politics was always something undertaken by critically thinking individuals. And whether or not it was accurate to speak of paying back a debt, as Zhitlovsky revealingly put it, this appears to be exactly what the critically thinking individuals thought they were doing.

CHAPTER 8

"We Are Americans"

WRITING IN ENGLISH

OF COURSE, there was little prestige attached to "the plain, unembellished vernacular of the Ghetto," and few Jewish intellectuals wanted the public to think this was the only language they knew. The ability to speak Russian eloquently was a *sine qua non*, a feature that set the thinking elite apart from the proletarian masses in America at the outset. "Another mark of her noble birth," says the hero of Abe Cahan's *The Rise of David Levinsky* as he speaks of an educated Jewish woman (who also knows how to play the piano), "was the fact that she often addressed her husband and her older children, not in Yiddish or English, but in Russian."[1] Speaking Russian, and speaking it without a Yiddish accent (or, better still, not even knowing how to speak Yiddish), was enough, even if you could not play the piano.

Still, the mark of a true Jewish intellectual in America, an intellectual who already possessed a multilingual background but also had the sophistication to learn a new language and learn it well, was proficiency in English *in addition to* Russian.

John Spargo, a socialist writer and editor of the radical literary monthly *The Comrade* (1901–1905), showed a keen sensitivity to this system of values, though he himself was not a Russian Jewish immigrant. Here is the picture he draws of life on the Lower East Side of New York during an election campaign: "There is little advertising of the ordinary kind, but the word is passed cheerily from passerby to passerby that there will be a meeting, and the hall is soon crowded; or, if it be in the open, an audience soon gathers. That young Russian there, speaking in fearful and wonderful English—if he spoke in Yiddish they could better understand him but he loves to demonstrate his linguistic attainments—is the candidate of his party. He hisses out the names of his opponents; they belong to the hated capitalist class. And how they cheer him!"[2]

LEARNING ENGLISH

To be a "young Russian," not a Jew, speaking English, not Yiddish—this was the aspiration of many a Russian Jewish intellectual. Unless you were one of the relatively few admirers of Zhitlovsky's Yiddishism, what could be more cosmopolitan, more antinationalist than the ability to participate in a culture and a political scene that was not intrinsically Jewish? Abe Cahan knew this, knew that a solid grasp of English would give him influence that few other immigrants could hope to attain. Soon after his arrival, he set out to master English grammar and an authentic American pronunciation, including those banes of every Yiddish-speaking immigrant, the American *r* and *th*. He even went so far as to attend classes in a public primary school so that he could learn as American schoolchildren did.[3]

There can be no doubt about the power a good command of English could give an immigrant Jew in public, political life, even outside the journalistic activities associated with that life. Progressive newspapers and magazines in various languages were always running English-language advertisements for the professional services of many members of the Jewish left (often those whose names appear elsewhere in the same publication), a sign that many had gained at least some form of acceptance in the civic life of the majority population.

Frank Rosenblatt occupied positions in the federal and state government as a labor economist.[4] Many members of the intelligentsia found the time to pursue legal studies after their arrival in America, earn a law degree, and practice law, in addition to carrying out more purely political activities in the labor movement. Nicholas Aleinikoff, Morris Hillquit, Louis Miller, and Isaac Hourwich were among the best known members of the intelligentsia who had careers as attorneys. Henry L. Slobodin, who became active in the socialist movement and wrote extensively for the English-language radical press, was at one point Morris Hillquit's partner in a law practice and appears to have opened up his own office later.[5] I have already mentioned the role of Simon O. Pollock in the extradition case. Louis Boudin had a long and illustrious career as a labor attorney.

Those with the most influence, however, were the ones who entered electoral politics, like the typical figure in Spargo's literary portrait, and the ones who worked their way from the Yiddish-speaking sections of socialist and labor organizations to the national, English-speaking sections. Undoubtedly the most spectacular example of the first type was Meyer London (1871–1927), an immigrant from Poland who carefully cultivated the skill of public speaking in English, earned a law degree, and devoted himself to the socialist cause as an activist and a union lawyer for the rest of his life. His most remarkable accomplishment was his election to Congress, on the Socialist ticket, as the Representative from New York's Ninth District (the Lower East Side) in 1914, 1916, and 1920.

The most notable example of the second type was probably Morris Hillquit, also a labor lawyer and also many times a candidate, though an unsuccessful one, for public office. Hillquit's claim to fame, however, is his role in the socialist movement. He had helped organize the United Hebrew Trades in 1888 and had become one of the most active members of the Socialist Labor Party. When that party split at the end of the 1890s, Hillquit helped put together the coalition of moderate groups that was finally organized as the Socialist Party in 1901. Hillquit became perhaps the leading member and chief spokesman of the new party. The height of his prominence both inside and outside the Jewish community came during World War I, to which he adopted a highly public stance of unbending, pacifist opposition. During this era, one reads of Hillquit's many public statements and his speeches at mass rallies for peace and against the draft. He was also a respected authority on socialism and the labor movement. And of course, his *History of Socialism in the United States* (1903) was one of the most highly regarded books on the subject and went through many printings.

No Russian Jewish immigrant intellectual had such a high stake in her mastery of English, or rose so high through it, as did Emma Goldman. In many ways Goldman is an anomaly in the story of the immigrant Jewish intelligentsia in America. She came at an earlier age and received more of her political education in America than many others, even though the intellectual sources of her worldview were primarily Russian. This worldview set her apart from the better known immigrant political leaders, most of whom embraced a form of socialism for most of the period of mass immigration.

It is true that Goldman found inspiration for the broader outlines of her political philosophy in Chernyshevsky, as she explains in her memoirs, and Chernyshevsky had much to do with her first political awakening.[6] She went so far as to set up a dressmaking cooperative (which failed almost immediately) in New Haven in 1890, in imitation of a similar venture undertaken by the heroine of *What Is to Be Done?* But Goldman was an anarchist, and the dominant forces in the shaping of the political program she carried out for most of her life were the Russian anarchists Bakunin and Kropotkin, together with a number of other figures she encountered in America. In addition, more than almost any other immigrant intellectual, she widened the arena of her political activity almost from the very start, reaching out to a population that was not exclusively Jewish, whose ethnic identity, in fact, was irrelevant.

She lost patience early on with the workers' movement, mostly, she said, because she lost patience with the workers themselves. Abe Cahan reported her sentiments on the subject as she left for a trip to Europe in 1899. Anyone who has read Dostoevsky's *The Devils* and remembers the character of Peter Verkhovensky, the proudly unscrupulous apostle of an anarchistic Nihilism carried to a monstrous extreme of utter senselessness, will hear an echo in the cynical disdain that Goldman professes for the humanitarian compassion central to socialist politics. Such disdain was typical for Russian anarchists. This is what she said, as Cahan reported it:

> In my experience with the American workingman, during more than ten years, I have found him to be the most contemptible creature on earth. Even the ignorant Russian peasant, downtrodden and stupid as he is, will revolt some time when the outrages committed upon him become great. Here, in this country, the government is more despotic than that of the Czar. Crime after crime, outrage after outrage, is perpetrated in the name of 'law and order,' and the workingman goes on voting for his oppressors. . . . Talk of liberty! Why, there is more of that in Russia than you have here.[7]

These sentiments may have been the expression of a heartfelt political conviction. But a glance at the list of topics Goldman lectured on shows a mind that could never have been satisfied with the inner politics of the Jewish labor movement in New York. She lectured on birth control, sexuality, marriage, free love, atheism, Russian culture, free speech, countless topical political matters, and, of course, anarchism. Speaking was truly the center of Goldman's life. She often spent many months of the year on the road giving public lectures around the country. Free speech, in fact, was probably the single most important cause of her life-long political struggle. Though she was an accomplished speaker in Russian, German, and Yiddish, English allowed her to reach the widest audience, and she devoted a tremendous amount of effort to perfecting her command of her adopted language.

English was thus clearly a vehicle by which the immigrant intellectuals could propel themselves from the confined world of the Jewish ghetto into the broader, "American" world of business and politics. Still, in most cases they retained their sense of identity as Russians (hence David Levinsky's emphasis on his acquaintance's Russian, not her English). Emma Goldman wrote a letter to Petr Kropotkin in 1913, in which she expressed a sentiment that many of her fellow immigrant intellectuals shared (and showed that her English spelling still needed work): "While my whole life is rapt up in the American struggle, almost as if I had been born here, still my soul is in Russia, and probably will never be anywhere else."[8] Though many, especially after the turn of the century, devoted much of their energy to political and intellectual pursuits that were not directly connected with either Russian or Jewish cultural life, many remained committed to the ideas they had learned in the old country. Native-born Americans, of course, were not prepared to overlook the ethnic and cultural differences that separated them from Cahan, Hillquit, and others, but, to judge from the treatment the most influential immigrants received in the English-language press, Americans were often just as inclined to view them as Russians as they were to view them as Jews. And since Americans at the end of the nineteenth century were showing a budding fascination with Russian culture, they frequently treated members of this group as curious artifacts whose qualities could supplement the translated stories of Chekhov and Tolstoy they were already reading in mainstream magazines.

AMERICANS LOOK AT RUSSIA AND THE "RUSSIANS" IN AMERICA

Russophilia caught on in the United States. To some extent, it was independent of the Russian Jewish radicals. Among the earliest and most fervent Russophiles were American-born radicals, especially anarchists. Kropotkin's and Bakunin's names appear with some frequency in the American radical press from as early as the 1880s. There are stories by Chekhov, because he was a realist, and by Gorky, because he was a revolutionary and a proletarian. Above all, there is Tolstoy, because he was viewed as a socialist (by some), a supporter of the peasants, a martyr of Russian oppression (as when the Russian Orthodox Church excommunicated him in 1901), and a victim of international persecution (as when the Postmaster General of the United States banned editions of the *Kreutzer Sonata* from the mails). Progressive American periodicals published stories by Tolstoy and also kept their readers abreast of important happenings in his life.

Few Americans were as inspired by Russian revolutionary culture as Benjamin Tucker (1854–1939), the translator of Chernyshevsky's *What Is to Be Done?*. His biweekly, *Liberty*, started publishing material about the heroes and heroines of the Russian revolutionary movement in its very first year, 1881, before almost any of the Jewish radicals had arrived.[9] By 1882, there had already been a poem about Sofiia Perovskaia, a profile of Bakunin, and an article about ten Russian Nihilists who had been sentenced to death.[10] It was in *Liberty* that Tucker's translation of Chernyshevsky's novel first appeared, in serial form, from May 1884 to May 1886.[11] Tucker published a serialized translation of a work by the famous terrorist Stepniak (pseudonym of Sergei Mikhailovich Kravchinskii), numerous articles on Tolstoy and Chernyshevsky, and many articles on members of the Nihilist generation.[12]

But the Russian Jewish immigrants played a significant role in arousing interest in things Russian among native-born Americans in large part because Americans so often viewed the immigrants as Russians. Some even wrote about them in the periodical press and in books. Hutchins Hapgood, a young reporter for the *New York Commercial Advertiser*, was no doubt the best known of these. In the 1890s, Hapgood's older brother Norman, also a journalist, had discovered New York's ethnic enclaves and written about them, and Hutchins had struck up a friendship with Abe Cahan, who wrote in English for the *Advertiser* from 1897 to 1902. The younger Hapgood pursued his brother's interest and focused specifically on the Jewish ghetto, writing a series of sketches for the *Advertiser* and other publications between 1898 and 1902. He then collected the sketches and brought them out in book form as *The Spirit of the Ghetto* in 1902.

Hapgood knew that the human subjects of his investigation were Jews, and much of what he describes on the Lower East Side has to do with Jewish life. And yet when he comes to speak of the more influential members of the immigrant community, it is to their Russianness that he directs our attention. His editor at the *Advertiser*, the future muck-raking journalist Lincoln Steffens, viewed Abe Cahan as "an East Side Russian socialist," and Hapgood seems to have picked up on this dominant ingredient in the cultural and intellectual make-up of Cahan and his fellow immigrant intellectuals.[13]

It is astonishing how deeply Hapgood penetrated into the political and cultural worldview of his subjects. He did so apparently with little knowledge of the Russian sources of the ideas and attitudes he describes, for his acquaintance with Russian culture seems confined to the classics that were available in English translation at the time he wrote. His description of "the modern type" of women in the ghetto could have come from the pages of a work on Chernyshevsky's impact on Russian society. "As we ascend in the scale of education in the Ghetto," he says, having already described those traditional "Jewesses" who live their lives strictly by Talmudic principle, "we find women who derive their culture and ideas from a double source—from Socialism and from advanced Russian ideals of literature and life." They know Russian better than Yiddish, he says, they read Tolstoy, Turgenev, and Chekhov, and they "put into practice the most radical theories of the 'new women,' particularly those which say that woman should be economically independent of man." He tells us that many of the "new women" have pursued professional careers as dentists, doctors, writers, and lawyers. He describes certain "Nihilists" among the women immigrants, and mentions their preference for realism in art. There is even a drawing of "a Russian girl-student" that contains all the elements we find in Leo Deutsch's humorous description of Russian Nihilist students.[14] The student's appearance is severe and unglamorous: she wears small spectacles like the ones Chernyshevsky himself had worn, her hair is close-cropped, and her hat is ungainly and awkward.[15]

The distinctive feature of almost all the writers and artists in the Jewish community, as Hapgood sees it, is their fidelity to Russian models. Abraham Liessin is a man whose entire view of the world changed after his exposure to Russian literature, and Hapgood sees him as one who continues to like Russia better than America.[16] The writings of Jacob Gordin,

9. The Nihilist style in America. "A Russian girl-student," as drawn by Jacob Epstein for Hutchins Hapgood's *The Spirit of the Ghetto*.

David Pinski, and the influential drama critic and Yiddish playwright Bernard Gorin (pen name of Yitskhok Goydo), as Hapgood describes them in a section called "American Life through Russian Eyes," are all "Russian not only in form, but also in material."[17] The sketch of the Yiddish playwright and fiction writer Leon Kobrin is all about the Russian traditions that are carried on in his work.[18]

The intellectuals as a group are, in Hapgood's words, "neither orthodox Jews nor Americans." "Coming from Russia," he says, "they are

10. "Interesting People: A Jew who wields tremendous power over his people." Abe Cahan featured in *American Magazine*, 1912.

reactionary in their political opinions, and in matters of taste and literary ideals are Europeans rather than Americans." The word "reactionary" is strange in this context, but Hapgood appears to mean not "ultraconservative," but "tending to react against things politically," because a few sentences later he says that the ghetto as a whole (meaning the masses) has not yet learned enough about the conditions of American life to "react against them."[19]

Those writing in Yiddish newspapers, he goes on, "produce realistic sketches of the life in the quarter, underlying which can be felt the same kind of revolt which is apparent in the analogous literature of Russia."[20] And in a passage that acknowledges the Jewishness of the young intellectuals of the Lower East Side, he says this: "In their restless and feverish eyes shines the intense idealism of the combined Jew and Russian—the moral earnestness of the Hebrew united with the passionate, rebellious mental activity of the modern Muscovite."[21]

Hapgood's sketch of Abe Cahan, to whom he devotes more space in *The Spirit of the Ghetto* than to any other individual, shows how essential Cahan's Russian education and outlook were to the position Hapgood thought this man, identified in the title to the sketch as "A Novelist," held in his community. Cahan had taken "an early and overpowering interest in the Russian language and ideas," despite his *kheyder* education.[22] During Cahan's tenure as editor of *Arbayter Tsaytung* the paper sought "to educate the people to an appreciation of the best realistic Russian writers, such as Tolstoi, Turgenieff and Chekhov."[23] But this was because of the overarching belief Cahan had about writing, a belief that is as Russian as can be, though Hapgood does not connect it with Cahan's Russian background: "Literature, however, was at that time to Cahan only the handmaiden of education. His career as an east side writer was that primarily of the teacher. He wished not merely to educate the ignorant masses of the people in the doctrines of Socialism, but to teach them the rudiments of science and literature."[24] "Love of truth," he says, "is the quality which seems to a stranger in the Ghetto the great virtue of that section of the city. . . . And after all, the great passion of the intellectual quarter results in the consciously held and warmly felt principle that literature should be a transcript from life. Cahan represents this feeling in its purest aspect. . . . This passion for truth is deeply infused into his literary work."[25] Nothing could be more characteristic of the era of Russian Nihilism than this.

CAHAN AND CO., PURVEYORS OF RUSSIAN CULTURE AND POLITICS

So in the eyes of many Americans, a man like Abe Cahan was a Russian socialist, as Lincoln Steffens described him. He could also be "a Jew who wields tremendous power over his people," as he was described in the popular *American Magazine*. This second description was written in 1912, when the American reading public was perhaps a bit more receptive to the idea of including an immigrant Jew in a column called "Interesting People" than it had been a few years earlier.[26] But the first description was far more common, and once the immigrant intellectuals discovered the rewards of publishing in English, it was on their status as Russians that they almost always focused attention.

Many clearly saw an opportunity to capitalize on an existing fascination with Russia and its culture by serving as conduits for the exotic settings they had seen and the perilous deeds they had witnessed or performed in the movement. Others used their new forum for political propaganda. And still others wrote fictional pieces borrowed from or set in their native culture.

Morris Winchevsky, who wrote plenty of propaganda but whose great love appears to have been literary writing, was one of the third group. He contributed a number of short literary sketches to left-wing periodicals, always using the ornate, stilted English prose style that he and other immigrants borrowed from their favorite British novelists. He published a number of his stories originally in English magazines, republished some of these in the American press, and then, in 1908, published a collection of fifteen of these stories in a little volume called *Stories of the Struggle*.[27] Many of Winchevsky's sketches are oddly put together, with curiously unbalanced story lines and truncated endings, possibly in imitation of Chekhov. What almost all of them have in common is a Russian setting and characters who are clearly Jewish but presented primarily as Russian.

Winchevsky was a member of the editorial board of *The Comrade* (1901–1905), a socialist monthly, as it described itself on the masthead, whose express purpose was to be specifically a literary publication. To this journal Winchevsky contributed such pieces as "Why he did it," a story set partly on the Lower East Side. The characters speak Russian, have Darwin and Spencer at the "fingers' tips," have "a good deal to say about Gorki," gather around a samovar ("the one thing every man and woman born on Russian soil either loves or affects to love"), talk of anarchism, terrorism, and the assassination of Alexander II—in short, they make a very Russian gathering, except that on the Lower East Side everyone is Jewish, and anyone speaking Russian is almost certain, in reality, to be a Jewish intellectual.[28]

Winchevsky's fiction also appeared in the *International Socialist Review* (1900–1918), the journal most closely associated with the American socialist movement in its heyday. In early 1908, Winchevsky published "The Knout and the Fog," which had originally appeared in England and was also published in *Stories of the Struggle*. Here Winchevsky dramatizes the lives of Jewish intellectuals in Russia. His heroine is Nellie, who, like many other Jewish and non-Jewish young women in the Russian intelligentsia, had taken up medicine. Owing to official anti-Jewish measures, she is forced to abandon her studies and her hopes of a profession, is denied permission to reside in the two big cities, registers as a prostitute in order to remain legally in Moscow, and flees Russia (the "knout") for London (the "fog"). There, in a bathetic ending worthy of the early Dostoevsky, she dies homeless and hungry on a doorstep. Winchevsky, who in his youth had been unable to pass a *bes medresh* (Jewish house of study) without gnashing his teeth in anger, concludes with bitter sarcasm: "But Russia was purged of one moral monster, of one Jewess, at all events."[29]

Simon O. Pollock was especially active in the English-language press, publishing literary pieces and commentary, all centered on Russia. In one early instance, he published a story that, as the editor explains in a footnote, he had heard from the lips of the critic and activist Mikhailovsky in St. Petersburg years earlier and had set down from memory. "The Singer" is a typical bargain-with-the-devil tale about a young Russian man who is offered the opportunity to sing in an inhumanly beautiful voice—but only three times; after the third time, he will perish. What Pollock, and presumably Mikhailovsky, did with the *Trilby*-like story was to place it in the setting of Russia's and Europe's great revolutionary struggles, so that each time the hero sings, the power of his song stirs his listeners to some form of valiant action: "devotion to the cause of all for all" in Russia, a determination to combat tsarism, even a brave counterattack on the battlefield, as the hero fights alongside Garibaldi's troops against the Austrians during Italy's war for independence.[30] Pollock later published this story in *The Young Socialists' Magazine* in 1918.[31]

In 1904, the famous heroine of the Russian revolutionary movement, Ekaterina Breshkovskaia, was in the United States seeking aid for the movement. Pollock devoted an acclamatory article to her in *The Worker*, the official organ of the Social Democratic Party. George Kennan had written about Breshkovskaia in *Siberia and the Exile System*, and now, at the time of her visit and for years afterward, the radical press was full of articles by and about this "grandmother" of the Russian revolution.[32] As in so many similar articles appearing in the English and Yiddish press, Pollock was obliged to review the history of the radical movement in Russia, in this case starting from the emancipation of the serfs in 1861. The reader thus learned about Lavrov, Bakunin, the "going to the people" movement, *Narodnaia volia*, and similar matters, in addition to reading of the horrendous torments that Breshkovskaia underwent in her twenty-two years of penal servitude.[33]

No doubt Pollock's most stirring contribution to the English-language press was a piece called "The Russian Bastille," which came out in the *International Socialist Review* in 1907. He devoted this article to a grim description of one of Russia's most notorious symbols of tyranny and political repression, the hated Schlüsselburg Fortress near St. Petersburg, where many famous revolutionaries were imprisoned. Once again, Pollock reviews the major moments of the Russian revolutionary movement and lists many of its heroes and heroines, including those who had been imprisoned in this "Russian Bastille."[34] Charles Kerr, the publisher of

International Socialist Review, must have considered Pollock's article either a great success or a promising piece of propaganda, because he brought out an expanded version of it as a small book in 1908.[35]

Left-wing readers after the turn of the century were no doubt just as eager to read about the ordeals of political prisoners and exiles as mainstream readers had been a decade or two earlier, when George Kennan published his series on Siberia, and there was no shortage of such material in the American radical press. Leo Deutsch, whose hardships in Siberia rivaled those of almost any other revolutionary, contributed reminiscences to the English-language press. In 1904, when his *Sixteen Years in Siberia* came out in New York, *The Comrade* brought out an excerpt from it, and *The Worker* reviewed it.[36]

One of the most thoughtful contributions to the radical English-language press by a Jewish intellectual is a series that Jacob Milch published in the *International Socialist Review* called "New Movements Amongst the Jewish Proletariat."[37] The series is particularly valuable to the historian of Jewish immigration because it combines three focal concerns of the Russian Jewish intelligentsia in America: the Russian revolutionary movement, the specifically Jewish movement in Russia, and the importation to America of ideas central to those movements. This last concern, in fact, appears at the outset to be Milch's reason for writing his series. Where formerly East Side Jews were interested almost exclusively in socialism, he says, events in Russia have now led to the emergence of many different political theories among Russian Jews. The latest persecutions and resulting stream of Jewish immigration have meant that the new theories "have now been transplanted to our shores."[38]

Like the majority of politically progressive Jews in America at this time, Milch was a confirmed foe of Zionism. His article "What is to be done?" in *Di Tsukunft* in 1903 had proclaimed his views on this theory, and he wastes no time here in blasting all its latest versions. He is as unwilling as ever to allow that the Jews are truly a nation. Everything about the Jews that is distinctive, he insists, is a product of their exile, which means that they can be understood not in relation to the land of their origin, Palestine, but in relation to the lands where they have settled, primarily Russia.

So it is not surprising that Milch correctly locates the origins of Zionism in Russia, in the writings of Leo Pinsker, the author of the proto-Zionist pamphlet *Auto-Emancipation* (1882), and Moses Leib Lilienblum. It was no accident that two Russian Jews were the first to give clear expression to what came to be called Zionism, Milch explains. Their views were a direct response to the pogroms and the anti-Jewish legislation that followed the assassination of Alexander II, when it became natural for Jews to think that their status as *foreigners* (not Jews) was responsible for their sufferings and that the sooner they found a country of their own, the sooner they would cease to be foreigners.[39]

In keeping with his view, as expressed in the *Tsukunft* article, that the Russian Jewish immigrants are spiritually still in Russia and only bodily in America, Milch devotes the final part of his discussion to the future of the Jewish proletariat—not in America, but in Russia only. He addresses what he sees as the only authentic political theory regarding the Jews, namely the historical materialist one, which explains the current position of Jewish workers by referring to the late arrival of capitalism in Russia and the absence, until recently, of a Jewish working class.[40]

All these views may very well have been transplanted to "our shores," but Milch is not really interested in what happens to them in their new home. It is only their original context that interests him, and that context is one in which the Jews are distinctive, not because of any innate religious characteristic, but just because they are perceived as "foreigners." When Milch had said such things in *Di Tsukunft*, it had been in an attempt to stir his fellow Jews to an antinationalist political struggle of the sort that he and like-minded intellectuals had wanted to wage in the Russian Empire and its territories (he was from Warsaw). But when he says such things in an English-language publication for a readership that necessarily includes many non-Jews, he is clearly attempting to persuade his readers that, when it comes to a political struggle, Jewishness is not a mark of ethnic distinctness but a conduit for Russian radical ideology (or Marxist ideology as applied to Russia).

No Russian Jewish intellectual, however, was so prolific and influential a contributor to the English-language press as was Abe Cahan. In 1897, Lincoln Steffens took over the city editorship of the New York *Commercial Advertiser*, a staid newspaper that had been around since 1793, and set out to transform it into an attention-grabbing popular publication with an emphasis on the everyday life of the city. Since he was interested in New York's burgeoning immigrant enclaves, Steffens hired Cahan. Cahan's short English novel *Yekl* had garnered stupendously good reviews the year before and had brought him considerable fame. Between 1897 and 1902, he wrote regularly for the *Advertiser* and also for such mainstream English-language publications as the *Atlantic Monthly*, *Harper's Weekly*, and *Cosmopolitan*.[41]

But he did not confine himself to writing local-color pieces on life in the Jewish ghetto. The identity Cahan adopted in the world of English-speaking journalists was, not surprisingly, that of a Russian artist and intellectual, culturally superior to his American colleagues and committed to the tenets of literary realism that had been firmly established in the West as the essential features of Russian fiction. So, while Cahan was able to roam the city and find entrancing slices of ethnic life, while he had a chance to boost the standing of the immigrant Jewish community by explaining to American readers the quaint customs of the socially humble (that is, still religious) members of this community, he also had a chance to provide all Americans with an education in Russian culture and politics.

The American reading public was bound to be relatively ignorant of the history of the Russian revolutionary movement, so Cahan and other "Russians" writing in the American press had to fill in many details for their readers. For example, when the *Commercial Advertiser* asked Cahan to write an article about the Kishinev pogroms in May of 1903, describing him in the editorial introduction to his article as "probably the best known Russian writer now in this country," Cahan rightly felt compelled to set the context by referring to events that had occurred in preceding decades.[42] He speaks, for example, of *Narodnaia volia*, the assassination of Alexander II, and the anti-Jewish riots of 1881. What is curious about the piece is that, though it is in part designed to engage American sympathy for a group that Americans have never been especially fond of and though Cahan refers touchingly to "the history of my unhappy people," he begins by directing our attention to the broader political situation in Russia. "Russia is quivering on the brink of a revolution," he says and repeats the sentence almost verbatim later in the article. The revolutionary movement is particularly important to the matter of anti-Semitism because, in Cahan's view, it harbors no racial hostility. "Indeed," he says," in every place where [the revolutionary] movement has obtained a firm footing, the two races live in perfect harmony and good feeling."[43]

It was undoubtedly owing in part to Cahan's efforts that the word "Nihilism," in the Russian sense, gained a certain currency in the English language around the turn of the century. In 1900, Cahan writes of a speech that Vladimir Stoleshnikov had given on East Broadway in honor of Petr Lavrov, who had died a couple of weeks earlier. The article is titled "Nestor of Nihilism" (Cahan's name for Lavrov), and in it, Cahan repeatedly uses the word "Nihilist" in a broad sense to refer to anyone now or previously connected with the Russian revolutionary movement. He never sees the need to define the term.[44] Two years later, Cahan writes about a certain unnamed Russian "Nihilist" who is visiting New York and who has brought with him news of the movement in Russia. The Nihilist's report is full of information about the revolutionary movement of the previous two decades.[45] Once again, Cahan sees no need to define "Nihilist" for his American readers.

Cahan did not limit his treatment of Russia to politics. He used his podium at the *Advertiser* to introduce American readers to his favorite authors, some of whom were practically unknown before these articles appeared. There are translations from Potapenko and Chekhov, articles on

Tolstoy, and even a translation from a set of memoirs on Dostoevsky, at a time when Dostoevsky was not well known in the United States. Cahan was a natural at playing the pedagogue—as he put it, Americans were mere "children" when it came to art, and he was there to teach them.[46]

This is not to suggest that Cahan in his years as an English-language journalist completely turned his back on his fellow Jews in order to advance the cause of Russian culture or socialist cosmopolitanism. One of his most stirring contributions to the press and to an important national debate was "The Russian Jew in America," published in the *Atlantic Monthly*.[47] This is the article in which he told one of his versions of the story about the repentant Jewish Nihilists. After he tells the story, Cahan focuses much attention on the intellectuals among Jewish immigrants, referring at one point to the "educated Russian-speaking minority forming a colony within a Yiddish-speaking colony" in most American cities. But Cahan's purpose is to make a plea to American readers for the dignity of the ordinary Jewish immigrants.

What impelled him to write this defense of his fellow Jews—and a circumstance that might expose Cahan to the charge that he was nothing more than a foul-weather friend to his own people—were the proposals that the United States Congress frequently took up to limit immigration. Proponents of these measures would cite such factors as illiteracy, crime, and poverty among the recent immigrants, together with the tendency of immigrants to depress the wages of native-born workers. Cahan uses his article and his standing in the larger community of educated Americans to refute one by one the arguments of the anti-immigrationists. What emerges is an eloquent, surprisingly "nationalistic" paean to the Jews as a people. He even gets in a scarcely disguised dig at the Irish and Italian immigrants when he says of "the Essex Street Jew" (by which he means the typical Jew from the Lower East Side) that "he strives to live like a civilized man, and the money which another workman perhaps might spend on drink [Irish] and sport [Italian] he devotes to the improvement of his home and the education of his children."[48]

Hutchins Hapgood had felt that Yiddish theatre presented the spectacle of "American life through Russian eyes," since he believed that such playwrights as Gordin, Pinski, and Gorin were essentially Russians writing in Yiddish. One could say that Cahan's contributions to the English-language press present the same spectacle, except that Cahan is able to bring the Russian perspective to readers who know neither Yiddish nor Russian. And the same could be said for all of Cahan's fellow immigrants who joined the progressive movements and published in English. But there are other voices besides those of Cahan, Morris Hillquit, Louis Boudin, and Louis Miller.

One of these, of course, belonged to Emma Goldman. Another be-

longed to her friend, sometime lover, and fellow Russian Jewish anarchist, Alexander Berkman (1870–1936). Berkman's story more chillingly
than almost anyone else's during the era of mass immigration illustrates
the art-into-life ideology of Russian Nihilism (and anarchism). Berkman
had come to the United States as a young man in 1888 (he was born in
1870), after devoting his student years in Russia to Nihilist and Populist
causes. Like Goldman, he quickly became involved in the anarchist movement in America, forming a close friendship with the German leader of
that movement, Johann Most. In 1892, he decided to assassinate Henry
Clay Frick, the plant manager of the Carnegie Steel Company in Homestead, Pennsylvania, near Pittsburgh. Frick had proved to be a hard task-
master in his negotiations with striking workers at the plant. His most
egregious act was to call in a battalion of Pinkerton guards, who engaged
the workers in a series of armed skirmishes early in July and killed nine of
them (several guards were killed, too).

In his memoirs, which have a clear place in the annals of radical Jewish
publications in English, Berkman tells of the train ride to Homestead and
gives a kind of stream-of-consciousness presentation of the thoughts that
went through his mind. The scene shifts continually between the present
and Berkman's past in Russia. An English-speaking reader who picked up
Berkman's book after it was published in 1912 and read no farther than
the opening pages would have been treated to a brief course on nineteenth-century Russian radical politics. For example, this:

> In my mind I see myself back in the little Russian college town, amid the
> circle of Petersburg students, home for their vacation, surrounded by the
> halo of that vague and wonderful something we called "Nihilist." The rush-
> ing train, Homestead, the five years passed in America, all turn into a mist,
> hazy with the distance of unreality, of centuries; and again I sit among supe-
> rior beings, reverently listening to the impassioned discussion of dimly un-
> derstood high themes, with the oft-recurring refrain of "Bazarov, Hegel,
> Liberty, Chernishevsky, *v naród*." To the People! To the beautiful, simple
> People, so noble in spite of centuries of brutalizing suffering! Like a clarion
> call the note rings in my ears, amidst the din of contending views and ob-
> scure phraseology. The People![49]

Berkman never loses sight of the position he occupies in the Populist
struggle, though he consistently uses the word "Nihilist" generically for
all Russian revolutionaries. "The Nihilists!" he exclaims.

> How much of their precious blood has been shed, how many thousands of
> them line the road of Russia's suffering! Inexpressibly near and soul-kin I
> feel to those men and women, the adored, mysterious ones of my youth, who
> had left wealthy homes and high station to "go to the People," to become

11. Alexander Berkman, at the time of the Homestead Strike.

one with them, though despised by all whom they held dear, persecuted and ridiculed even by the benighted objects of their great sacrifice.[50]

Much of Berkman's reverie appears to come from Mikhail Bakunin and Sergei Nechaev. Nechaev was an infamous terrorist who served as a real-life model for Peter Verkhovensky in Dostoevsky's *The Devils*. The most renowned forum for Bakunin's and Nechaev's ideas was their *Catechism of a Revolutionary*, written in 1869. This impassioned screed presents a picture of the ideal revolutionary as one who places the cause above all personal interest and physical well-being, the cause being the earliest possible destruction of the state and all its institutions. So, as Berkman sits in the train on the way to enacting his bold plan, he muses about how a revolutionary is "a being who has neither personal interests nor desires above the necessities of the Cause."[51]

His thoughts then turn to Chernyshevsky, or, to be more precise, the super-human hero of *What Is to Be Done?*, Rakhmetov. After reflecting that Rakhmetov's burdensome efforts to "steel his nerves and harden his body" (efforts, remember, that Abe Cahan and his friends had mimicked by sleeping on the hard floor) suggested a certain measure of self-doubt, Berkman concludes that he can dispense with such efforts. But his admiration for Rakhmetov is intact, as we see. "My own individuality is entirely in the background; aye, I am not conscious of any personality in matters pertaining to the Cause," he thinks to himself. "I am simply a revolutionist, a terrorist by conviction, an instrument for furthering the cause of humanity; in short, a Rakhmetov. Indeed, I shall assume that name upon my arrival in Pittsburgh."[52]

He did. And, flush with the assumption of this inspiring identity, he tracked down his prey and shot and stabbed him. Perhaps he had, in fact, underestimated the need to steel his nerves, because he did not succeed in killing Frick. He was immediately arrested.

To judge from his own account, though, his nerves were sufficiently hardy to allow him to face down the police chief who interrogated him. The ghost of Chernyshevsky was present here, too, as we see in the grimly comical scene that Berkman describes. The chief attempts to play both parts of a god-cop-bad-cop routine, alternately coaxing and threatening. He wants his prisoner to reveal his true identity, though Berkman has done so. The chief does not believe him, so he plays his trump:

> "You can be quite frank with me," the inquisitor is saying. "I know a good deal more about you than you think. We've got your friend Rakmetov."
>
> With difficulty I suppress a smile at the stupidity of the intended trap. In the register of the hotel where I passed the first night in Pittsburgh, I signed "Rakhmetov," the name of the hero in Chernishevsky's famous novel.
>
> "Yes, we've got your friend, and we know all about you."[53]

THE "RUSSIANS" IN AMERICA SPUR AN INTEREST IN RUSSIA

If only for pragmatic reasons—most labor leaders, after all, wanted to inspire America's workers, not compare them unfavorably with the "downtrodden," "stupid" Russian peasants and then abandon them in disgust, as Emma Goldman had done—Russian Jewish intellectuals in America used Russia as a model in political discussion: an inspiring model when they spoke of the revolutionary movement and its heroes, a cautionary model when they spoke of the tsarist tyranny that made this revolutionary movement necessary.

There quickly developed in the English-language radical press a cultural and political exchange between the Russian Jews and the native-born Americans. If such leaders as Hillquit and Miller became involved in a political movement that was at least in some part an indigenous creation, their American comrades quickly learned the benefits of keeping an eye on Russia's political past and present. After the era when Benjamin Tucker was almost a lone native-born voice in the cause of propagating the culture of Russian radicalism in America, other nonimmigrant radicals disseminated their views on Russia in a press that they shared with Jewish immigrants from that country. It can be no accident that dozens of articles on Russian politics and culture, signed by writers bearing non-Russian and non-Jewish names, appear in the same journals as articles signed by such writers as Winchevsky, Boudin, Hillquit, and Milch.

The Americans appear to have had their own legion of Russian political and cultural heroes, one that differed from that of the émigrés largely by the emphasis the Americans placed on certain figures. Kropotkin was a continuing source of fascination, though it must be said that, like Mikhail Bakunin, he seems to have established an international reputation that was no doubt partly independent of the efforts of Russian Jewish émigrés. Still, the anarchist movement in the United States had attracted considerable attention, and many of its most attention-getting figures, like Emma Goldman, were Russian Jews. This, no doubt, helped keep non-Jewish anarchists like Kropotkin in the news.

When Kropotkin's masterpiece, *Mutual Aid*, came out in 1902, it was immediately hailed in the socialist press as a signal work for the cause. *Mutual Aid* attacks traditional evolutionary theory to advance the notion that cooperation is as important a factor in the development of a species as is the struggle for survival. Kropotkin's thesis thus represents an advance over the simplistic evolutionary thinking of Russian Nihilism, which focused on the brutal reality of the survival of the fittest. John Spargo, editor of *The Comrade*, reviewed the book and claimed that its arguments were "an invincible armament for the Socialist propagandist."[54] Kropotkin, after all, had given socialism a powerful tool by claiming that cooperation, not (capitalist) competition, is a natural instinct. Algie M. Simons, the editor of *International Socialist Review*, devoted a substantial review article to Kropotkin's book in his journal.[55]

The Young Socialists' Magazine printed a short piece by Kropotkin and an account of Kropotkin's daring escape from prison.[56] This magazine started out in 1908 with the title *The Little Socialist Magazine for Boys and Girls* and billed itself as the "organ of the American Socialist Sunday Schools and Young People's Federation," before becoming affiliated with the Young People's Socialist League in 1918. It regularly published articles by members of the Russian Jewish émigré intelligentsia, as well as articles about Russian politics and culture. Its unabashed purpose was to propagandize among the country's very young and, later, among the country's slightly older "youth." The reader who thumbs through the pages of this journal will find selections by and about such Russian Jews as Morris Hillquit, Morris Winchevsky, Meyer London, Simon O. Pollock, and Yiddish writer Z. Libin. There are also many selections by and about such Russians as Tolstoy, Gorky, and Lenin.

Gorky received a great deal of notice. After he first became known, in the first year or two of the century, the radical English-language press published many of his short works in translation and reviewed the large number of translations that began coming out in book form. In August of 1901, *The Worker* ran an unsigned review of a forthcoming English translation of Gorky's novel *Foma Gordeev*. The review was titled "The Young Giant of Russian Literature," and its author described Gorky's life and his intellectual pedigree, including the names of such individuals as Chernyshevsky, such publications as *Sovremennik* and the Russian Social Democratic *Iskra* (The spark), and such trends as Nihilism.[57]

The Comrade published one of the first English translations of Gorky anywhere, the author's "Twenty-six and One," in December of 1901, in the same issue as an early essay on Gorky, called "Gorky and his Philosophy."[58] His name appeared frequently in the pages of *The Comrade* for the remainder of the journal's short existence.

The *International Socialist Review* frequently featured Gorky. As early as 1902, one can read a review of a collection of Gorky's stories in translation. The *Review* published one of the most thoughtful discussions of Gorky in this era, and though it was not written by an American, the decision to publish it indicates a commitment to the cause of disseminating radical Russian culture. This was in June of 1906, shortly after a disastrous visit Gorky paid to the United States at the invitation of progressive publisher Gaylord Wilshire. The radical press, especially the Yiddish press, had built up this visit for months before Gorky's arrival, but after he arrived, it was discovered that the "wife" who was accompanying him was not legally married to him, a scandal ensued in the mainstream press, and Gorky left the country in disgrace.

The Yiddish press was willing to overlook Gorky's little sin, however, and so, apparently, were the editors of some radical English-language publications. The essay in the *International Socialist Review*, by the Dutch socialist Henrietta Roland-Holst (Henriëtte Goverdina Anna Roland Holst-van der Schalk, 1869–1952), concerned Gorky's literary criticism and was titled "Gorky as a Proletarian Literary Critic."[59] It had originally appeared in the Stuttgart-based social democratic journal *Die Neue Zeit*, and Simons had translated it for the *Review*. Roland-Holst uses the article to establish an early version of a Marxist literary theory, calling for authors to impart an understanding of the class character of literature ("the peculiar spirit of the literature of any epoch is but the living reflection of that class to whose views and conceptions, hopes and aspirations the author gives expression") and then saying that Gorky has succeeded in this enterprise while his countryman Kropotkin has not.

Later, Gorky's name appears frequently in the radical press, but this is scarcely surprising, since the international reputation he had built was so substantial that he is published and mentioned without any help from the Russian Jewish intelligentsia. *The Little Socialist* and *The Young Socialists' Magazine*, always eager to spread the word among the country's budding young socialists, printed a biography and quite a few stories by Gorky, including two in German translation. And after the October Revolution, Gorky appears in the pages of *Class Struggle*, which was very much an affair of immigrant Jewish intellectuals.

It is difficult to discover the agency by which Gorky's name became known in America. One thing appears certain, though, and that is that Jewish intellectuals were paying attention to Gorky before non-Jews writing in the English-language press. In September of 1899, Cahan published an article in English on the most recent generation of young Russian writers, speaking primarily of Gorky, Chekhov, and Vladimir Korolenko (and giving an excellent account of Russian realism in which he quotes from Dobroliubov).[60] I have not been able to find any earlier reference to Gorky in English in the United States. A few years later he would bring out another article on the same generation, in the mainstream *Bookman*, this time with a remarkably disparaging treatment of Gorky, whose writing he regarded as "un-Russian" and unduly suggestive of Nietzsche.[61]

The same month as the first of Cahan's two articles, the *Arbayter Tsaytung* printed an article about Chekhov and Gorky. The author, Khaim Aleksandrov, assumes that his readers have never heard Gorky's name before.[62] The following year, the *Arbayter Tsaytung* brought out several translations from Gorky. In the next couple of years, translations of works by him and articles about him become fairly frequent in the Yiddish press. S. Yanovsky, for example, was already serializing *Foma Gordeev* in 1902 for his anarchist *Fraye Arbayter Shtimme*. In the same year, the *Forward* printed a piece called "Maxim Gorky. A page from his biography," and the following year it printed two articles on Gorky's play *Burghers*.[63]

The earliest articles on Gorky in the English-language periodical press—those not written by Jewish immigrants like Cahan—appear in 1901, since 1901 is the year when the first English translations of his works were published in book form in the United States.[64] Whether or not the Yiddish-speaking radicals discovered Gorky and then actually passed his name on to their American-born counterparts, if we look at the history of Gorky's reception in America, we see that both groups promoted his reputation, and we know that the first group often served as mentors to the second, in matters of Russian culture and politics.

There were other documents and articles relating to Russian politics and the Russian revolutionary movement that appeared in the radical English-language press as well. In *The Comrade*, for example, one could find a translation of the speech that the assassin of Viacheslav Plehve (Russia's hated Minister of the Interior under Nicholas II) had prepared to deliver in his own defense at his trial.[65] This is followed by an article on the two primary revolutionary parties in Russia and a series of political cartoons on Russia from publications around the world. William English Walling, the white Southerner who helped found the NAACP, wrote of socialism in Russia in an article for the *International Socialist Review*. Though the piece is short, it is well informed, including a reference to the Jewish Bund and another to Lenin, who was not much talked about in the United States at this early date.[66] This, of course, is in addition to the regularly featured updates on the political situation in Russia that the *International Socialist Review* included in its "Socialism Abroad" column.

THE RUSSIAN INTELLECTUAL AS CULTURAL AMBASSADOR

Naturally, there were many educated Russian Jewish immigrants who did not become socialists, union leaders, or newspaper editors and who wanted nothing more than to learn English, dress like Americans, and assimilate themselves into complete inconspicuousness as fast as possible. Once again, the ads in the Yiddish press are a powerful social indicator, since they show a demand for true, American-style, middle-class respectability. The properly attired gents who appear in the clothing ads, the cozy, single-family dwellings on Long Island (beyond Brooklyn, beyond even Queens!) that are pictured in the real estate ads, the elegant passenger attended by an appropriately servile black waiter in the fashionably appointed dining car of the express train from New York to Philadelphia— all this was meant to appeal to the strivings of immigrants rich and poor, educated and uneducated, Russian-speaking and only Yiddish-speaking.

Many immigrant intellectuals did stay in the movement, remained committed to the political aspirations they had learned in their clandestine reading groups in Vilna or Minsk, but widened the base of their politics so that it was no longer exclusively Jewish or no longer Jewish at all. Louis Boudin is a perfect example. After a period of involvement in the Yiddish press, when, it must be said, the mark of his Jewishness was the Yiddish language and little more, Boudin became a sort of general Marxist intellectual and labor lawyer, writing books and articles that clearly disdained anything so particularizing as a commitment to the needs of his ethnic group.[67] *The Theoretical System of Karl Marx*, which was originally serialized in the *International Socialist Review* before appearing as a book, is exactly what the title suggests, an abstract and theoretical approach to Marxian economic theory. *Government by Judiciary* is a study of American constitutional law.[68] These are the works of an *American* intellectual. Boudin's cosmopolitanism paid off: of those today who have heard of him, few know that he ever contributed to the Yiddish press.

Others remained in the movement, adopted an English-language forum for much of their political and cultural activity, but dedicated some or most of this activity to causes that primarily benefited Jews. Even a figure with a substantial reputation, like Morris Hillquit, who spent so much of his time after the turn of the century in the national arena, still knew that he had a powerful political base in the Lower East Side and continued to appeal to that base by, for example, publishing articles in *Di Tsukunft* as late as World War I. The man who had played the role of the Russian intellectual so typically in the 1890s, writing articles in Yiddish on Marxism and various scientific topics, was still playing that role two decades later, informing *Di Tsukunft*'s readership of important developments in American socialism.

And then, of course, there was Abe Cahan, who established a sound reputation as an author of fiction in English ("ethnic" fiction, to be sure), retained his connection with the Jews by editing the *Forward* until he died, and all the while considered himself, as many Americans considered him, a "Russian" intellectual. Of Russian intellectuals who had learned English, none was more willing than he to use his mastery of the new language to tell native-born Americans about his two cultures, as in numerous pieces in *Commercial Advertiser* that explain Jewish holidays; or in the one that gives a picture in miniature of two pushcart women selling fish for Yom Kippur and quarreling with each other over a customer; or in one that introduces a new Russian author to the American reading public. Of Russian intellectuals, none was as willing as he to teach his countrymen about their new land, as when he worked furiously to produce a Yiddish-language history of the United States.

All of these types contributed to the picture that emerges when we look at the periodical press in the early decades of the twentieth century. It is there that we can see the interaction between the Jewish intellectuals and American-born intellectuals in the area of culture and political theory, and this interaction took place because of the efforts of people like Boudin, Hillquit, Cahan, Goldman, and Berkman.

CHAPTER 9

American Realism

LIFE, THOUGHT, AND ART

"I COULD NOT see why people should quarrel over mere stories." Abe Cahan puts those words into the mouth of his semiautobiographical hero, David Levinsky, as the hero describes the impassioned arguments some Russian (Jewish) acquaintances have over books.[1] To the extent that David Levinsky is a projection of Cahan, nothing could be more implausibly disingenuous than this observation. It would be as though the same hero, after growing up in his classic *shtetl* in Lithuania, had exclaimed that he could not figure out why the men in his home town always wore hats.

Of course, the naive perspective here is nothing more than a device that allows Cahan to show his American readers something that was as easy for him to understand as it was to understand why devout Jewish men covered their heads. Cahan and other Russian intellectuals, Jewish or not, knew that the sort of thing the characters in Cahan's novel argued about could never be described as "mere stories." *The Kreutzer Sonata* was no "mere story." *What Is to Be Done?* was no "mere novel." The poems of Nekrasov were no "mere" poems, just as God's Torah was no "mere book" to the residents of Levinsky's home town.

"Mere stories!" No, Mr. Levinsky should have known better. Maybe he himself had not grown up "in Chernyshevsky's *kheyder*," and maybe his dazzling success as a shameless capitalist businessman had made him forget about the sanctity of ideas, but he must have known plenty of young men and women, besides those he is talking about here, who had lived and died for those ideas. This was the generation of young men and women who had slept on the floor so they could be like Rakhmetov, a "mere" character in a book. These were the young students who had "gone to the people" because they had read Populist theory in a "mere" book. They were the ones who had heeded Liberman's call to "go to the aid of the proletariat," to "go to the [Jewish] people," because of a "mere" idea in a "mere" pamphlet. Anyone who had ever heard of propaganda, agitation, and the link between the two would have been astonished at Levinsky's response to the behavior of his "Russian" friends.

Naturally, Cahan and his own friends were busy leading the life that "developed" intellectuals were meant to lead, writing books and articles, organizing workers. As the intelligentsia saw it, the entire Jewish labor movement was a sort of "going to the people," both because there were workers to be led and leaders to do the leading and because the theoretical foundation for relations between workers and leaders was taken from Lavrov.

The intellectuals were also writing *about* the life they were leading. The articles that Pinski and others published on Lavrov in the *Arbayter Tsaytung*, for example, introduced Yiddish-speaking readers, not only to a great Russian thinker and revolutionary, but also to the notion of a "thinking realist," to the power of Lavrov's publications, in short, to the very possibility of a life where ideas and action are confused to the point of becoming practically indistinguishable. The material that Cahan and his fellow editors printed in the Yiddish press about Russian politics and culture was thus a kind of supplementary rationale for what Cahan and the others were doing when they published newspapers; it was the epic story of their own intellectual class and how it came to serve its readers by offering them this newspaper or magazine.

Nowhere is that story better told, however, than in the articles explicitly devoted to literature, whether or not the literature is Russian. Since so many Russian editors and writers had accepted the notion that books are to live and die by, that "realism" is more than just a name for a literary school, that the writer controls the destiny of peoples and nations, the literary pages in their publications were not just *femili riding* ("family reading" spelled in Yiddish and pronounced with a Yiddish accent), as Cahan contemptuously put it in a broadside on the hypocrisy of American literature.[2] They presented the view of the interaction between literature and life that was so fundamental to the Nihilist generation. They promoted realism because of the attitude toward the world that it implied, an attitude founded on the dual tendency to seek the truth and to respond to that truth politically. Perhaps the greatest contributions the Russian Jewish intelligentsia made specifically to cultural life in America was the education in critical realism—*the* Russian view of literature, in their eyes—that they gave their Yiddish-speaking and non-Yiddish-speaking readers.

LIFE AND ART, REALISM

No one among the Russian Jewish immigrants had more to say about realism than Abe Cahan. He had been in the United States barely seven years when he delivered a public lecture on the subject—in English—and then published the lecture in a progressive paper called *Workmen's Advocate*. The lecture was called "Realism," and it is a perfect adaptation of his Russian theory to the American idiom.[3] Cahan speaks of the "imitating faculties" as the source of the fine arts. Like any good Russian Nihilist, he cites Herbert Spencer, whose theory of evolution and principle of the survival of the fittest (a phrase Spencer invented) served as the basis for so much Russian social thought of the 1860s. Most of all, of course, he offers his Russian literary theory.

Cahan had been in the United States long enough to learn a thing or two about the native culture, and he devotes much of his article to celebrating the virtues of the man he thought best represented realism in American letters. This was William Dean Howells (1837–1920), author of *The Rise of Silas Lapham* (whose title Cahan would paraphrase in *The Rise of David Levinsky*) and for much of his career perhaps the most prominent and successful writer in America (with the possible exception of Mark Twain). Howells was a mentor to Cahan and a valuable sponsor, helping, for example, to find a publisher for the novella *Yekl* in 1896 and helping to insure its surprising success thereafter.

But even before Howells became personally and professionally useful to Cahan, Cahan found Howells interesting for at least two reasons. The first was that Howells himself had long espoused a version of literary realism, one whose primary feature was its demand that literary authors avoid moral interventions in their stories. The second was that, in the 1880s, Howells underwent a political conversion of sorts that made him look very much like a socialist, though he resisted political labels. The result of the conversion was that Howells's realism began increasingly to resemble *critical* realism of the sort that Belinsky and his followers had favored.

In fact, Cahan admired Howells's writing precisely because it was not dominated by any tendentious viewpoint but still managed to point up the radical failings of American society. This is how Cahan says it:

> Mr. Howells is not a socialist, and yet, unconsciously, free from the pressure of partisan passion, merely at the bidding of his realistic instinct, he accentuates in his works . . . a fact in American life which lays bare the fictitiousness of American equality. The same public-spirited American citizen who sets down critical socialism for the cranky babble of foreigners 'unacquainted with our institutions' takes pride in the great American novelist, whose pen makes a more dangerous assault on the present system than the most eloquent speeches of the most rabid 'foreign socialist.' . . . As a true realist he cares little for ideas; and yet it is just because he is such, because of his fidelity to the real, that he cannot help embodying an idea in his works.

And what is the idea that he embodies in his works? Cahan names it in the next sentence. "The rottenness of capitalistic society inevitably lends color to every work of realistic fiction."[4] Cahan has thus shown American readers the two essential ingredients of a theory of critical realism: the demand for "fidelity to the real" and the political critique of society. The two elements are, of course, inseparable. The suggestion is that the rottenness of capitalistic society is a necessary part of reality and therefore a necessary part of any truthful representation of reality.

Cahan would retain this conception of literature for his entire career, though it is to his credit that he shied away from a rigidly doctrinaire version of it. Over the years, he contributed many articles on fiction to the Yiddish press, and the pattern was almost always the same: an assertion that fidelity to "truth" was paramount, followed by an often unmotivated discussion of social criticism, usually from a specifically Marxist or generally socialist point of view. In a pair of articles on the novella *Nedda*, by Italian *verismo* novelist Giovanni Verga (1840–1922), Cahan shows that good novels must always be truthful and contain a "bit of criticism."[5] They should have a moral, he thinks, and the moral should have to do with "the social sickness that surrounds the author."[6] Cahan praises Verga for his truthfulness and then, without warning, says that *Nedda* "expresses an indictment of the whole social order, which requires that [people like Verga's characters] should be made so miserable and should work so hard all their lives for a few pennies a day. Verga's sketch," Cahan triumphantly concludes, "is thus a bit of socialism."[7]

Cahan turned his attention to his native tradition in a lengthy review of a story by Mendele Moykher Sforim (Sholem Abramovich, 1835–1917), often described as the founding father of modern Yiddish literature.[8] Cahan did not share the Yiddish-speaking public's enthusiasm for Mendele, and, in order to justify his disappointment, he wrote a theoretical preface that outlined his position. The subject of the preface was criticism, not fiction. It was called "A Few Words on Criticism in General," and in it Cahan set out the principles that he thought any good critic should observe.[9]

The principles are essentially the same as for a writer of fiction, and what Cahan presents is, once again, the classic theory of Russian realism. "Criticism of good novels is a social as well as a literary study," he says. Examples? Chernyshevsky, Dobroliubov, and Pisarev, who represent the only national literature that can proudly claim to have produced a criticism based on the precepts Cahan has laid out. Only Russian criticism has understood the true role of the critic, as these three men demonstrate. "By writing criticism about the works of a Turgenev, a Pisemsky, or an Ostrovsky, for example," Cahan says, "they were writing criticism about the social life of their fatherland."[10] Cahan, ever the faithful socialist, bluntly defined the critic's duty as "writing socialism, criticizing capitalism by criticizing novels."[11] Mendele's fiction fails, in Cahan's view, because the Yiddish author appears to care more about giving his readers pleasure ("a *mekhaye*") than about fulfilling his duty as a realist or a critic of capitalism.

Louis Boudin, who would later elaborate one of the first versions of a

Marxist literary theory ever to be published in the United States, started out like Cahan, reiterating the reigning principles of the age of Nihilism. He was already contributing to the development of literary theory in Yiddish when he was twenty-four years old and had been in the country only six years. An essay by Bernard Gorin promoting a theory of literature based on the notion of pleasure (*fergnigen* or *fergenigen*, like the German *Vergnügen*) inspired a spirited response from Boudin in *Arbayter Tsaytung*. The response came in the form of a two-part article called "Tendentiousness in Literature," whose purpose was to show that tendentiousness, in the sense in which Boudin understands the term, is a desirable quality in literature.[12] Where Gorin felt that the central function of literature was to stimulate pleasure in the reader, Boudin felt it was to instruct and cultivate. Where Gorin felt that an author should aim above all to be true to nature, since fidelity to nature is in itself a source of pleasure, Boudin felt that fidelity to nature was not enough. It must be combined with a lesson, a moral, in short, with tendentiousness. In fact, Boudin insists, fidelity to nature should be the very reason that good literature instructs us, since life is actually the best teacher, and images that an author has carefully chosen from life will instruct us better than simple moralizing.

The influence of Russian Nihilism could not be clearer. In fact, in one place, Boudin betrays his intellectual heritage when, without further comment or a trace of irony, he cites Chernyshevsky's *What Is to Be Done?*, next to Aristotle's *Politics* and Plato's *Republic* as an example of a great work of world literature that would fail to meet Gorin's requirement (as Boudin describes it) that good literature contain no thoughts. When we read that it is not *how* an author paints a scene but *what* he chooses to paint, that life, not art, is the source of the moral lessons we can learn, and finally that, among the lessons that life has to offer us, it is the social ones that matter the most—all of this is a direct, though somewhat simplistic application of the aesthetics that Belinsky introduced and that Chernyshevsky further developed. Chernyshevsky would certainly object to the suggestion that the author should do no more than draw images from life, but Boudin's demand that good literature contain lessons about social life introduces the same element of subjective authorial intervention as Chernyshevsky's requirement that art should render life "as it ought to be according to our conceptions."[13]

Contributions to the continuing conversation on realism often came in surges, undoubtedly because an article by one author would inspire others to respond or simply to add their own views. One surge, after the turn of the century, showed with particular clarity how thin the line was that separated literary art and life. This is when the Yiddish press took up the subject of contemporary Yiddish drama. Nowhere did passions run so high, nowhere was personal involvement so intense, nowhere did one's views on art more clearly reflect one's entire worldview so much as in the wars that were waged in the Yiddish press (and, for that matter, in the streets and cafes of the Ghetto) over the Yiddish theatre.

When it came to the theatre, a new pair of terms arose. They were "realism" and "romanticism." Actually, this opposition had been around for a few years in the Yiddish press (Moyshe Katz, for example, a critic who wrote for the *Forward,* used it in a series of articles in 1899), but it was not until the early years of the twentieth century that it came to define two warring camps in a pitched battle that ended friendships and appeared to eclipse what any outsider would consider the truly important issues of the day (like wages, working conditions, and union organization).[14]

The dominant figure in Yiddish theatre in America was Jacob Gordin, who had immigrated in 1891 and quickly established a reputation for himself. Even an outsider like Hutchins Hapgood, writing in *The Spirit of the Ghetto* a decade after Gordin's appearance on the scene, easily saw what the major issues were among patrons of this art form. "Realism, the Spirit of the Ghetto Theatre" is the title of Hapgood's section on the subject, where he describes the immense popular success of the realist credo among common Jewish theatre-goers.[15]

Not long after Gordin's arrival in the United States, the theatre world—and the entire Jewish community in New York, it would seem— was divided into two factions: followers of Gordin, who favored "realism," and followers of rival playwrights Joseph Lateiner and Moshe Horowitz, known as proponents of "romanticism." Each camp had its own theatre and its own favorite actors, and each appears to have been equally passionate about its preference.

The realists looked down upon the romantics, whom they regarded as purveyors of trash to ignorant *proste* (boors) from the old country. The realists also had the full force of Russian progressive political and cultural theory on their side, so it is easy to see how the debate shaped up in the press. No significant intellectual case was made for the romantics, since a taste for this style of theatre showed less a philosophical commitment than a preference for diversion, so the realists were free to direct their fire against their less sophisticated opponents. After disagreements broke out in their own midst, they directed it against each other, too.

But the debate showed how what might otherwise have been an obscure cultural theory, buried in the inside pages of Yiddish newspapers, made its way into a public forum. Ordinary Jewish immigrants went to see plays and, to judge by the account of another outsider, Lincoln Steffens, took sides—with a vengeance. "A remarkable phenomenon it was," Steffens writes in his autobiography, "a community of thousands of people fighting over an art question as savagely as other people had fought over political or religious questions, dividing families, setting brother against brother, breaking up business firms, and finally, actually forcing the organization of a rival theater with a company pledged to realism against the old theater, which would play any good piece."[16] In a community whose cultural direction was so firmly guided by "Russians," art questions *were* political questions.

Cahan had said that literature should always have some other purpose than to give the reader a *mekhaye*, and this is the tenet of his continuing advocacy of realism in art and his attacks on whatever he chose to call its opposite—romanticism, *shund* (trash), or the name of a particular theatre. All the issues associated with realism came out in a series of articles in the *Forward* in late 1903 and early 1904 and in *Di Tsukunft* in 1904 and 1905. The motivating factor in this continuing discussion appears to have been the theatre, but the participants, Cahan especially, often sought higher ground and addressed broader issues of literature and the arts.

Cahan used the *Forward* to offer Yiddish-speaking readers his wisdom on the subject of literature, giving them a definition of realism, distinguishing between realism and romanticism, discussing the difference between literature and science, and even addressing the question whether authors are entitled to interject themselves into their own works. In response to an article in a rival Yiddish newspaper calling for more attention in realist drama to the relations between men and women, Cahan brings out an international array of his favorite authors to prove that good realist literature shows little interest in this subject.[17] He attacks romanticism in literature by saying that it is based on a dream world and that the curiosity interest that is common in romantic literature is not one of the true interests of art.[18]

The title of one of Cahan's articles was "Realist Literature." It was not by coincidence that a little announcement by him appeared in a box next to the conclusion of the article. "Send us interesting true novels," it begins, inviting readers to send real-life stories for publication in the *Forward*. Cahan's "True Novels" feature never got off the ground in this format, but it shows a desire to publish writing that would be realist in the most literal sense of the word. One could easily argue that the famous column called *A Bintel Brief* (a bundle of letters) was the ultimate fulfillment of Cahan's realist philosophy. *A Bintel Brief* presented letters from ordinary readers, together with responses from the wise editor. After its inauguration in early January 1906, it became a lasting and cherished institution of Jewish life on the Lower East Side.

In the middle of the journalistic dialogue on realism—in fact, what may have been responsible for some of it—came the performance of a new play by Gordin. It was called, appropriately, *The Truth* (*Di vahrhayt*). The *Forward* ran a front-page article on the event, using its prime news section for a cultural subject, not only because Gordin's play was such an important contribution to artistic realism, but also because it presented the *Forward* with an opportunity to thumb its nose at a rival Yiddish paper commonly associated with the opposing theatrical style. The *Forward* article reports how Gordin had come on stage between the acts, as was his frequent practice, to give a highly politicized speech on his play and in this instance had used the occasion to proclaim a moral victory over Kasriel Sarasohn's *Tageblat*, which he accused of slandering him. But his weapon was the ideal of political Nihilism and it was named in the title of his play, so he was able to announce gleefully that, while the *Tageblat* had printed lies, he had "come out with the truth (*vahrhayt*)."[19]

Gordin had a chance to express himself in writing on the subject, in *Di Tsukunft*, where the discussion was taken up early in 1904 and where Gordin published his own article on "Realism and romanticism."[20] Gordin was undoubtedly a better playwright than theoretician of literature. His rambling article adds little to our understanding of realism, but it does put him squarely in the realist camp, at least as he defines it. It also contains some memorable thoughts and shows that Gordin was still very much the Russian intellectual he was eleven years earlier, when he was editing *Russkie Novosti*. Because realism focuses on the present, he says, it is "the only force that can make us think about a better future." To illustrate his point, he draws a distinction between a "realist" cobbler, one who has all the supplies he needs to make a nice pair of boots later (thus making a "better future"), and a "romantic" one, who considers boots to be a trifling matter, given that children love to run barefoot through puddles.[21]

Not long after the articles of 1903 and 1904 (and there were many in addition to the ones I have mentioned), discussion of the Yiddish theatre in the *Forward* degenerated into an ugly personal vendetta between Cahan and Gordin. The conflict reached its peak several years later, in 1908, when Cahan used his newspaper to wage a relentless war of words against Gordin, railing against his plays, accusing him of plagiarism, and otherwise attacking him at every opportunity. Gordin was dying of cancer at the time, and the entire affair does Cahan, who certainly knew that his rival was ill, little credit. It also adds little to the discussion of realism, despite the immense publicity it received, since it was so thoroughly infected by motives that had nothing to do with larger questions of culture and politics.[22] But it did show how Cahan continued to have a powerful voice in such questions, at least within the Jewish community.

LIFE AND ART: MARXISM À LA RUSSE

To the historian of literary criticism and theory, especially to one who knows about the Russian tradition, little that was published in the Yiddish press on the subject of realism will look especially original. Different writers showed different degrees of knowledge and sophistication, and a number had some valuable and insightful things to say, especially on the subject of their Russian intellectual forebears. But most of the debate about realism was precisely a continuing dialogue with those forebears, a dialogue to which the Yiddish writers added little besides occasionally an American context and their popularized Marxist conceptual apparatus. This does not mean, however, that the debate was insignificant. The part of it that was carried out in the world of the Yiddish theatre shows that even if the intellectual and cultural vanguard in the immigrant community was excessively beholden to a group of Russian masters, the ideology they had borrowed was a powerful one indeed, particularly as measured by the extent to which it affected the masses.

A handful of Yiddish writers, however, had something fairly new and different to contribute. It was a Marxist theory of literature, probably the first to make an appearance in America under that name. The theory may not appear extraordinarily fancy if it is held up to other, subsequent theories. It was never developed beyond a fairly rudimentary stage and can thus be likened to the early theories of Plekhanov (who may well be one of its sources) and Franz Mehring. What was remarkable about it was that it arrived long before any of the important Marxist cultural theories written in English. Though it is impossible to pin down the origins of Marxist criticism in the Yiddish press with complete certainty, it is probable that those origins are closely connected with the Russian intellectual heritage we have examined, something that makes its originality difficult to assess. But even if the Yiddish writers borrowed elements of their Marxist theory from elsewhere, at the very least it represented something new in the world of Yiddish-language cultural criticism.

Not all Russian Jewish émigrés learned Marxism itself primarily in Russia or from Russian sources. Those who left Russia as late as the turn of the century, after the establishment of the Bund and a Jewish labor movement, certainly might have been indoctrinated in the old country. We know that Aron Liberman and others who were close to Lavrov had incorporated some Marxist principles into their thinking, and we know that Abe Cahan had first read Marx before he left Russia. But at the time when the first wave of Jews left Russia after the pogroms of 1881, Marxism was still not the major force in Russian political thought that it would become over the next two decades. Though *The Communist Manifesto* was translated into Russian as early as 1869 and *Das Kapital* as early as 1872, Russia's own native brand of Marxism did not really develop until the 1880s, with the first writings of Georgy Plekhanov. Many Jewish immigrants, it appears, learned Marxism for the first time in America.

So even if many of the intellectuals who came to the United States knew something of Marx's thought before they emigrated, they generally did not embrace Marxism until they were already in their new home, in many cases because of contact with the German-speaking radical community and its publications. When Cahan says that many of his fellow immigrants learned German in order to read the Marxist *New Yorker Volkszeitung*, he is speaking of comrades who went through a process of soul-searching like his own. This means they had started out as anarchists or Nihilists, with perhaps some casual knowledge of Marx, and then incorporated into their largely Russian views the elements of Marxist thought they picked up from the *Volkszeitung* or from such charismatic figures as Sergei Schevitsch.

There were many publications in America whose editorial outlook could be described as Marxist, including some that were published by immigrant Jews, and most of these publications included various amounts of cultural material. Still, there is little before the early years of the twentieth century that even looks like a true Marxist cultural critique. It was not uncommon to find writers who wrote about cultural matters— mostly literature—and who used Marxist terms to describe, say, the backdrop of a book or what they saw as the book's message. Cahan did plenty of this in his early critical articles, where he commonly judged the book on its truthfulness and then gave an account of its "truth" that was clearly constructed in socialist terms and that strongly suggested a Marxist outlook.

But this was not something one could call a Marxist literary theory. Abe Cahan used his literary reviews as a forum for lambasting American capitalism and advancing a Marxian socialism, he focused attention on class struggle, and yet he never said or even suggested that what he was practicing was "Marxist literary criticism." There were two factors that, in combination, distinguished the Marxist trend in literary criticism from the sort of criticism that Cahan wrote. The first was the view, stated or implied, that art must be examined in an historical context. This view, to be sure, was a cornerstone of Belinsky's theory of literature and had been present *by itself* in much of the criticism the Jewish émigrés wrote. The second was an inquiry, inspired by Marxist analysis, into the economic circumstances that produced that historical context.

Several things happened that may have encouraged the development of a Marxist trend in literary criticism in the Yiddish press. One is that a Marxist literary criticism sprang into existence in Russia, above all with the publication of Plekhanov's *Letters Without Address* from 1899 to 1900 and also with scattered remarks Plekhanov had made in earlier writings. In *Letters Without Address* Plekhanov formulated the following description of art: "The art, whatever its type, of a given people is defined by the psyche of that people; its psyche is created by its position, and its position is conditioned in the last analysis by the state of its productive forces and its relations of production."[23]

This description is constructed from two sources. One is easy for a student of Marx to see: it is the preface to the *Contribution to the Critique of Political Economy* (1859), where Marx describes the conflict between the productive forces of society and the existing relations of production and explains how this conflict generates revolution, moving history dialectically from one stage to a succeeding stage. This is also where Marx wrote the famous statement that social life determines consciousness.

The other source is Hippolyte Taine, whose theory of *la race, le moment*, and *le milieu*, enunciated in the introduction to his *History of English literature* (1863–1864), had provoked a dual response from Plekhanov. On the one hand, Plekhanov was inspired by the notion that art is embedded in its historical situation, while, on the other, he contested Taine's notion of a national psyche that generates literary production. Plekhanov's assertion that a people's psyche is created by its historical situation is his effort to purge Taine of the dangerously idealist notion that the human psyche has an existence independent of history and society.

Another circumstance that might have helped to raise the general Marxist consciousness of the Jewish intelligentsia was the increasing prominence of the Bund, starting a few years after its founding in 1897. The Yiddish press in America followed the Russian organization closely, since news of the Bund touched on two themes of fundamental importance: Russian politics and Jewish identity. *Di Tsukunft*, for example, ran a series on the Bund in 1903 and an article on the Bund and the Kishinev pogroms in 1904.[24] The *Forward* featured the Bund prominently in its pages starting in 1905.

The formation of an explicitly Marxist literary theory took place largely in the pages of *Di Tsukunft*, from 1905 to 1906. Two events appear by their timing to have had a significant impact on literary theory in the Yiddish press. One was Gorky's visit in April of 1906; the other was the publication of the first complete edition of Upton Sinclair's *The Jungle*, in February of the same year.

I have already described Gorky's reception in the English-language press in America and in the Yiddish press before and immediately after the turn of the century. In the weeks preceding his visit in 1906, he was the subject of frequent, often front-page articles in the Yiddish press. The *Fraye Arbayter Shtimme* hailed his upcoming visit in a front-page feature titled "Gorky as Envoy of the Russian Revolution."[25] The *Forward* was running articles on Gorky early in 1906, and by the time the celebrated proletarian writer arrived, Cahan, who had deprecated him in his *Bookman* essay only a few years earlier, was publishing daily articles and editorials on him.

The most noteworthy of the *Forward* articles was an unsigned editorial called "Maksim Gorky as Poet and Socialist," in which the author sets Gorky apart from all other contemporary writers who might be considered socialists in the broad sense of the word (a sense so broad as to embrace such diverse figures as Tolstoy, Anatole France, Shelley, and Ibsen). Gorky alone, this "poet," "thinker," and "fighter," is a true socialist, the author says, because he alone understands the scientific nature of Marxism. He thus understands Marx not at all the way a poet does, but in a way that places him on an equal footing with such respected theoreticians as August Bebel and Wilhelm Liebknecht.[26]

In June of 1906, Gordin wrote an essay on Gorky for *Di Tsukunft*.[27] The man who had written two years earlier on the superiority of realism over romanticism now praises the Russian writer for combining both trends in his writing. "Gorky," Gordin says, "has the realist power to describe reality as it is and possesses the romantic fantasy to poeticize the soul of reality."[28] It is just this independence that distinguishes Gorky from other writers. But Gordin makes clear that Gorky does more than simply describe and poeticize reality; like all great artists, he is a teacher.

Gorky thus presented the Jewish intellectual community with a model of the revolutionary artist-intellectual-activist, like such heroes of the 1860s as Chernyshevsky, Dobroliubov, and Pisarev. But he was also a Marxist—a *true* Marxist, at that, since his admirers seem to agree that he possessed an understanding of scientific socialism that set him apart from most mere poets. A group that had been raised on the idea of fusing activism with the artistic life and had then adopted a Marxist approach to politics was now confronted with living proof that all these things could be combined.

The other forceful proof was *The Jungle*. Sinclair's novel exposing the brutal character of the meat industry created an instant sensation, especially among Jewish intellectuals. Here, after all, was a novel that openly took aim at American capitalism and openly held up socialism as a favorable alternative to it. Abe Cahan immediately recognized the power of this book, so he translated it into Yiddish and ran his translation in the *Forward* from June to August of 1906.[29]

The most powerful review of Sinclair's book to appear in the Yiddish press, and the one that most clearly shows the movement toward a Marxist literary theory, is one that Louis Boudin wrote for *Di Tsukunft* the year *The Jungle* came out in book form.[30] It would be hard to mistake Boudin's tone and point of view in this passage from his opening paragraph:

> Only in America, where capitalism is, at least in some places, more developed than in any other country in the world; where the country has an old-fashioned form of government that makes the struggle with the natural outgrowths of capitalism more difficult even when there is someone who can serve this struggle; and where the power that should lead this struggle is not yet developed; only in this country can the "jungle" that Sinclair describes

exist in its full savagery and rawness; and only in this country of sensation, publicity, and the almighty dollar, where the greatest literary talents are leased out and sold, body and soul, to capitalist publishers and advertisers; where advertisements are written as literature and literature is written as advertising; where the greatness of a writer is measured by the number of his readers and the literary worth of a book is measured by the number of dollars it makes for the author; where capitalists make a business out of socialism and socialists get their ideals from capitalist businesses; only in this country of sensation, publicity, and the almighty dollar has *The Jungle* been able to find the reception and achieve the "success" that it has.[31]

As the strident style suggests, Boudin is every bit as enraged by American capitalism as Sinclair is, and much of his article is devoted to echoing, in overtly Marxist language, Sinclair's condemnation of the economic order and the social ills it has created. But this passage also shows that Boudin has extended his view beyond the beef trust, with its hideous corruption and inhuman exploitation of workers, to the literature "industry," which means that he is thinking of literature as a form of production and thus something susceptible to Marxist analysis. To be sure, Boudin thinks, Sinclair's novel falls short of being a true socialist novel, but this is because Sinclair is describing a state of socialism in a country where socialism has not yet developed. The author cannot be blamed for existing in an inadequate state of historical development.[32]

By 1907, Boudin had taken the rudimentary conceptions he had presented in his review of *The Jungle* and elaborated them into a true Marxist theory. In the meantime, some important changes had taken place in the management of *Di Tsukunft*. Jacob Milch took over as editor from January through June of that year and, in the first issue under his supervision, announced a new editorial policy. "*Di Tsukunft* will be a Marxist journal," he said flatly, though he insisted that it would be open to other viewpoints.[33] When Morris Winchevsky replaced Milch as editor in July, he announced a policy of greater tolerance toward non-Marxist viewpoints, but it is clear that Marxism would dominate the journal ideologically for years to come. So it makes sense that the writers contributing literary criticism and theory to *Di Tsukunft* under the new editorial policy would have come up with something that could be described as Marxist.

And they did. In the very first issue of the year, Boudin published an article called "Life and Art."[34] This could very well be the first article published in the United States that presents a Marxist theory of literature and actually calls it that. One could not, for example, be much more explicit than Boudin was in this declaration: "I am a Marxist, as the readers of *Di Tsukunft* know. . . . I intend to write literary criticism from my Marxist viewpoint."[35]

Boudin supplies a theoretical foundation for this new criticism and actually suggests a methodology, though he does not have the space to develop either at any length. The key elements of this theoretical foundation are Taine's theory of culture and history, on the one hand, and the placement of literature in a set of social and economic circumstances, on the other. The insight from Taine, as Boudin puts it, is that we can understand literature in particular and art in general only if we understand "all human development," since life and art are part of a "process of development."[36]

It is possible that Boudin came to Taine by way of Plekhanov.[37] Whether or not he knew Plekhanov's writings on the subject of art, Boudin took an approach similar to that of the Russian Marxist, even when it came to the foundation of his theory. As Boudin phrased it, Marx's contribution to the discussion is his idea that "the social [sotsyaler] structure of society [gezelshaft], with all its institutions and ideas, is the result of economic circumstances." This is what defines the method.[38] Plekhanov had expressed the principle in similar terms: "the art of a given people," he says in Letters Without Address, "always bears the closest causal connection to its economy."[39] Boudin points out, incidentally, that Marx's method cannot be false—only conclusions drawn in its improper or incomplete application can be false—since it is based not on dogma but on the injunction to investigate (forshen, like the German forschen).

If Boudin was following Plekhanov, though, he was not following him in every particular. Plekhanov, who valiantly attempted to reconcile a Marxist, materialist conception of art with a Kantian view of the autonomy of artistic activity, believed that proper literary criticism had not only the right but the duty to judge the artistic merits of a work.[40] For Boudin, Marxism in the field of literary studies is above all a method, and because that method, based as it is on purely dispassionate investigation, is thoroughly scientific, a literary criticism that applies it can have no predilections and must not judge. "All tendencies and schools—classic, pseudo-classic, romantic, realist, naturalist, symbolist, impressionist—are for [the Marxist critic] the same thing, namely, phenomena to be studied and explained," Boudin says. "For the Marxist literary critic and historian, even so-called art for art's sake is not a thing to be denounced and condemned, but an object for study and explanation."[41]

Boudin's article was admittedly a cursory and rudimentary introduction to the subject. The Yiddish press at this time could afford to offer little more than short articles on subjects like this, and Boudin himself was no doubt interested more in writing The Theoretical System of Karl Marx than in being a literary theoretician. But "Life and Art" clearly had an impact, since it immediately stirred a minor debate in the Yiddish press. First came a sharp response from the Fraye Arbayter Shtimme. The anarchist newspaper had been busy attacking *Di Tsukunft* and its new editor for the entire month of January 1907, and now the unnamed author of the article, seeking to promote the virtues of freedom, predictably takes exception to the deterministic features of Boudin's theory. He is offended above all by the notion that life and art are the results of certain causes. If it is true that they are, he asks, how can we account for the appearance of, say, Wagner in Germany and not in England? Marxist theory cannot explain this, he says, because economic circumstances alone do not produce artistic genius. Artistic genius, in fact, a concept for which there is no room in Marxist theory, is greater precisely when an artist frees himself from his surroundings. Nor is there room in Marxist theory for the concept of aesthetic pleasure. Art, after all, in the view of this critic, is something that speaks primarily to our feelings.[42]

With his journal and editorship under attack, Milch responded with what is probably the first article printed in America under the title "Marxist Literary Criticism."[43] Milch's article is less an attempt to propose his own Marxist theory of literary criticism, as his title might suggest, than an effort to comment on the polemic between Boudin and the *Fraye Arbayter Shtimme* critic. What his title does, however, is acknowledge the existence of something called "Marxist literary criticism," which Boudin had introduced, the anarchist writer had attacked, and Milch now seeks to modify. Milch agrees that the model of economic circumstances and their causal relation to the production of art (and life) is flawed. He agrees that such a model cannot reveal to us why England did not produce any Wagners. But he is not ready, as the anarchist critic was, to reject Marxism as the foundation for a literary theory.

On the contrary, he thinks Marxism has the answer and that Boudin has simply not found it. Boudin, relying on both Marx and Taine, has placed all the emphasis on economic circumstances, or, as Milch renders Taine's set of factors, "race, climate, and surrounding circumstances."[44] But in Marxism, Milch says, these three factors are subordinated to another, more basic factor, something he calls *dos ekonomishe tsuzamenleben* (a term he seems to have taken from the German *ökonomisches Zusammenleben*, literally "economic living-together"). Unfortunately, Milch does not really say what this term means or where it comes from, but it appears to suggest an economic description of social life that is less strictly deterministic than the one Boudin employed in his article. As Milch puts it, "Try, for example, to use economic circumstances to demonstrate the decline of philosophy in Greece, and two lifetimes of investigation [*forshen*] and study won't be enough."[45]

In the next few years, *Di Tsukunft* published further examples of criticism that may be called Marxist. Nothing could be more orthodox, for example, than the opening of an article that Zivion (pen-name of Ben

Tsion Hofman, 1874–1954), a prominent Bundist, published in 1908, under the title "The People and Art":

> The economic conditions in which we live, the form of production, the productive forces through which human society carries on the struggle for its existence call forth in us certain ideas, thoughts, and convictions. With a change in economic conditions and forms of production, comes a change also in our ideas, views, and convictions. Man's intellect is nothing more or less than a product of the external material milieu in which he finds himself. We think we shape history, whereas in reality it is history that shapes us.

Zivion follows this with the *locus classicus* of all Marxist cultural theory: "It is not the consciousness of men that determines social being, but on the contrary social being determines the consciousness of men."[46]

And in 1914, *Di Tsukunft* published a piece by the painter Saul Raskin on an exhibition of works by Constantin Meunier, a Belgian painter who devoted much of his work to exalting the activity of common laboring people.[47] Raskin is hardly a Marxist theoretician in any strict sense of the term, and yet his review of Meunier's works is decidedly Marxist in orientation. He sees fit to point out, for example, that the well-to-do residents of upper Manhattan who come to see Meunier's paintings at Columbia University are the very people who will be vanquished by the social class that Meunier portrays. He says that Meunier's work is the first truly proletarian art we have had and goes on to lend support to the notion that true proletarian art must not be tendentious.

Finally, *Di Tsukunft* brought out a number of articles on Plekhanov in 1918, the year he died, among them a study of his literary criticism. The author of this study speaks favorably of Plekhanov's interest in literary descriptions of the lower levels of society and points to the fundamental aspect of his criticism, namely his emphasis not on the writer but on the social situation of the writer.[48]

There is no doubt that, no matter what its origins, the Marxist literary theory developed in the Yiddish press owed a great deal to Russian intellectual history of the nineteenth century. The central impulse to examine the historical context of a work of art had been around since Belinsky, and even though it would appear to be implicit in any Marxist cultural theory, Plekhanov himself, a true child of his century, was a critical realist in the Belinskian tradition before he was a Marxist. If the Yiddish-speaking intellectuals in New York borrowed their theory from Plekhanov, they were simply borrowing from the same tradition that had shaped both him and them. And if they were not borrowing from him, there is every probability that they came to the Marxist viewpoint in precisely the same way as he did, that is, by melding a Marxist approach to history with the historical contextuality of Russian critical realism. How original was this? We have seen that Boudin and Milch differed from each other on how to apply Marxism to literary criticism, and we have seen that both differed from Plekhanov in their refusal to recognize an autonomous form of artistic merit. In addition, even if this Marxist literary theory represents a continuation of the existing, realist view of literature, it has still added a level of sophistication that had been lacking in much of the cultural criticism in the Yiddish press. This is not to say, of course, that Boudin and Milch should be ranked with Lukács, Benjamin, and Adorno; it is to say that they deserve credit for proposing something new and relatively original in their own context.

THE REAL REALISM

By 1918, when *Di Tsukunft* ran its series of articles on Plekhanov, the "historical spirit of one's time," as Belinsky put it, had changed in a way that would alter Jewish radical culture and politics in the United States for good. The Bolshevik Revolution had taken place the previous year, the once relatively obscure figure of "Nikolai" Lenin, as he had been known for many years, was now thrust onto the international stage, as was Trotsky, and a major realignment of the European powers was in progress. Suddenly, *Marxism, Russian political thought,* and *proletarian revolution* were no longer topics of partly abstract, though impassioned discourse in radical periodical publications. Now they were real, commanding the attention of the entire world and forcing many members of the Russian Jewish intelligentsia in America to carry out a serious reexamination of their own political beliefs. From now on, especially for Marxists, participation in radical politics would mean taking a stand on issues of broad consequence, and political work of both a practical and an intellectual nature (if the two could be separated) would never be purely local and domestic any more.

Literature would play a central role in the new radical political scene, for Jews and non-Jews. For those who declared themselves followers of such Russian political figures as Lenin and Trotsky, this could hardly be surprising. Lenin and Trotsky were as much a part of the legacy of Belinsky and Chernyshevsky as were Abe Cahan and Morris Hillquit, so for them, "literary work," which was broadly construed to comprise not only *belletristika* (from *belles-lettres*), as the Russians call imaginative literature, but all serious written expression, plays an essential role in the birth and survival of the Revolution. As Stalin said a few years later, echoing in his own characteristically blunt way the sentiments of almost a century's worth of Russian radical belief, "Print [the press] is the sharpest and strongest weapon of our party."[49]

The new Soviet leaders were "realists," too.

Conclusion

WHERE IT WENT

What happened to the Russian radicalism that the Jewish intellectuals brought with them? There can be no doubt that 1918 or 1920 marked the beginning of a new era for the radical Jewish intelligentsia in America. This was partly owing to the significance of the Great War and the Bolshevik Revolution. The war had split the Jewish community like few other events, as former subjects of the Russian Empire tried to establish a hierarchy for such conflicting sentiments as hatred for the tsar, hostility toward the imperial ambitions of Germany, and opposition to war in general. And it was not long before the October Revolution created profound divisions in the Jewish left. It was largely a question of when disenchantment set in. For some it came early in the 1920s, and for others it came in response to news of the purges in the 1930s. In any case, in the 1920s there were at least two camps at war over an issue that was as defining as any that had ever confronted the Jewish left.

There were other factors, too, that brought about change over the next generation. The simplest and most obvious was the circumstance that a great many of the dominating figures in this group died in the 1920s and 1930s, while a number of others disappeared from the central arena of immigrant radical activity. Consider the four founders of the *Arbayter Tsaytung*. Philip Krantz died in 1922, Louis Miller died in 1927, and Morris Hillquit, who had carried his political ambitions onto a larger platform as early as the turn of the century, died in 1933. Abe Cahan, who died in 1951, having edited the *Forward* (at least nominally) until his death, is the only one who lived through the Great Depression and World War II. And the other immigrant intellectuals? Jacob Gordin had died early, in 1909. Leo Deutsch left the United States in 1916, returned to Russia after the February Revolution, and essentially gave up all overtly political activity after that. Isaac Hourwich died in 1924, as did M. Baranov. Morris Winchevsky died in 1932, Adella Kean Zametkin in 1931, Mikhail Zametkin in 1935, Karl Fornberg in 1937, and Abraham Liessin in 1938. Louis Boudin lived until 1952, but even though he remained involved in left-wing political causes for his entire life, he did not confine his activities to the circle of Russian Jewish intellectuals.

Chaim Zhitlovsky lived until 1943, but came increasingly to adopt political positions that isolated him from both the American Jewish mainstream and the American Jewish left. During World War I, for example, when the Jewish left initially rallied to the support of Germany (any enemy of Russia was a friend of the Russian Jew), Zhitlovsky remained resolutely neutral. In the mid-1930s, during the famous show trials in Moscow, he took it into his head to express support for the Soviet Union, because of the rising threat of Nazism, but at the same time he offered the suggestion that Hitler's policies toward the Jews stemmed in part from the Jews' past exploitation of workers.

And Emma Goldman, though she remained a highly visible political activist and continued to devote her energies to American causes, was deported to Russia with Alexander Berkman in December of 1919, and was obliged to conduct her activities almost entirely outside the United States for the rest of her life. She died in Toronto in 1940.

Another factor promoting change was the legislation passed in the 1920s restricting immigration. By the end of the 1920s, Jewish immigration had been reduced to a mere fraction of its former levels, with the result that the United States no longer received large influxes of young, Yiddish-speaking Jews to sustain the movement that had begun in the 1880s. The older generation was replaced more and more by members of a generation that was born in America. This next generation was brought up speaking American English in society and Yiddish mostly at home. Many of its members, in fact, did not really *speak* Yiddish at all; Yiddish became a source of folk sayings and funny, earthy expressions, something that one could refer to fondly as the *mame loshn* (mother tongue) but without being able to construct a proper sentence in it.

Yiddish journalism did not by any means die, however. Abraham Liessin's successful editorship of *Di Tsukunft* lasted from 1913 to 1938, and the magazine continues to appear today, though it is naturally aimed at a very small group of aficionados who do not view it is a primary source of enlightenment. And while the *Forward* went into a period of slow decline after reaching its peak circulation in the early 1920s, it continued to come out every day until 1983, when it changed over to a weekly format. Even as recently as 1992, the Yiddish version claimed some fifteen thousand readers.[1] *Der Tog*, which first came out in 1914, merged in 1918 with a paper Louis Miller had founded, and continued publication until 1971.

But the Yiddish press after the early 1920s would never again be what it had been in its glory days, from the founding of *Arbayter Tsaytung* through World War I. This was not only a function of the decline in readership and the resulting decline in influence. It was also a function of the change in the political scene. Take the *Forward*, for example. After the Bolshevik Revolution, Abe Cahan briefly lent his paper's support to the new Russian regime, but he soon recoiled in horror from it, remaining a fierce anti-Bolshevist for the remainder of his life. The focus of his paper was no longer the struggling union movement and the travails of newly arrived immigrant Jews. By the twenties and thirties, that base of support and the ideology on which the movement had stood were a thing of the past. The *Forward* continued to have wide appeal to readers of Yiddish, but its scope was more cosmopolitan and less tendentious. The other large-circulation Yiddish newspaper, *Der Tog*, had never been a voice of radical reform in the first place, and the elite *Tsukunft* remained a high-brow journal with a limited circulation even in its best days.

So by the time of the Great Depression and the new radical movements in American politics, the torch had necessarily been passed to a different generation. The question is whether the old generation passed the light of its own knowledge with the torch, or whether the new generation started afresh, with ideas that originated from elsewhere.

It is important to remember that many of the offspring of the Jewish radical left, even those who grew up to lead highly public lives, had never shown much interest in the political struggles of their parents and did nothing to continue their parents' work. Laura Hobson comes to mind. The author of *Gentleman's Agreement* spent her childhood dimly aware that her father, Michael Zametkin, worked on a newspaper (the *Forward*) and all too painfully aware that both her parents professed strange beliefs whose primary purpose, she felt, was to embarrass her. On the occasion of the Triangle Shirt Waist fire in 1911, for example, the young Laura was mortified to find that her parents had draped the entire porch of their house with black bunting, to honor the dead. Yiddish? Her mother presented her with a copy of *Der froys handbukh* (The woman's handbook, an edited collection of the columns she wrote for *Der Tog*) for her birthday in 1930. This is how Hobson describes the book, whose title she does not even appear to know:

> In any case, that heavy book my mother inscribed to me on my birthday, and which I could never read, was a collection of her own pieces for the newspaper, *The Day*, printed in Yiddish, which is why I can't read it. But I can read its page numbers, ordinary English numbers, and, leafing backwards from that title page to its last page, I come at last to 648.[2]

As for Russian, that was the language her parents spoke to each other, and the children were not taught it any more than they were taught Yiddish.

> To think that I might have been a linguist! But the whole purpose of their moving away from New York in my earliest childhood, first to Brooklyn, and then to a small town on Long Island, away from their colleagues and friends, away from their co-workers on newspapers and in labor unions—the whole point was to bring up their children as total Americans, with no trace of foreign accent, no smallest inflection or gesture that was not native to this their beloved country.[3]

But many members of the new generation did follow the path of their parents' generation, at least in the sense that they became involved in radical politics. These are the people I mean when I speak of the "new generation." It is the generation of Jewish intellectuals who joined radical politics as early as the late twenties and were active, above all, in the thirties. This generation includes the group that is often referred to as the "New York Intellectuals," a group that counted among its members Irving Howe, Lionel Trilling, Irving Kristol, Sidney Hook, Alfred Kazin, Meyer Schapiro, Daniel Bell, and *Partisan Review* co-founders Philip Rahv and William Phillips.[4] Though there were non-Jews among the "New York Intellectuals," the identity of this group was very much wrapped up in Jewishness. As Irving Howe put it in a retrospective essay in 1968, "by birth or osmosis, they are Jews."[5]

There are some obvious reasons to see a continuity of political spirit from one generation to the next. Almost all the New York Intellectuals were born in the United States to Yiddish-speaking parents (though not necessarily to members of the intelligentsia), and almost all had some exposure to radical politics at an early age. One exception was Philip Rahv, who was born in the old country and arrived in the United States in 1922, at the age of fourteen. Many of the New York Intellectuals wrote of their childhood in the ghettos of New York and recalled how they were surrounded by socialist ideas. Sociologist Daniel Bell, for example, tells of giving socialist street-corner speeches when he was a teenager.[6] Art historian Meyer Schapiro's father had learned his socialist ideas through the Bund before immigrating to America.[7] Sidney Hook, the historian and philosopher of history, writes about "devouring" socialist literature at a young age.[8]

But any Jewish child born into a working-class immigrant family in the ghetto in those days, one who had not been taken to a safer environment, as Laura Hobson was, was bound to come into contact with the political culture that Abe Cahan and his fellow immigrant intellectuals had established in the previous generation or two. The labor movement, or at least the memory of it, was very much alive, and almost no Yiddish-speaking home was without its daily copy of the *Forward*, *Der Tog*, or some other more or less progressive Yiddish-language publication. This does not mean that a child born in Brownsville or the Lower East Side in 1920 grew up knowing the Marxist literary theories that Louis Boudin had published in *Di Tsukunft* a decade and a half earlier. In fact, if there was a single factor that prevented the political ideology of the immigrants from being passed down more successfully to their children, it was no doubt the linguistic gap that separated one generation from the other. But it does mean that such a child was likely to grow up with some exposure to political activism. Activism, after all, was visible on the streets. Where else would the young Daniel Bell have discovered the art of street-corner speech making?

What is striking is the similarity between the ideas of the Jewish New

York Intellectuals and their Yiddish-speaking predecessors, especially when it came to culture and the relation between culture and politics. They had found an early model in another New York Jewish intellectual, Mike Gold, one of the first proletarian literary critics to write in English in the United States and, later, author of the proletarian novel *Jews Without Money* (1930). In 1921, he had taken his knowledge of Nietzsche, Walt Whitman, Russian literature, and the Bolshevik Revolution, tossed it all into a mixing bowl, and produced the essay "Towards Proletarian Art." This visionary cry for a post-apocalyptic culture created by workers and farmers, so that "in every American factory there is a drama-group of workers, when mechanics paint in their leisure, and farmers write sonnets," boisterously pointed ahead to the theory of culture that the New York Intellectuals would elaborate in the 1930s.[9]

In the 1930s, Mike Gold was still developing his proletarian theory of literature. What could be more evocative of the Russian Nihilist and Populist view of life, literature, and the role of the intellectual elite than this call to arms that Gold issued at the American Writers' Congress in 1935 (a year, that is, after the First All-USSR Writers' Congress formally mandated for Soviet writers the literary style known as "socialist realism")? "It is our main task," he said, "to see that a strong working class is developed in the United States to lead the revolutionary vanguard. We may not lead it. So I think one of the basic tasks of every writer is to stimulate and encourage and help the growth of proletarian literature which is written by workers."[10] We see here, just as in Lavrov, the hesitation between the urge to entrust the guidance of the revolutionary movement entirely to the beneficiaries of that movement and the urge to entrust at least some of it to a professional class of leaders.

Even two years before the Congress, Philip Rahv had come up with his own version of the role of literature in the political struggle. His theory is a conscious reworking of Aristotle's theory of tragedy, but it is also a perfect amalgam of Marxism, Lavrovian Populism, and Russian realism. To the Aristotelian categories of pity and fear Rahv adds a "synthesizing third factor," which he calls "militancy, combativeness." "The proletarian katharsis is a release through action—something diametrically opposed to the philosophical resignation of the older idea. Audaciously breaking through the wall that separates literature from life, it impels the reader to a course of action, of militant struggle; it objectifies art to such a degree that it becomes instrumental in aiding to change the world."[11]

Something like this credo became a guiding editorial principle of the *Partisan Review* at its founding in 1934. *Partisan Review* was designed to be a specifically literary journal that would fill a gap left by such other radical journals of the time as the more purely political *New Masses*. In the inaugural issue, the editors made this statement: "We propose to concentrate on creative and critical literature, but we shall maintain a definite viewpoint—that of the revolutionary working class. Through our specific literary medium we shall participate in the struggle for the workers and sincere intellectuals against imperialist war, fascism, national and radical oppression, and for the abolition of the system which breeds these evils."[12] A few months later, Rahv and Phillips (signing himself Wallace Phelps) co-wrote an article for the *Review* titled "Problems and Perspectives in Revolutionary Literature," in which they defined the role of the literary critic. "The critic is the ideologist of the literary movement," they said.[13]

The New York Intellectuals underwent a number of changes in political outlook, the most significant of which was the one that took many of them from their early support for Stalin and the Soviet Union (the editorial statement in the first issue of *Partisan Review* had listed the defense of the Soviet Union as one of the principal tasks of the fledgling journal) to a fierce rejection of Stalinism in favor of Trotskyism or a milder form of liberalism. The *Partisan Review* underwent further changes, too, and individual members of the New York Intellectuals took off in a variety of different directions.

But there is one element that all the New York Intellectuals, Jews and non-Jews, appear to have had in common, and that is the inspiration that they initially found in Soviet Communism after the Bolshevik Revolution. In fact, Daniel Bell (born 1919) reports that he had no knowledge of the Yiddish literature of the previous generation.[14] William Phillips (born 1907), a product of an immigrant Jewish household, denies that the Russian-Jewish émigrés played any role in shaping his views, says that the same is probably true of other New York Intellectuals, and insists that the early views of this group "came from thinking associated with the revolutionary tide that came from the Soviet Union." Moreover, he says, this phase was brief.[15] In a retrospective he wrote in the 1970s on the *Partisan Review*, Phillips claimed that, intellectually, he was "born in the 30's," having avoided all politicization up until that time. He also said that *Partisan Review* was intended to represent a "new approach to literature and politics."[16]

But then Phillips had believed from the outset that the entire political-cultural enterprise of which his magazine was a part was new. This is certainly an exaggeration. And to suggest that the Soviet Union was the sole source of inspiration for all the New York Intellectuals or that others besides Phillips were "born in the 30's" would be wrong, too, since we know that many learned at least some of their left-wing politics from elsewhere. But there is no doubt that Lenin, Trotsky, and Stalin were key figures in the rise of this generation of progressive American Jewish intellectuals.

And this is the element that complicates the task of assessing the role of the earlier generation. Anyone taking inspiration from Lenin, Trotsky, and Stalin was knowingly or unknowingly taking inspiration from the same tradition that served as a legacy for the Yiddish-speaking émigrés. There is a famous story about a conversation Lenin had in Switzerland, in 1904. His friend Nikolai Valentinov, it seems, made the mistake of deprecating Chernyshevsky and describing *What Is to Be Done?* as "primitive and talentless." Lenin flew into a rage. "It's impermissible to call *What Is to Be Done?* primitive and talentless," he shot back. "Under its influence hundreds of people became revolutionaries. Could this have happened if Chernyshevsky had written talentlessly and primitively? He captivated my brother, for example, and he captivated me, too. *He completely made me over.*" Lenin went on to say that it was "not by chance" that the famous pamphlet he wrote in 1902 bore the same title as Chernyshevsky's novel.[17]

In fact, the pamphlet *What Is to Be Done?*, which gives one of the earliest and most complete statements of Lenin's program, is permeated with pre-Marxist Russian revolutionary doctrine that is, not surprisingly, the same as what so many Russian-Jewish intellectuals brought with them to the United States. Lenin's separation of the revolutionary movement into a class of workers and a professional class of revolutionaries—the basis for his conception of the party—is pure Lavrov. His desire to establish a powerful press ("print [the press] has long been a force among us," he says) bespeaks a Nihilist's faith in the impact of the printed word.[18] He mentions Pisarev and uses terms from his works.[19]

As for Lenin's views on culture, nothing could be clearer than the account his wife, Nadezhda Krupskaia, gave after his death. She speaks of her late husband's admiration for Chernyshevsky, she mentions his description of the era of Chernyshevsky as an era when "every socialist was a poet and every poet was a socialist," and she offers this view of his attitude toward literature:

> Vladimir Il'ich read literature, studied it, loved it. But one thing was true with Vladimir Il'ich—for him the social approach [to reality] and the artistic reflection of reality merged into one. These two things he somehow could never separate from each other, and just as Chernyshevsky's ideas were reflected entirely in his artistic works, so Lenin, in his choice of literary works especially liked books in which social ideas of one sort or another were clearly reflected in the artistic production.[20]

It was an easy step from views like these to the view of a literature—broadly conceived as written expression—placed in the service of the party, the sort of view that is expressed in Stalin's admonition to make print (the press) "the sharpest and strongest weapon of our party."[21] In his 1905 essay, "Party Organization and Party Literature," Lenin urged his fellow revolutionaries to link all literary activity with the movement.

"All Social-Democratic literature," he says, "must become party literature. All newspapers, journals, publishing houses, and so forth must immediately get down to the task of reorganizing, of preparing for this situation, so that on the basis of one set of principles or another they can
enter into one party organization or another."[22]

Trotsky and Stalin presented variations on the basic set of premises
that Lenin—and the Nihilist generation before him, including the Jewish
intellectuals—adopted, Trotsky favoring considerably more autonomy
for artistic activity, Stalin favoring the most direct subordination of art to
the needs of the political professionals. But the underlying culture was
essentially the same. It was a culture that was adopted from nineteenth-
century Russian Nihilism and Populism, one on which Marxism represented an almost casual accretion. In fact, one of the clearest signs that the
Soviet approach to culture was more "Russian" than Marxist is the
speech that Leningrad Party Chief Andrei Zhdanov gave at the First All-
USSR Writers' Congress in 1934. In his remarks to the future socialist
realists, he mentioned Belinsky, Chernyshevsky, and Dobroliubov nineteen times, and never once mentioned Marx.[23]

This is why the political approach to culture that the New York Intellectuals took, even if it had been derived entirely from Soviet sources and
from nowhere else (a dubious notion), would have borne the resemblance
it did in fact bear to the approach that the Yiddish-speaking generation
took. It is also why it is so difficult to determine to what extent the culture
of the 1930s was a legacy of the earlier immigrant generation and to what
extent it stemmed from developments that were largely independent of
that generation.

It is hard not to see some connection, even if the connection is based on
nothing more than an ill-defined notion of political and cultural activism
that was communicated from one generation to the next. If Phillips was
exaggerating when he said that *Partisan Review* represented a new approach to literature and politics, he may not have been exaggerating
when he followed this claim with the observation that the magazine he
helped found "was itself to influence writing and thinking for a long time
and to set an intellectual pattern for literary publications."[24]

If this is true, then we can see at least a continuity of *purpose* from the
days of the early Russian Jewish immigrant intellectuals to the trends in
political criticism that have been fashionable in more recent times. Cahan
had admired the Russian critics for "criticizing the social life of their father land" by criticizing the works of famous authors. He had said that
"criticism of good novels is a social as well as a literary study." This view
is not much different from a statement like "Through our specific literary
medium we shall participate in the struggle of the workers and sincere
intellectuals against imperialist war, fascism, national and racial oppression, and for the abolition of the system which breeds these evils" (*Parti-*

san Review). And it is but a small leap from there to the rhetoric of recent times, which, too, appears convinced of its absolute freshness and novelty: "The point is not only to interpret texts, but in so interpreting them, change our society." "The literary act is a social act" (Frank Lentricchia).[25] "It therefore falls to literary criticism to continue to compare the inside and the outside, existence and history, to continue to pass judgment on the abstract quality of life in the present, and to keep alive the idea of a concrete future. May it prove equal to the task!" (Fredric Jameson).[26] "Not until the profession [of literary critics] begins to see through the discourse of humanism and to understand some of the material functions of the institutions it embodies as these relate to the hegemony can criticism begin to wrest the knowledge-producing apparatus away from the interests it now serves" (Paul Bové).[27]

This is not to say that modern critics on the left can trace their origins directly to Abe Cahan and a generation of Yiddish-speaking, Russian-born intellectuals. Nor is it to overlook the role that a multitude of other thinkers, Marxist and non-Marxist, have played in constructing the progressive tendency in recent literary studies, thinkers as diverse as Nietzsche, Lukács, Heidegger, Derrida, Foucault, and Adorno, to mention only a few. But a look at the contributions of the Yiddish-speaking generation will show that they deserve to be a part of the history just as much as do the New York Intellectuals and later writers.

We must be careful, on the one side, not to overstate the sophistication and originality of the contributions the émigré Jewish intellectuals made. If only because the available medium (mostly the Yiddish press), the readership (mostly immigrant Jews with little education), and political priorities (building a labor movement, educating workers) imposed such formidable constraints on the style, length, and content of written work in their world, there was little possibility the Jewish intellectuals in the era of mass immigration could ever move far beyond a translation, transportation, and very modest transformation of the political theories that had shaped them in their Russian youth. Those like Zhitlovsky who tried to do more and tried to do it in Yiddish found very few readers.

But, on the other side, we must be careful to acknowledge the contribution these men and women made. Even if we put to one side all the very conspicuous achievements that have been the subject of so many scholarly and popular books—the labor union movement, the Yiddish theatre, the political careers of such visible figures as Meyer London and Morris Hillquit, Emma Goldman's role in the strengthening of First Amendment rights—there was an undeniable contribution to American intellectual life. The style of political and cultural activism that Cahan and his fellow immigrant intellectuals brought with them to this country had never before existed in just this form. Whether it was passed on from a Yiddish-speaking generation to a non-Yiddish-speaking generation by force of example, by casual conversation (with a Yiddish accent on one side and a native-born New York accent on the other), or by actual contact with the written texts of the immigrant generation, the ideologies of the parents' generation did not die out with the parents. That is why it is so easy to hear echoes of this generation in the language of the left in recent years. Whether or not their mode of activism, the one they adopted in their homeland and brought with them, was passed on directly, in this country it was the one that came first.

KIBETS GOLYES

What of the impact this generation of Jewish intellectuals had not just on the left, but on all American Jewry in the twentieth century? And what of the question of Jewish identity, to which so many Jewish radicals returned time and again, grudgingly or willingly? Assessing this is complicated, too.

If there is a single, dominating theme in the writings and political activities of the radical Jewish intellectuals from the era of mass immigration, it is the abandonment of traditional Judaism, with its foundation in religious faith and its many constraints on everyday life, in favor of a secular and cosmopolitan worldview. What most radical intellectuals wanted was a rejection of Judaism as a religion. What better evidence of this than the didactic articles appearing in the *Arbayter Tsaytung* from time to time explaining the meaning of such fundamentally important holidays as Passover (with a socialist slant, of course), as if the editors' wishes had come true and their readers had actually forgotten the meaning of these observances?

One might have predicted that secularism and cosmopolitanism, so much a part of the Russian heritage of the radicals, might have led to a rejection of *Jewishness*. After all, the clearest concession to Jewishness that the intellectuals made, namely their use of Yiddish, was often little more than a tactic adopted for the sake of convenience and expediency. From its earliest use in the modern press, Yiddish appeared destined to write itself out of existence. The first weekly Yiddish-language newspaper in Russia had as one of its aims to educate the Jewish masses until they would no longer need to use Yiddish, and this was clearly on the minds of many contributors to the Yiddish press in the United States, too.[28] It was on Abe Cahan's mind when he spoke of Yiddish newspapers as "preparatory schools from which the reader is sooner or later promoted to the English newspaper."[29]

But the Yiddish weekly in Russia did not achieve its aim as soon as its editor would have liked. It was immensely popular for its decade-long life and in no way appears to have furthered the decline of Yiddish among

Russian Jews. The same thing was true of American papers, for if they had anything to do with the very real decline of Yiddish, they certainly did not achieve this aim as quickly as one might have predicted. If they had, there would have been almost no Yiddish press by the late twenties, and yet Yiddish papers continued to reach a remarkably large readership for several generations.

In part, this was owing to the longevity and the loyalty of readers who had arrived in America during the era of mass immigration and grown to depend on the *Forward*, *Der Tog*, or *Di Tsukunft*. Many Jewish immigrants who had been born in Russia at the turn of the century or later and had come to the United States before World War I were still around to subscribe to their favorite Yiddish publications well into the 1970s. That is why the *Forward* still had the surprisingly large readership of over fifty thousand in the middle of that decade.[30]

It was also owing to a culture that the *Forward* and other publications created, perhaps unwittingly. Find an American Jew who has a first- or even second-hand acquaintance with early twentieth-century Yiddish culture, ask about "Khaye Tsipe" or "Yente Telebende," and you will see what I mean. These satirical characters, the creation of B. Kovner (pseudonym of Yankev Adler), appeared for many years in the *Forward* in cartoons and short prose sketches. They were *olraytnitses*, that is, women *olraytniks* (all-right-niks), meaning fatuous and self-adoring immigrant Jews who fancied that they had "made it" in American society. Khaye Tsipe and Yente Telebende were both overbearing women who drove their husbands mad. And both were so well known to readers of the *Forward* that references to them were a commonplace of ordinary conversation. One could *make up* a story about Yente Telebende, and if it fit her character, no one would be shocked at the piracy, so much a part of the culture had she become.

A respectable number of immigrants from that era sought to preserve the heritage of *Yidishkayt* for their children. The Workmen's Circle (*Arbeyter ring*), founded in 1892, set up schools for children in 1916. The curriculum was vintage Jewish labor movement: the children learned Yiddish and a variety of subjects that hesitated between strictly secular and culturally Jewish. A few years earlier another group had founded the Sholom Aleichem Folk Schools, dedicated to much the same goal as the Workmen's Circle schools. Thus a small number of second-generation immigrants and even a few members of the baby boom generation were brought up speaking Yiddish. Predictably, it is not unusual for these American Jews to speak a *mame-loshn* replete with the Hebraisms that are part of the Yiddish lexicon and yet to be almost totally ignorant of both Hebrew as a language of prayer and, for that matter, Jewish ritual in general.

The efforts of the Russian Jewish intellectuals to reject *Judaism* as a

religion certainly met with some success, though it is impossible to separate the role of individuals like Cahan from a host of other factors in
American life. If Judaism as a religion in America would never again be
what it had been in Poland and the Pale of Settlement, no doubt American
life, with its many impious temptations, had as much to do with this as
the writings and activities of Abe Cahan and Morris Winchevsky. In fact,
Abe Cahan himself had shown this vividly in his stories about immigrants
who give themselves over to the worldly delectations of their new home
(going bare-headed, riding the streetcar on Saturday, eating non-kosher
food) and do so with no help from intellectuals like Cahan himself.

In any case, one thing is certain, and that is that even those intellectuals
who adopted an attitude of hostility toward the traditions of their people
and continued to present themselves as Russians did not bring about a
wholesale rejection of *Jewishness*, either in the era of mass immigration
or afterwards. Initially, it was because such a rejection would have lost
those intellectuals their popular base. This was the lesson they had
learned in the Russian phase of their immigrant life. Later it was because,
having already helped sustain an interest in Yiddish culture, Yiddish-
speaking intellectuals like Cahan realized that their own survival as leaders required them to remain tapped into the Jewish community and its
issues. No Jewish intellectual later in the twentieth century could ever
endure—and retain an identity as a specifically Jewish figure—without
recognizing the two primary Jewish issues of the twentieth century (after
the mass immigration itself): Zionism and the Holocaust. It is a mark of
Cahan's own growth, or perhaps only of his pragmatism, that, after years
of doctrinaire hostility to a movement that he and his comrades had always considered too inherently tied to Jewish messianism and nationalism, he finally reached an accommodation with Zionism, one that allowed him as early as the end of the 1920s to avoid calling himself a
Zionist while showing support for the cause of building a Jewish homeland in Palestine. And the rise of Fascism in Europe aroused in Cahan and
his newspaper a sense of Jewish nationalism that would have been un-
thinkable a generation earlier.[31]

If the Jewish radicals created a sense of community among other Jewish immigrants and helped sustain that sense of community in later generations, was it in spite of themselves? Their penitent protestations of loyalty to their people after the pogroms notwithstanding, many upon arriving in America quickly began to see themselves once again as citizens of
Russia, not as members of a Jewish "nation." They had sought, first, to
use their new home as a distant base of operation for the revolutionary
struggle in their homeland and, then, to wage a struggle in their new
home like the one they had helped wage in their homeland. Over and over
again they had asserted their status as Russians and been so successful
that native-born Americans thought of them primarily as Russians. Over

and over again they had shied away from acknowledging the Jewishness of their readers, even when those readers were reading them in a language that almost no one except Jews could understand. When they had moved into the world of English-language publishing, many of them abandoned all traces of their Jewish identity.

Can memory have been so short? "We have striven to adopt the language and manners of our Christian fellow countrymen; we have brought ourselves up to an ardent love of their literature, of their culture, of their progress," Aleinikoff had said before the sobbing congregation in Kiev. "We have tried to persuade ourselves that we are children of Mother Russia. Alas! we have been in error." How have we been in error? "We are Jews, just like you. We are sorry that up till now we have thought of ourselves as Russians and not as Jews. . . . Yes, we are Jews."

There is another blessing that has formed part of the Jewish liturgy for more than two thousand years. It is called, in Yiddish conversational pronunciation, *Kibets Golyes* (*Kibuts Galuyot*), the "ingathering of exiles." It serves one of the many occasions in religious life when Jews pray for the return to Israel and the restoration of the Temple. It goes like this:

> Sound the great shofar for our freedom,
> Lift up a banner for the ingathering of our exiles,
> And gather us together from the four ends of the earth.
> Blessed art Thou, O Lord, Who gathers the outcasts of His people Israel.

"To America!" may have been inspired initially by nothing more exalted than a fear of further political oppression and physical violence. But the first pogroms, with their reminder that Jews were Jews and not citizens of some other nation, were not far behind. Nor was the collective memory of exile and the often repeated prayers for the reestablishment of Jerusalem. For Aleinikoff and his fellow students as they stood in the synagogue, this was no farther away in time than their own *kheyder* days, no farther away in distance than the worshipers sitting before them. "To America!" at that moment meant a chance to fulfill a national destiny. Once they got to the other shore, try as they might, they could not entirely forget.

Notes

Introduction

1. Abraham Cahan, "The Russian Jew in America," *Atlantic Monthly*, 82 (1898): 128–39. The quoted passage appears on pp. 128–29.

2. See A. I. Gertsen (Herzen), *Sobranie sochinenii v tridtsati tomakh* (Moscow: Izdatel'stvo Akademii Nauk SSSR, 1954–64), 6:493.

Chapter 1
"We Were Not Jews"

1. Simon Dubnow, in his classic history of Russian and Polish Jewry, cites Polish census figures from 1764–66 that show 621,000 Jews in Poland before the Partitions. See *History of the Jews in Russia and Poland from the Earliest Times Until the Present Day*, trans. I. Friedlaender (Philadelphia: The Jewish Publication Society of America, 1916–20), 1:187n1. When Russia annexed White Russia in the First Partition (1772), she acquired about 200,000 Jews (Dubnow, *op. cit.*, 1:307). In the generation or so after the Polish census of 1764–66, however, the Jewish population in what was left of Poland seems to have grown by roughly the amount that went over to Russia in 1772, for Dubnow reports that the official figure for Jews living in Poland in 1788 was 617,032. But Dubnow points out that official figures are almost certainly low (because the Jewish population had an interest in being undercounted) and says that the actual figure for 1788 was probably closer to 900,000 and maybe even 1,000,000 (Dubnow, *op. cit.*, 1:263–64). Most estimates of the total number of Jews that Russia acquired through all three Partitions range between 900,000 and 1,000,000. Louis Greenberg, citing a Russian source from early in the twentieth century, says that the total Jewish population in Russia after the last Partition (1795) was 900,000, including, of course, the small number that had been there before the first Partition. See Greenberg, *The Jews in Russia* (New Haven: Yale University Press, 1944–51), 1:8.

2. There is a remarkable lack of agreement among Yiddishists about the origins of both the Jews who first spoke Yiddish and the language they spoke. Whether Yiddish first came into being in the Rhineland or somewhere else, one can certainly say that by 1,000 CE there was a significant number of Jews in this part of Germany and that an ancestor of modern Yiddish was their principal vernacular language.

3. On Jewish education in the Polish era and later, see Zvi Halevy, *Jewish Schools under Czarism and Communism: A Struggle for Cultural Identity* (New York: Springer, 1976).

4. Irving Howe, *World of Our Fathers: The Journey of the East European Jews to America and the Life They Found and Made* (New York: Harcourt, Brace, Jovanovich, 1976), Chapter 1, "Origins," pp. 11–12.

5. Lev Grigor'evich Deich (Lev Deutsch), *Rol' evreev v russkom revoliutsion-*

nom dvizhenii (The role of the Jews in the Russian revolutionary movement) (Berlin: "Grani," 1923), p. 17.

6. For figures on Jewish enrollments in the universities, see Il'ia Trotskii, "Evrei v russkoi shkole," in Frumkin et al., eds., *Kniga o russkom evreistve ot 1860-kh godov do revoliutsii 1917 g.* (New York: Soiuz russkikh evreev, 1960), p. 357; English translation: "Jews in Russian Schools," in Mirra Ginsburg, trans., *Russian Jewry (1860–1917)* (New York: Thomas Yoseloff, 1966), pp. 411–12.

7. See Steve J. Zipperstein, "Haskalah, Cultural Change, and Nineteenth-Century Russian Jewry: A Reassessment," *Journal of Jewish Studies*, 34 (1983): 191–207. This study is designed to correct and enrich the standard treatments of the subject, above all the one by Dubnow in *History of the Jews in Russia and Poland*. Zipperstein's principal contribution is to show that the Haskalah and its impact on Russian Jews are considerably more complicated than Dubnow's account suggests. Dubnow's account falls short, Zipperstein thinks, largely because he favored a view of his own people as relatively homogeneous, ignoring such factors as cultural diversity from one region to another.

8. On the Haskalah in general, see Dubnow, *History of the Jews in Russian and Poland*, 2:125; Greenberg, *The Jews in Russia*, 1:12–28; and Nora Levin, *While Messiah Tarried: Jewish Socialist Movements, 1871–1917* (New York: Schocken, 1977), pp. 9–10.

9. For accounts of the law of 1844, see Dubnow, *History of the Jews in Russia and Poland*, 2:57–59; and Greenberg, *The Jews in Russia*, 1:33–41.

10. On the reforms of this era and how they affected the Jews, see Dubnow, *History of the Jews in Russia and Poland*, 2: 154–83; and Greenberg, *The Jews in Russia*, 1:74–80.

11. For figures on university enrollments, see Martin Malia, "What Is the Intelligentsia?", in Richard Pipes, ed., *The Russian Intelligentsia* (New York: Columbia University Press, 1961), pp. 1–18. The figures appear on p. 14. As Malia shows, there were never more than a few thousand university students per year, in a population that ranged (according to his figures) from around forty million in the 1840s to around seventy-five million in the 1870s (other sources would give a higher figure for the 1840s, but the point remains essentially unchanged).

12. F. Krants (Philip Krantz), "Nastoiashchee pole deiatel'nosti" (The present field of activity), in the New York–based, Russian-language socialist newspaper *Znamia*, February 15, 1890, pp. 1–2. See Chapter 6.

13. Shmuel Niger and Yankev Shatski, eds., *Leksikon fun der nayer yidisher literatur* (Lexicon of modern Yiddish literature) (New York: Congress for Jewish Culture, 1956–81), 6:554–63. This *Leksikon* is the source for much of the biographical information in the section that follows. Irving Howe claims that Edelstadt taught himself Yiddish. See *World of Our Fathers*, pp. 420–21.

14. Laura Z. Hobson, *Laura Z: A Life* (New York: Arbor House, 1983), p. 22. Hobson is best known as the author of *Gentleman's Agreement* (1947), the best-selling novel about the experiences of a Gentile who poses as a Jew in order to investigate American anti-Semitism. The story was made famous by the movie version (1947), starring Gregory Peck and directed by Elia Kazan.

15. On *Progress*, see Chapter 6.

16. Abraham Cahan, *Bleter fun mayn leben* (Pages from my life) (New York: Forward Association, 1926–31), 1:104–105; English translation in Leon Stein,

Abraham P. Conan, Lynn Davison, trans., *The Education of Abraham Cahan* (Philadelphia: The Jewish Publication Society of America, 1969), pp. 38–39.

17. Cahan, *Bleter fun mayn leben*, 1:110–11; *The Education of Abraham Cahan*, pp. 41–42.

18. See Emma Goldman, *Living My Life* (New York: Knopf, 1931), 1:27–28.

19. Ibid., 1:13.

20. Morris Winchevsky, *Erinerungen* (Memoirs), in *Gezamlte verk* (Collected works), ed. Kalman Marmor (New York: Farlag "Frayhayt," 1927), 9:155–56. The reference to Joshua is from Joshua 10:12–13. The Talmudic saying is from Berakhot 58A.

21. Winchevsky, *Gezamlte verk*, 9:151.

22. Chaim Zhitlovsky, *Zikhroynes fun mayn lebn* (Memoirs of my life) (New York: Dr. Chaim Zhitlovsky Jubilee Committee, 1935), 1:236–37.

23. There is considerable difference of opinion on the date of Liberman's birth. Tcherikower (with coauthors) lists four sources for the biographical sketch he gives in *The Early Jewish Labor Movement in the United States* (New York: YIVO, 1961), each source giving a different date. See pp. 32–33n9. Jonathan Frankel seems to have accepted 1845 as the year of Liberman's birth, since he puts Liberman's age at thirty-five in 1880, the year of his death. See *Prophecy and Politics: Socialism, Nationalism, and the Russian Jews, 1862–1917* (Cambridge: Cambridge University Press, 1981), p. 28.

Chapter 2
"In Chernychevsky's *Kheyder*"

1. Belinskii, "Rech' o kritike" (Discourse on criticism), *Polnoe sobranie sochinenii* (Moscow: Izdatel'stvo Akademii Nauk SSSR, 1955), 6:267–334. The article is a review of a work by literary historian and censor A. V. Nikitenko. The quoted phrase appears on p. 268. This edition will be abbreviated as *PSS*.

2. Belinskii, *PSS*, 6:270.

3. Ibid., 6:280, 284.

4. Ibid., 6:287.

5. Ibid., 6:318.

6. Irina Paperno asserts that Chernyshevsky "has had the greatest impact on human lives in the history of Russian literature." See her *Chernyshevsky and the Age of Realism: A Study in the Semiotics of Behavior* (Stanford: Stanford University Press, 1988), p. 4. Joseph Frank refers to Chernyshevsky's novel *What Is to Be Done?* as the nineteenth-century novel "that has had the greatest influence on Russian society." See Joseph Frank, "N. G. Chernyshevsky: A Russian Utopia," *The Southern Review*, no. 1 (1967): 68–84; reprinted as "Nikolay Chernyshevsky: A Russian Utopia," in Joseph Frank, *Through the Russian Prism: Essays on Literature and Culture* (Princeton: Princeton University Press, 1990), pp. 187–200.

7. Nikolai Gavrilovich Chernyshevskii, *Polnoe sobranie sochinenii* (Moscow: Goslitizdat, 1939–1953), 2:14. This edition will be abbreviated as *PSS*.

8. Chernyshevskii, *PSS*, 2:10. Emphasis added.

9. Chernyshevskii, *Ocherki gogolevskogo perioda russkoi literatury* (Essays on the Gogol period in Russian Literature) (Moscow: "Khudozhestvennaia literatura," 1984), p. 268.

10. Ibid., p. 329.

11. Ibid., p. 378.

12. See Paperno, *Chernyshevsky and the Age of Realism*, pp. 89–158, for an excellent account of Chernyshevsky's views on marriage. See p. 130 for his views on sexual abstinence and marital infidelity.

13. Ibid., pp. 133–35.

14. Dobroliubov, *Sobranie sochinenii* (Moscow: Goslitizdat, 1961–64), 6:309.

15. Ibid., 6:98–99.

16. Pisarev, *Sochineniia* (Moscow: Gos. Izd. Khud. Lit., 1955–56), 3:367.

17. Ibid., 3:419.

18. See P. Nikolaev, "Razvitie teorii realizma v russkoi kritike serediny XIX v." (The development of the theory of realism in Russian criticism of the mid-nineteenth century), in K. N. Lomunov et al., eds., *Razvitie realizma v russkoi literature* (The development of realism in Russian literature) (Moscow: "Nauka," 1973), 2:343.

19. This is the date René Wellek gives in his essay "Realism in Literary Scholarship." See Wellek, *Concepts of Criticism* (New Haven and London: Yale University Press, 1963), pp. 226–27. For a history of the term *réalisme* in France, see the classic work of Harry Levin, *The Gates of Horn* (New York: Oxford University Press, 1963), pp. 64–73.

20. Pisarev, *Sochineniia*, 3:20.

21. Ibid., 3:67.

22. P. Nikolaev, in Lomunov et al., *Razvitie realizma v russkoi literature*, 2:345.

23. Irina Paperno has an excellent section called "Living Merged with Writing," which shows how Chernyshevsky's life exemplified the fusion I have been describing here. See *Chernyshevsky and the Age of Realism*, pp. 48–53.

24. Leo Daytsh (Deutsch), "Beti Kaminski: Di ershte idishe studentke un propagandistke" (Betty Kaminskaia: The first Jewish woman student and propagandist), *Di Tsukunft*, 1915, pp. 930–33. The quoted passage appears on p. 931. The same story, with minor changes, appears in *Rol' evreev v russkom revoliutsionnom dvizhenii*, pp. 138–39.

25. Deutsch, *Rol' evreev v russkom revoliutsionnom dvizhenii*, p. 31.

26. Zhitlovsky, *Zikhroynes fun mayn lebn*, 1:220.

27. Tcherikower, "Yidn-revolutsyonern in rusland in di 60er un 70er yorn" (Jewish revolutionaries in Russia in the 1860s and 1870s), in Tcherikower et al., eds., *Historishe shriftn* (Paris-Vilna, 1929–39), 3:79–80.

28. *Di Tsukunft*, 1913, p. 440. See also Deutsch, *Rol' evreev v russkom revoliutsionnom dvizhenii*, p. 73.

29. Leo Daytsh (Deutsch), "Di iden in der rusisher revolutsyonerer bevegung" (Jews in the Russian revolutionary movement), *Di Tsukunft*, 1913, pp. 248–57. The reference to the three authors appears on p. 253.

30. Deutsch, *Rol' evreev v russkom revoliutsionnom dvizhenii*, p. 37.

31. Ibid., p. 32n.

32. Ibid., p. 280.

33. Cahan, *Bleter fun mayn leben*, 1:241–45; *The Education of Abraham Cahan*, pp. 95–97.

34. Cahan, "Kritishe studyen iber zhargonishe mayster-verk" (Critical studies on masterpieces in Yiddish), *Di Tsukunft*, 1896, pp. 53–56, 56–59, 153–60, 178–87, 223–29, 485–91, 523–28, 594–96. The general study of criticism is called "A por verter vegen kritik in algemeyn" (A few words on criticism in general). It appears on pp. 53–56. The quoted passage appears on p. 54. See Chapter 9.

35. Sh. Agurski, ed., *Di sotsyalistishe literatur af yidish in 1875–1897* (Socialist literature in Yiddish, 1875–97) (Minsk: Vaysrusisher Visnshaft-Akademye, 1935), pp. 402–401, 401n (original Russian, paginated backwards); pp. 59–60, 60n (Yiddish). Cited in Ezra Mendelsohn, *Class Struggle in the Pale: The Formative Years of the Jewish Workers' Movement in Tsarist Russia* (Cambridge: Cambridge University Press, 1970), p. 122.

36. John Mill, *Pyonern un boyer: Memuarn* (Pioneers and builders: Memoirs) (New York: "Der Wecker," 1946), p. 33.

37. Ibid., pp. 45–51.

38. Winchevsky, *Gezamlte verk*, 9:159. A version of these memoirs was published in *Di Tsukunft*. See *Di Tsukunft*, 1906, p. 734. The phrase that I have translated as "sentimental socialist" literally means "feeling-socialist" (*gefil-sotsyalist*).

39. Goldman, *Living My Life*, 1:27–28.

40. Zhitlovsky, *Zikhroynes fun mayn lebn*, 1:223.

41. Ibid., 1:223.

42. Ibid., 1:224.

43. Ibid., 1:225.

44. Ibid., 1:232–36.

45. Ibid., 1:224.

46. Cahan, *Bleter fun mayn leben*, 1:396; *The Education of Abraham Cahan*, p. 144.

47. Deutsch, *Rol' evreev v russkom revoliutsionnom dvizhenii*, p. 74.

48. Ibid., p. 320.

49. Cahan, *Bleter fun mayn leben*, 1:445; *The Education of Abraham Cahan*, p. 162.

50. Cahan, *Bleter fun mayn leben*, 1:477; *The Education of Abraham Cahan*, p. 173.

51. For additional information on reading, see Mendelsohn, *Class Struggle in the Pale*, pp. 116–25; and "The Russian Roots of the American Jewish Labor Movement," *YIVO Annual of Jewish Social Science*, 16 (1976): 157–58, 173n25.

52. Levin, *While Messiah Tarried*, pp. 26–27.

53. Frankel, *Prophecy and Politics*, p. 33. On *Vpered!*, see Chapter 3.

54. Cahan, *Bleter fun mayn leben*, 1:464; *The Education of Abraham Cahan*, p. 168.

55. Lev Deich (Deutsch), *Kak my v narod khodili* (How we went to the people) (Davos, Switzerland: "Za rubezhom," 1910), p. 5.

56. *Di Tsukunft*, 1913, p. 440. Deutsch tells this story in *Rol' evreev v russkom revoliutsionnom dvizhenii*, pp. 74–75, in a passage that is almost a word-for-word translation of the one I have quoted from *Di Tsukunft*. Curiously, though, in the book, he omits the names Chernyshevsky, Dobroliubov, and Pisarev, using the phrase "our advanced press" (*nasha peredovaia pechat'*) instead.

57. *Di Tsukunft*, 1913, p. 254. See also Deutsch, *Rol' evreev v russkom revo-*

liutsionnom dvizhenii, pp. 33–34, for a nearly identical version of the quoted passage.

58. See Chapter 8.

59. Paperno's observation has specifically to do with marriage in the age of Nihilism, but it could easily be extended to other aspects of life in the same era. See *Chernyshevsky and the Age of Realism*, pp. 89–91.

60. Zhitlovsky, *Zikhroynes fun mayn lebn*, 1:236

61. Cahan, *Bleter fun mayn leben*, 1:412–13; *The Education of Abraham Cahan*, pp. 149–50.

62. On the Yom Kippur balls, see Tcherikower, *The Early Jewish Labor Movement in the United States*, pp. 253–71.

Chapter 3
"Critically Thinking Individuals"

1. Andrzej Walicki, *The Controversy over Capitalism: Studies in the Social Philosophy of the Russian Populists* (Oxford: Oxford University Press, 1969), pp. 3–5. Walicki uses as his point of departure an essay by Richard Pipes, "Narodnichestvo: A Semantic Inquiry," *Slavic Review*, 23 (1964): 441–58. On the background to Russian Populism, see also Richard Wortman, *The Crisis of Russian Populism* (Cambridge: Cambridge University Press, 1967), pp. 1–34.

2. Lavrov, *Istoricheskie pis'ma* (Historical letters) (St. Petersburg: Tipografiia A. Kotomina, 1870), pp. 65–66; English translation in *Historical Letters*, trans. James P. Scanlan (Berkeley and Los Angeles: University of California Press, 1967), p. 141.

3. Lavrov, *Istoricheskie pis'ma*, pp. 74–75; *Historical Letters*, p. 147.

4. Lavrov, *Istoricheskie pis'ma*, p. 30; *Historical Letters*, p. 111. Emphasis in original.

5. Lavrov, *Istoricheskie pis'ma*, p. 63; *Historical Letters*, 140. Emphasis in original.

6. Lavrov, *Istoricheskie pis'ma*, p. 91; *Historical Letters*, p. 161. Emphasis in original.

7. Lavrov, *Istoricheskie pis'ma*, p. 118; *Historical Letters*, p. 180.

8. Lavrov, *Istoricheskie pis'ma*, p. 120; *Historical Letters*, p. 181.

9. *Vpered!* was published in two formats, a "nonperiodical" format and a periodical format. The nonperiodical *Vpered!* was issued in five volumes of several hundred pages each. Volumes I and II were published in Zurich in 1873 and 1874, respectively, and volumes III through V were published in London from 1874 to 1877. The periodical *Vpered!* was published as a newspaper in forty-eight issues, from 1875 to 1876, all in London. It is usually referred to as a fortnightly (*dvukhnedel'nyi* in Russian), although in fact it was a semimonthly, coming out on the first and fifteenth of each month. I will cite the nonperiodical volumes using a roman numeral for the volume, a section number, and a page number. I will cite the periodical issues using an arabic numeral for the issue, a date, and a column number. The quoted material from the programmatic article, "Vpered! Our Program," is from I, sect. 1, p. 12. The scholar who did more than anyone else to bring out reprints of *Vpered!*, establish the authorship of the arti-

cles printed in it (almost all of which were unsigned), collect and publish related documents, and investigate the details of Lavrov's life and career is Boris Sapir. For a brief history of *Vpered!*, see Sapir's introduction to the first volume of *Vpered!* (The Hague: Mouton, 1969). For a more detailed history, see his "Osnovnye etapy istorii 'Vpered'" (The basic stages in the history of *Vpered!*), in Boris Sapir, ed., *"Vpered!" 1873–1877: Materialy is arkhiva Valeriana Nikolaevicha Smirnova* (*Vpered!* 1873–1877: Material from the archives of Valerian Nikolaevich Smirnov) (Dordrecht: D. Reidel, 1970), 1:19–159. The same text appears in English, under the title "The Main Stages in the History of *Vpered*" on pp. 225–363. For a list of contributors to *Vpered!*, with the articles they wrote and the issues in which those articles appeared, see pp. 160–74 of the same volume.

10. *Vpered!*, I, sect. 1, p. 14.

11. "Nevozmozhnye i vozmozhnye puti k sotsial'noi revoliutsii" (Impossible and possible paths to social revolution), ibid., 28 (March 1, 1876), 97–108. The quoted material appears on p. 106.

12. On the Jews associated with *Vpered!*, see Boris Sapir, "Jewish Socialists Around *Vpered*," *International Review of Social History*, 10 (1965), 365–84. On spurning anti-Semitic attitudes, see pp. 368–70. See also Tcherikower, "Der Onhoyb fun der yidisher sotsyalistisher bavegung" (The beginning of the Jewish socialist movement), *Historishe shriftn*, 1:469–532, for a discussion of early Jewish involvement in the revolutionary movement and for the Lavrovist phase. This article contains a number of errors, which Sapir has exposed and corrected, especially in "Liberman et le socialisme russe," *International Review for Social History*, 3 (1938), 25–88. See below. Tcherikower has more on the Lavrovist phase in "Yidn revolutsyonern in rusland in di 60er un 70er yorn," *Historishe shriftn*, 1:124–36.

13. See Tcherikower, "Peter Lavrov and the Jewish Socialist Émigrés," *YIVO Annual of Jewish Social Science*, 7 (1952): 132–45. Tcherikower claims that the translator of the Paris speech is unknown. Jonathan Frankel, however, says unequivocally that it was Morris Winchevsky. See *Prophecy and Politics*, p. 567n137.

14. These references are scattered throughout Lavrov's memoirs of the populist movement, *Narodniki-propagandisty 1873–78 godov* (Populist-propagandists from 1873 to 1878) (Geneva, 1895–1896; rpt. St. Petersburg: Tipografiia "T-va Andersona i Loitsianskogo," 1907). Lavrov mentions, among others, Nikolai Utin, Arkadii Finkelshtein, Lazar Goldenberg, Lidiia Figner, Vera Figner, Beti Kaminskaia, V. A. Gol'shtein, Aron Zundelevich, Aron Liberman, Pavel Akselrod, and Leo Deutsch.

15. For general material on Liberman, see Tcherikower, "Der Onhoyb fun der yidisher sotsyalistisher bavegung," *Historishe shriftn*, 1:469–532; Sapir, "Liberman et le socialisme russe," *International Review for Social History*, 3 (1938): 25–88; Levin, *While Messiah Tarried*, pp. 38–46; and Frankel, *Prophecy and Politics*, pp. 28–48.

16. Sapir offers what he calls indirect evidence of the influence of the Lavrovists on Liberman before Liberman's involvement with *Vpered!* See "Liberman et le socialisme russe," *International Review for Social History*, 3 (1938): 28–29.

17. See Kalman Marmor, ed., *Arn Libermans briv* (Aron Liberman's letters) (New York: YIVO, 1951). For references to Chernyshevsky's *Prolog* (Prologue), see pp. 133, 171 (Russian); 137, 174 (Yiddish translation); 140n35, 175n11 (ed-

itor's footnotes). For a reference to Chernyshevsky's *Pis'ma bez adresa* (Letters without address), which, incidentally, was published in the second volume of the nonperiodical *Vpered!* (1874), see pp. 146 (Russian); 151 (Yiddish translation); 154n23 (editor's footnote). And for a reference to *What Is to Be Done?*, see pp. 205 (Russian); 208 (Yiddish translation); 211n2 (editor's footnote).

18. *Belostok* is the Russian form of *Białystok*, the name of a town in Grodno province (today in northeastern Poland) with a large Jewish population. Different sources give different accounts of which articles in *Vpered!* were the work of Liberman. The definitive version at this point appears to be that of Boris Sapir, who in the two volumes of documentary material on *Vpered!* (published in 1970) gives a complete list of articles published in *Vpered!*, together with the authors (or, in some cases, the most likely authors). Research in the archives of Smirnov allowed Sapir to correct a number of errors in the account that Tcherikower gives in "Der onhoyb fun der yidisher sotsyalistisher bavegung," *Historishe shriftn*, 1:512n3. One discrepancy remains between the list Sapir gives in the documentary material and the list of Liberman's publications he gives in his article "Liberman et le socialisme russe" (published in 1938). The list in the article (p. 33) contains one item that does not appear in the documentary material (1:167).

19. *Vpered!*, 16 (September 1, 1875): 505.

20. Ibid., 21 (November 15, 1875): 660–61.

21. Ibid., 27 (February 15,1876): 84.

22. Ibid.

23. Liberman had written an appeal to the Jewish youth in November 1875 (that is, before the article "From Belostok"), and had torn it up after Lavrov and Smirnov criticized its excessive emphasis on two of Liberman's obsessions, namely the Bible and rabbis. See "Liberman et le socialisme russe," *International Review for Social History*, 3 (1938): 38–39, where Sapir describes the appeal of November 1875, and 60–61, for a first-hand account by Smirnov of the conversation that led Liberman to destroy that appeal. It is not clear whether this earlier appeal can be considered a version of the manifesto. The Hebrew version of the manifesto dates from July 1876. See Tcherikower, "Der onhoyb fun der yidisher sotsyalistisher bavegung," *Historishe shriftn*, 1:517.

24. The statutes are printed as part of an article titled "Osnovanie sotsial'no-revoliutsionnogo obshchestva evreiskikh rabotnikov v Londone" (The founding of a social-revolutionary society of Jewish workers in London), *Vpered!*, 37 (July 15, 1876): 453–55. The statutes appear on pp. 454–55. Tcherikower, in "Der onhoyb fun der yidisher sotsyalistisher bavegung," *Historishe shriftn*, 1:479, says the article accompanying the statutes is by Liberman, but Sapir has shown that Smirnov was the author. See Sapir, "Liberman et le socialisme russe," *International Review for Social History*, 3 (1938): 34. For the Hebrew and Yiddish versions of these statutes, see *Historishe shriftn*, 1:541–44

25. *Vpered!*, 38 (August 1, 1876): 475.

26. Ibid.

27. Ibid.

28. Tcherikower, "Der onhoyb fun der yidisher sotsyalistisher bavegung," *Historishe shriftn*, 1:532.

29. Frankel, *Prophecy and Politics*, pp. 6, 47.

30. Cahan, *Bleter fun mayn leben*, 1:254–55; *The Education of Abraham Cahan*, p. 101.

31. *Di Tsukunft*, 1906, p. 734. Also in Winchevsky, *Gezamlte verk*, 9:159.

32. *Di Tsukunft*, 1906, p. 673.

33. See Lavrov, *Narodniki-propagandisty 1873–78 godov*, pp. 34–36.

34. Deutsch, *Kak my v narod khodili*, p. 5.

35. Ibid., p. 29.

36. See Deutsch, *Rol' evreev v russkom revoliutsionnom dvizhenii*, Chapter 8, "Uchastie evreev v narodnicheskom i terroristicheskom techeniiakh" (The participation of Jews in populist and terrorist trends), pp. 60–69. Tcherikower disputes the figures Deutsch offers in support of his claim, saying that Jewish participation and the impact of such participation were much greater than Deutsch suggests. Still, Tcherikower concludes that Jews did not play nearly so large a role in the Populist movement of the 1870s as they did in the workers' movement of the 1890s and after. He also diminishes the importance of Jewish participation in the Populist movement by explaining at length why Populist ideology was essentially alien to Jews: the Slavophile idealization of the Russian peasant, the sort of gentry penitence found among Russian landowners, the notion of a "debt to the people," the tradition of peasant uprisings on the model of those led by the famous Cossack rebels Emil'ian Pugachev in the eighteenth century and Sten'ka Razin in the seventeenth—all this, says Tcherikower, was utterly foreign to Russian Jews, who, after all, had been Russified for no more than ten or fifteen years at this point. See Tcherikower, "Yidn revolutsyonern in rusland in di 60er un 70er yorn," *Historishe shriftn*, 1:125–31. For more on the Jewish "going to the people" and the notion of a "debt to the people," see Chapters 4 and 7.

Chapter 4
A Crisis of Identity

1. Goldman, *Living My Life*, pp. 27–28. The details of this conversation are puzzling. Unless Goldman has confused several conversations, her mother must have been referring to pogroms that had taken place in Odessa in 1859 and 1871. The series of pogroms best known in the history of Russian Jewry began in April of 1881, six weeks after the assassination of Alexander II. See below, this chapter. Alexander II had already set the peasant serfs free in February of 1861, well before this conversation took place—well before Emma's birth, for that matter.

2. *Razsvet*, 10 (March 5, 1881): 366. The author of the editorial was one Iakov L'vovich Rozenfel'd, a law student from Galicia who was editor and publisher of the paper at this time. For the story of *Razsvet*'s response to the assassination and the pogroms, see Steven Cassedy, "Russian-Jewish Intellectuals Confront the Pogroms of 1881: The Example of *Razsvet*," *Jewish Quarterly Review*, 84 (1993–94): 129–52.

3. See Cahan, *Bleter fun mayn leben*, 1:419–35; *The Education of Abraham Cahan*, pp. 152–58. The quoted phrase appears on *Bleter*, 1:422, and *Education*, p. 153. Cahan transliterates the Russian words in the Hebrew characters of his Yiddish and then translates them into Yiddish.

4. See Chapter 7.

5. Deutsch, *Rol' evreev v russkom revoliutsionnom dvizhenii*, p. 7.

6. Ia. Rombro (Iaakov Rombro), "Kievskii komitet i vopros ob emigratsii" (The Kiev Committee and the emigration question), *Razsvet*, 32 (August 7, 1881): 1247–51. The quoted passage appears on p. 1250. Emphasis in original.

7. M. L. Lilienblium (Moses Leib Lilienblum), "Obshcheevreiskii vopros i Palestina" (The General Jewish Question and Palestine), *Razsvet*, 41 (October 9, 1881), pp. 1597–1600; and *Razsvet*, 42 (October 16, 1881), pp. 1637–42.

8. *Razsvet*, 42 (October 16, 1881): 1642.

9. Cahan, "The Russian Jew in America," *The Atlantic Monthly*, 82 (1898): 128–29. See Introduction.

10. Cahan, *Bleter fun mayn leben*, 1:500–501; *The Education of Abraham Cahan*, pp. 182–83.

11. Cahan, *The White Terror and the Red* (New York: A. S. Barnes, 1905), p. 321.

12. Aksel'rod, "O zadachakh evreisko-sotsialisticheskoi intelligentsii" (On the tasks of the Jewish-socialist intelligentsia), in V. S. Voitinskii, B. I. Nikolaevskii, L. O. Tsederbaum-Dan, eds., *Iz arkhiva P. B. Aksel'roda* (From the archive of P. B. Akselrod) (Berlin: Russisches Revolutionsarchiv, 1924), pp. 215–29.

13. Ibid., p. 221.

14. For an account of the publication of the proclamation, information about its author, and a text of the proclamation, see S. Valk, "G. G. Romanenko (Iz istorii 'Narodnoi Voli)'" (G. G. Romanenko [From the history of *Narodnaia Volia*]), *Katorga i ssylka*, 48 (1928), 36–59. The text of the proclamation is given on pp. 50–52.

15. *Iz arkhiva P. B. Aksel'roda*, pp. 219, 227.

16. On the *Am Olam* movement, see Abraham Menes, "The *Am Oylom* Movement," *YIVO Annual of Jewish Social Science*, 4 (1949): 9–33.

17. The editors of *Iz arkhiva P. B. Aksel'roda*, in a footnote to Akselrod's pamphlet on the pogroms, print a letter written by an unknown contemporary in response to the pogroms. The writer describes how Jewish students appeared in synagogue on the "day of fasting designated by the Jews" (undoubtedly Yom Kippur) and said that this was for them a "first going-out to the people" ("pervyi vykhod v narod"). See p. 228. Jonathan Frankel quotes from an article by M. I. Rabinovich, who came to be known under the pen-name Ben Ami, in which the writer describes the synagogue visits as a "first 'going to the people.'" See *Prophecy and Politics*, p. 54.

18. See Frankel, *Prophecy and Politics*, pp. 54–57, 112, 119, 268, 288, for further examples.

19. Abraham Menes, "Di yidishe arbeter-bavegung in rusland fun onheyb 70er bizn sof 90er yorn" (The Jewish workers' movement in Russia from the beginning of the 1870s to the end of the 1890s), in *Historishe shriftn*, 3:44–45. *Arbeter Tsaytung* is mentioned on 3:18.

20. Jonathan Frankel, "Socialism and Jewish Nationalism in Russia, 1892–1907," Diss. Cambridge, 1961, p. 237; quoted in Arthur Liebman, *Jews and the Left* (New York: Wiley, 1979), p. 133.

21. Henry J. Tobias, *The Jewish Bund in Russia From Its Origins to 1905* (Stanford: Stanford University Press, 1972), pp. 13–16.

22. Mendelsohn, *Class Struggle in the Pale*, pp. 154–55.

Chapter 5
Coming to Shore

1. On the early Russian immigrants, see Mark Efimovich Vil'chur, *Russkie v Amerike* (The Russians in America) (New York: First Russian Publishing Corporation in America, 1918), pp. 11–28.

2. Ibid., p. 11.

3. Morris Hillquit, *History of Socialism in the United States* (New York, 1903; rpt. New York: Russell and Russell, 1965), p. 177.

4. "Zum Beginn" (At the beginning), *Die New Yorker Volkszeitung*, January 28, 1878, p. 2.

5. Cahan, *Bleter fun mayn leben*, 2:87–88; *The Education of Abraham Cahan*, p. 227.

6. Cahan, *Bleter fun mayn leben*, 2:281–92; *The Education of Abraham Cahan*, pp. 330–37.

Chapter 6
"We Are Russian Workers"

1. Cahan, *Bleter fun mayn leben*, 2:193–94; *The Education of Abraham Cahan*, p. 281.

2. Most accounts of this period follow the one that Cahan gives in his memoirs. See *Bleter fun mayn leben*, 2:233–38; *The Education of Abraham Cahan*, pp. 303–306. See also Tcherikower, *The Early Jewish Labor Movement in the United States*, pp. 208–10. Cahan refers to the Russian-Jewish Workingmen's Association as simply the Jewish Workingmen's Association. Tcherikower has derived his more complete account from *Die New Yorker Volkszeitung* and from the early Yiddish newspaper *Nu-Yorker Yidishe Folkstsaytung* (New York Jewish people's paper). See *The Early Jewish Labor Movement in the United States*, p. 211n21.

3. For an excellent, concise account of the Russian Jewish intelligentsia in America and the transition from the use of Russian to the use of Yiddish, see Ezra Mendelsohn, "The Russian Roots of the American Jewish Labor Movement," *YIVO Annual of Jewish Social Science*, 16 (1976): 150–77.

4. On the Russian-language press in America, see Dirk Hoerder, ed., *The Immigrant Labor Press in North America, 1840s–1970s: An Annotated Bibliography* (Westport, CT: Greenwood Press, 1987), 2:107–43; and Vil'chur, *Russkie v Amerike*, pp. 101–17.

5. On *Znamia*, see V. Yu. Samedov, "'Znamia'—Russkaia gazeta sotsial-demokraticheskogo napravleniia v N'iu-Iorke (1889–1890 gody)" (*Znamia*—A Russian newspaper of social-democratic orientation in New York [1889–1890]), in A. I. Malysh, ed., *Iz istorii marksizma i mezhdunarodnogo rabochego dvizheniia* (Moscow: Izdatel'stvo Politicheskoi Literatury, 1973), pp. 295–332.

6. Ibid., p. 322.

7. "5,000 chel. sobralis' v Kuper Iunion, chtoby prokliast' tsaria, ego oprichnikov i vyrazit' sochuvstvie ikh zhertvam" (5,000 people gather at Cooper Union to curse the Tsar, his oprichniks, and to express sympathy for their [the Tsar's and

the oprichniks'] victims), *Znamia*, March 8, 1890, p. 5. The oprichniks were a gendarme corps in the service of the tsar dating from the sixteenth century.

8. Pavel Aksel'rod, "Otnoshenie revoliutsionnoi intelligentsii v Rossii k bor'be za politicheskuiu svobodu" (The attitude of the revolutionary intelligentsia in Russia toward the struggle for political freedom), *Znamia*, March 23, 1889, pp. 1–2.

9. Petr Lavrov, "Nashi zadachi. Pis'mo tovarishcham v Ameriku" (Our tasks. A letter to comrades in America), *Znamia*, January 26, 1890, pp. 1–3.

10. *Znamia*, January 26, 1890, pp. 2–3.

11. Ibid., p. 3.

12. F. Krants (Philip Krantz), "Nastoiashchee pole deiatel'nosti" (The present field of activity), *Znamia*, February 15, 1890, pp. 1–2.

13. See Chapter 1.

14. *Znamia*, February 15, 1890, p. 2

15. Ibid., January 26, 1890, p. 3. Krantz quotes the passage in *Znamia*, February 15, 1890, p. 2

16. Ibid., March 16,1889, p. 2.

17. Ibid., March 23, 1889, pp. 1–2.

18. Ibid., January 26, 1890, p. 1.

19. Ibid., February 15, 1890, p. 2.

20. Ibid., February 15, 1890, p. 2.

21. Even in a phase close to the era when *Znamia* was published, Lavrov maintained his faith in the power of the developed individual (and the importance of the party): "The developed individual at every historical moment, in the name of his development and his conviction, is obliged to direct all his forces toward the support of the party, which strives in the most direct manner to remove all obstacles to the many-sided development of all individuals and to unite the largest possible portion of mankind into a community with solidarity." See *Sotsial'naia revoliutsiia i zadachi nravstvennosti* (The social revolution and the tasks of morality) (1884), in P. L. Lavrov, *Filosofiia i sotsiologiia: Izbrannye proizvedeniia v dvukh tomakh* (Philosophy and sociology: Selected works in two volumes), ed. Okulov (Moscow: "Mysl'," 1965), 2:423.

22. On Hourwich, see Zalman Reyzen, *Leksikon fun der yidisher literatur* (Lexicon of Yiddish literature) (Vilna: Kletskin, 1928–1929), 1:812–19; and Niger and Shatski, *Leksikon fun der nayer yidisher literatur*, 3:93–97.

23. *Progress*, December 6, p. 8. On Cahan's acquaintance with Mashbir, see *Bleter fun mayn leben*, 2:36–39; *The Education of Abraham Cahan*, pp. 204–206.

24. "Russkaia gazeta na amerikanskoi pochve" (A Russian newspaper on American soil), *Progress*, December 6, 1891, p. 1.

25. Ibid. Toward the end of its second year of publication, *Progress* ran an article on Jewish revolutionaries. The occasion was the arrest of Emma Goldman for an inflammatory speech she had given in New York in August 1893. See "Evrei-revoliutsionery" (Jewish revolutionaries), *Progress*, September 15, 1893, p. 4.

26. *Progress*, December 13, pp. 1–2.

27. "Pis'mo P. L. Lavrova na Briussel'skii Mezhdunarodnyi Sotsialisticheskii

Kongress" (Letter from P. L. Lavrov to the Brussels International Socialist Congress), *Progress*, December 13, 1891; "Pis'mo v redaktsiiu" (Letter to the editor), *Progress*, March 4, 1892, p. 3. Immediately below the letter to the editor is an announcement of a new Russian edition of *Historical Letters*, with the comment that this work by Lavrov had the same meaning that Chernyshevsky's *What Is to Be Done?* had had for the preceding generation.

28. Reyzen gives this figure in his article on Hourwich. See *Leksikon fun der yidisher literatur*, 1:815.

29. *The People*, November 15, 1891, p. 2.

30. G. M. Prais (G. M. Price), *Russkie evrei v Amerike. Ocherki iz istorii, zhizni i byta russko-evreiskikh emigrantov v Soedinennykh Shtatakh Sev. Ameriki s 1881 g. po 1891 g.* (The Russian Jews in America. Essays from the history, life, and daily existence of the Russian Jewish émigrés in the United States of America from 1881 through 1891) (St. Petersburg: Landau, 1893). This book was translated into English by Leo Shpall. See "The Russian Jews in America," *Publications of the American Jewish Historical Society*, 48 (1958–1959): 28–62 and 78–133.

31. This story appears in the supplementary memoirs that were attached to the end of *Russkie evrei v Amerike*. See "Iz vospominanii emigranta" (From the memoirs of an émigré), p. 10. The memoirs were published in English translation as "The Memoir of Doctor George M. Price," trans. Leo Shpall, *Publications of the American Jewish Historical Society*, 47 (1957–1958): 101–10. The passage in question appears on p. 103.

32. "Russko-amerikanskoe obshchestvo vzaimnogo vspomoshchestvovaniia" (The Russian-American Mutual Aid Society), *Russkii Listok*, September 1892, pp. 1, 4; "Girshevskaia kolonizatsiia v Argentinii" ([Baron de] Hirsch colonization in Argentina), *Russkii Listok*, September 1892, p. 1; "Nekotorye evreiskie filantropicheskie uchrezhdeniia v N'iu Iorke" (Several Jewish philanthropic foundations in New York), *Russkii Listok*, September 1892, pp. 2–3.

33. Iankel' Mikhelevich, "Pis'mo evreia k Aleksandru III. (Shutka)" (Letter from a Jew to Alexander III. [Joke]), *Russkie Novosti*, February 5, 1893, p. 3. The announcement of the celebration for *Arbayter Tsaytung* appears in the issue of March 5, 1893, p. 3.

34. See Cahan, *Bleter fun mayn leben*, 2:236–37; *The Education of Abraham Cahan*, p. 305. The coeditor of *Russko-Amerikanskii Vestnik* advertises his services in an ad in his own paper under the name Mark J. Gretsch, but it is entirely possible that he had simply chosen a more American-sounding first name. The other coeditor, I. Rozental', apparently changed his first name, or at least his first initial, since he advertises his services under the name E. Rosenthal (in roman letters) and signs the ad I. Rozental' (in Cyrillic). See *Russko-Amerikanskii Vestnik*, November 15, 1893, p. 10.

35. *Ezhegodnik. Zhurnal Russkogo Sots.-Demokraticheskogo Obshchestva* (Annual. Journal of the Russian Social Democratic Society) (New York: Sotkin, 1898). The exception was Stoleshnikov, who wrote a poem using the pseudonym "Vedi-slova." It is Vil'chur who identified the poet as Stoleshnikov. See *Russkie v Amerike*, p. 114. I am assuming that the "I. G." who wrote an article on the socialist movement in 1898 is Isaac Hourwich ("Gurvich" in Russian). On the

Russian Social Democratic Society, see Abraham Ascher, *Pavel Axelrod and the Development of Menshevism* (Cambridge, MA: Harvard University Press, 1972), pp. 96, 159; and Vil'chur, *Russkie v Amerike*, pp. 119–20.

36. See Reyzen, *Leksikon fun der yidisher literatur*, 1:222–25; and Niger and Shatski, *Leksikon fun der nayer yidisher literatur*, 1:239–40.

37. M. Baranov, "Po povodu dramy v Iunion-Skvere" (Concerning the drama in Union Square), *Russko-Amerikanskii Rabochii*, May 1908, pp. 3–4.

38. M. Baranov, "Uspekhi sotsializma v Amerike" (The success of socialism in America), *Russko-Amerikanskii Rabochii*, June 1908, pp. 3–4.

39. M. Baranov, "Pis'mo v redaktsiiu" (Letter to the editor), ibid., September 1908, pp. 15–16.

40. See Hoerder, *The Immigrant Labor Press in North America*, 2:122. Hoerder does not give a source for this circulation figure.

41. L. Deich (Deutsch), "Po povodu obrashcheniia 'K soznatel'nomu trudiashchemusia naseleniiu Rossii' " (Concerning the appeal "To the conscious working population of Russia"), *Svobodnoe Slovo*, 1, no. 2 (November 1915): 65–71.

42. For a biography of Boudin and for his contributions to the Yiddish press, see Reyzen, *Leksikon fun der yidisher literatur*, 1:232–33; and Niger and Shatski, *Leksikon fun der nayer yidisher literatur*, 1:256–57. Boudin's book was *The Theoretical System of Karl Marx* (Chicago: Kerr, 1907).

43. L. B. Budin (Boudin), "Voina i amerikanskie sotsialisty" (The war and the American socialists), *Svobodnoe Slovo*, 1, no. 2 (November 1915): 81–84. The quoted passage appears on p. 82.

44. Letter to Boudin, September 23, 1912, in Boudin, *Catalogued Correspondence*, Rare Book and Manuscript Library, Columbia University. The journal to which Boudin had solicited Deutsch's contribution may have been *The International Socialist Review*, an English-language socialist journal that had published the series that became Boudin's book.

45. "Evreiskoi krov'iu" (By Jewish blood), *Volia*, August–September 1915, p. 1. A note in parentheses identifies this article as a reprint from another Socialist Revolutionary publication.

Chapter 7
"We Are Jews"

1. Cahan, *Bleter fun mayn leben*, 1:500–501; *The Education of Abraham Cahan*, 182–83; "The Russian Jew in America," *The Atlantic Monthly*, 82 (1898): 128–39 (story appears on pp. 128–29); *The White Terror and the Red*, p. 321.

2. There are several histories of the Yiddish press in America. See, for example, Mordecai Soltes, *The Yiddish Press: An Americanizing Agency* (New York: Teachers College, Columbia University, 1925); and Joseph Chaikin, *Yidishe bleter in Amerike: A tsushtayer tsu der 75 yoriker geshikhte fun der yidisher prese in di fareynikte shtatn un Kanade* (Yiddish newspapers in America: A contribution to the 75-year history of the Yiddish press in the United States and Canada) (New York: Farlag M. Sh. Shklarski, 1946). These two studies treat only the daily press. See also Hoerder, *The Immigrant Labor Press in North America*, 2:541–45;

Encyclopaedia Judaica, 13:1053–56; and Irving Howe, *World of Our Fathers*, pp. 518–51.

3. "Dos program fun di Arbayter Tsaytung Publishing Asosyeyshen" (The program of the Arbeiter Zeitung Publishing Association), *Arbayter Tsaytung*, March 7, 1890, p. 1.

4. "Unzer 'Tsukunft' " (Our *Tsukunft*), *Di Tsukunft*, January 1892, pp. 1–3.

5. Cahan, *Bleter fun mayn leben*, 2:292; *The Education of Abraham Cahan*, pp. 336–37. See Chapter 5.

6. Morris Hillquit, *Loose Leaves from a Busy Life* (New York: Macmillan, 1934), p. 3.

7. "Men zol shmaysen iden. Nikolay hot ge'khasm'et dem proyekt" (Whip the Jews. Nicholas has put his signature on the plan), *Forverts*, March 22, 1903, p. 1.

8. Yankev Milkh (Jacob Milch), "Vos iz tsu ton?" (What is to be done?), *Di Tsukunft*, 1903, pp. 271–75.

9. Yankev Milkh (Jacob Milch), "Unzer bevegung un di prese" (Our movement and the press), ibid., 1906, pp. 18–23.

10. See Moyshe Shtarkman, "Bashayners fun der 'Tsukunft' " (Luminaries of *Di Tsukunft*), ibid., March–April 1968, pp. 106–11. The story about the change from "Yiddish-speaking" to "Jewish" appears on p. 106. The text of the inscriptions telling the party affiliation of *Di Tsukunft* in its early years appears in the seventieth Jubilee edition. See ibid., November–December 1962, p. 504.

11. For example, on Jews in New York, see "Gor di ershte iden fun Nyu-York" (The very first Jews of New York), *Arbayter Tsaytung*, June 21, 1895, pp. 1, 6; "Der kampf fun di ershte Nyu-Yorker iden far zeyere rekhte" (The struggle of the first New York Jews for their rights), *Arbayter Tsaytung*, June 28, 1895, pp. 1, 6; "Di ershte poylishe iden fun Nyu-York" (The first Polish Jews of New York), *Arbayter Tsaytung*, July 12, 1895, pp. 1, 6; D. Brenson, "Di ershte iden in Nyu-York" (The first Jews in New York), *Forverts*, April 29, 1903, p. 4. On writing Yiddish, see L. Miller, "Vi men darf shrayben in idish" (How one should write in Yiddish), *Forverts*, November 5, 1899, p. 2; Abe Cahan, "Vi darf men shrayben idish?" (How should Yiddish be written?), *Di Tsukunft*, 1907, pp. 126–33, 189–93. Literary works and reviews of literary works are too numerous to cite.

12. Ronald Sanders tells this story in *The Downtown Jews: Portraits of an Immigrant Generation* (New York: Harper and Row, 1969), p. 217. It comes from Cahan, *Bleter fun mayn leben*, 4:187–88.

13. Abe Cahan, "Unzer inteligents" (Our intelligentsia), *Di Tsukunft*, 1910, pp. 39–42, 109–13.

14. Ibid., 1910, p. 42. Emphasis added.

15. Ibid., 1910, p. 111. In his essay "Reality" (The realists), Pisarev spoke forcefully for the necessity of popularizing science. "Society," he said, "already loves and respects science; but we must nonetheless *popularize* this science, and popularize it with great skill. One can say without the least exaggeration that the popularization of science is the most important, universal task of our age." See Pisarev, *Sochineniia*, 3:129. Emphasis in original.

16. Cahan, *Bleter fun mayn leben*, 3.354–55.

17. *Di Tsukunft*, 1910, p. 112.

18. Abe Cahan, "Folks-visenshaft. Di vilde indyaner velkhe Kolumbus hot gefunen in Amerika" (Popular science. The wild Indians that Columbus found in America), *Arbayter Tsaytung*, April 11, 1890, p. 5; "Folksvisenshaft—Di piramiden fun Mitsraim" (Popular science—The pyramids of Egypt), *Arbayter Tsaytung*, June 20, 1890, p. 5; "Di natur. Der krokodil" (Nature. The crocodile), *Arbayter Tsaytung*, November 28, 1890, p. 5.

19. "Aleksandr der driter un zayn korbm" (Alexander the Third and his victim), *Arbayter Tsaytung*, May 29, 1891.

20. For the story of the Russian Extradition Treaty, see Thomas A. Bailey, *America Faces Russia: Russian-American Relations from Early Times to Our Day* (Gloucester, MA: Peter Smith, 1964), pp. 156–59; and Tcherikower, *The Early Jewish Labor Movement in the United States*, pp. 234–38.

21. Abe Cahan, "Der shidekh tsvishen Amerika un Rusland" (The *shidekh* between America and Russia), *Arbayter Tsaytung*, February 17, 1893, p. 4; "Di ksube fun di amerikaner 'frayhayts' madam mit Aleksander'en" (The *ksube* between the American "freedom" madam and Alexander [III]), *Arbayter Tsaytung*, June 16, 1893, p. 1.

22. A[yzik] Ortman, "Di lebedig-begrobene. Di shreklikhe maternes fun di nihilisten, vos zaynen fershikt in Sibir. (Nokh Dzhordzh Kenan)" (Buried alive. The terrible torments of the Nihilists exiled in Siberia [from an account by George Kennan]), *Arbayter Tsaytung*, July 24, 1891, pp. 1–2, and July 31, 1891, pp. 1–2.

23. Kennan published a few preliminary articles on Siberia in *Century* as early as 1886. Since the book did not appear until December 1891, the *Arbayter Tsaytung* article has to have been based on the *Century* series. See *Siberia and the Exile System*, 2 vols. (London: James R. Osgood, McIlvaine and Co., 1891). For Madam Sigida's story, see 2:266–72. Kohan-Bernstein is mentioned only once in the book, but the story of his torture and execution is not told. That story appears to have been well known to Jewish intellectuals. At the YIVO photographic archives, in the Chaim Zhitlovsky files, there is a picture postcard, apparently the property of Zhitlovsky, with a photograph of Kohan-Bernstein. On the back of the card, one reads this handwritten note: "Geo[.] Kohan-Bernstein[.] Jewish student in the university of Dorpat [Tartu], sent to Siberia by administrative process for helping an escaped political exile whom he had previously known. Hanged from his hospital bed at Yakutsk in 1889 after trial & condemnation by a court-martial upon the charge of resisting the authorities." Kennan was considered by many to be the foremost American authority on Russia in his day. For a brief biography of Kennan, see George F. Kennan's introduction to the abridged version of *Siberia and the Exile System* (Chicago: University of Chicago Press, 1958), pp. ix–xix. The pictures that the *Arbayter Tsaytung* printed, which are not taken from Kennan's book or articles, had also appeared, together with some others on the same theme, in *Znamia*, March 8, 1890, p. 4, in a feature on the attitudes of the American press toward the Russian autocracy. The author of the feature says the pictures originally appeared in the *Morning Journal*.

24. For Liessin's biography, see Reyzen, *Leksikon fun der yidisher literatur*, 2:259–66; and Niger and Shatski, *Leksikon fun der nayer yidisher literatur*, 5:179–91. Liessins's real surname was Valt. Cahan came up with *Lyesin* (as it was spelled in Yiddish) by taking the Russian word for forest (*les*) and adding a standard Russian ending to it. *Valt* sounds like the Yiddish *vald* and is identical in

pronunciation to the German *Wald*, both of which mean "forest." See Cahan, *Bleter fun mayn leben*, 3:355. The pen name has been Anglicized in many different ways: Lessin, Liessen, Liesen, in addition to Liessin. I have used the form that appears in the Library of Congress Catalogue.

25. A. Lyesin (Abraham Liessin), "Di rusishe regirung un ihr ekonomishe politik" (The Russian government and its economic policy), *Forverts*, January 22, 1899, p. 3; "Di rusishe literatur un di tsenzur" (Russian literature and censorship), *Forverts*, February 26, 1899, p. 2; "Di pres-unterdrikung in Rusland" (Suppression of the press in Russia), *Forverts*, March 5, 1899, p. 2, and March 12, 1899, p. 3; "Di inteligents in Rusland" (The intelligentsia in Russia), *Forverts*, May 7, 1899, p. 3; "Di letste studenten unruhen in Rusland" (The most recent student unrest in Russia), *Forverts*, September 3, 1899, p. 2.

26. V. Zhuk, "Di revolutsyonere bevegung in Rusland far Aleksander I un Nikolai's tsayten" (The revolutionary movement in Russia before the time of Alexander I and Nicholas [I]), *Di Tsukunft*, June 1894, pp. 33–38, and July 1894, pp. 30–35.

. 27. Dovid Bernshteyn, "A nihilist's arbayt in rusishen kayzer's dvorets" (A Nihilist's job in the Russian tsar's palace), *Arbayter Tsaytung*, May 2, 1890, pp. 1–2, 5.

28. Dovid Bernshteyn, "I. I. Grinevitski der held fun 1 Merts 1881" (I. I. Grinevitskii, the hero of March 1, 1881), *Arbayter Tsaytung*, July 4, 1890, pp. 1–2, and July 11, 1890, pp. 1–2. This article is a translation of an article that had appeared in the Russian-language émigré journal *Na Rodine*.

29. Ph. Krantz, "Mayne erinerungen vegin Grinevitski" (My reminiscences about Grinevitskii), *Arbayter Tsaytung*, July 11, 1890, p. 2.

30. "Vyera Zasulitsh fond" (Vera Zasulich fund), *Arbayter Tsaytung*, October 31, 1890, p. 1; "Ver iz Vyera Zasulitsh?" (Who is Vera Zasulich?), ibid., November 21, 1890, p. 1.

31. Socius (Abraham Cahan), "Fier rusishe helden. Tsum ondenken fun monat April" (Four Russian heroes. In commemoration of the month of April), ibid., April 17, 1891, p. 1.

32. M. Boyman, "Sofya Perovskaya" (Sofiia Perovskaia), *Di Tsukunft*, 1895, pp. 401–409.

33. A. K. (Abraham Cahan), "Hesse Helfman" (Hesia Helfman), ibid., 1897, pp. 1–6.

34. *Arbayter Tsaytung*, April 17, 1891, p. 1.

35. L. [Louis] Miller, "Tolstoy's 'Kreytser Sonata'" (Tolstoy's *Kreutzer Sonata*), *Di Tsukunft*, 1895, pp. 480–85, 521–28.

36. D. Puls (David Pinski), "Peter Lavrov," *Arbayter Tsaytung*, May 6, 1900, p. 4; May 13, 1900, p. 4; May 20, 1900, p. 4; and May 27, 1900, p. 4. On Pinski's pseudonym, see Saul Chajes, *Thesaurus pseudonymorum quae in litteratura Hebraica et Judaeo-Germanica inveniuntur* (Thesaurus of pseudonyms occurring in Hebrew and Yiddish literature) (Hildesheim: Georg Olms, 1967), p. 244; and Reyzen, *Leksikon fun der yidisher literatur*, 2:888. Chajes, through the omission of a dot (dagesh) in the initial Hebrew letter, gives the pseudonym as "Fuls," *Puls* means "pulse." Pinski also used the Hebrew *dofek* (*doyfek* in Yiddish pronunciation) as a pseudonym, apparently since it can be constructed from some of the consonants in his name. It, too, means "pulse." See Chajes, *Thesaurus*, p. 97.

37. M. Vintshevski (Morris Winchevsky), "Erinerungen on Peter Lavrov" (Reminiscences about Petr Lavrov), *Forverts*, February 17, 1900, p. 4, and February 24, 1900, p. 4.

38. A. L. (Abraham Liessin), "Etvas iber Peter Lavrov " (Something about Petr Lavrov), ibid., March 20, 1900, p. 4.

39. C. Z., "Peter Lavrof (A kurtse byografishe skitse)" (Petr Lavrov [A short biographical sketch]), *Di Tsukunft*, February 1894, pp. 1–4.

40. "Peter Kropotkin (Byografishe skitse)" (Petr Kropotkin [Biographical sketch]), *Forverts*, April 2, 1901, p. 4; P. Kropotkin, "Rusland un di studenten-unruhen" (Russia and the student disturbances), ibid., April 6, 1901, p. 4; April 7, 1901, p. 4; and April 8, 1901, p. 4.

41. Leo Daytsh (Leo Deutsch), "Peter Kropotkin als mensh un denker" (Petr Kropotkin as man and thinker), *Di Tsukunft*, 1913, pp. 109–15.

42. Ibid., p. 111.

43. Ibid., pp. 112–13.

44. Kh. Aleksandrov, "Di rusishe korbones" (The Russian victims), *Arbayter Tsaytung*, July 8, 1900, p. 4.

45. The article, "N. Mikhaylovski als kritiker" (N. Mikhailovsky as critic), *Forverts*, February 17, 1904, p. 4, is signed "Bcn-Hilel." Both the Reyzen *Leksikon fun der yidisher literatur* (3:24) and the Niger-Shatski *Leksikon fun der nayer yidisher literatur* (7:314) list Ben Hilel as one of Fornberg's pseudonyms ("Karl Fornberg" itself was a pseudonym for Yeshaye Rozenberg), though neither mentions this article. Even though there was another Ben Hilel writing in the Yiddish press at around this time, it seems safe to conclude that the Ben-Hilel (with a hyphen) signing this article was Fornberg, first, because it appeared during the relatively brief time that Fornberg was affiliated with the *Forward* (he arrived in the United States in May of 1903, began writing for the *Forward* soon thereafter, then had a falling-out with Cahan and left in November of 1905) and, second, because it displays the same extraordinary intellectual prowess he displayed in other writings.

46. For Rosenblatt's biography, see Reyzen, *Leksikon fun der yidisher literatur*, 4:106–10; and Niger and Shatski, *Leksikon fun der nayer yidisher literatur*, 8:330–31.

47. F. Rozenblat (Frank Rosenblatt), "Mikhaylovski's filozofye" (Mikhailovsky's philosophy), *Di Tsukunft*, 1904, pp. 353–56; and "Mikhaylovski's polemik mit marksisten" (Mikhailovsky's polemic with Marxists), *Di Tsukunft*, 1904, pp. 580–82.

48. F. Rozenblat (Frank Rosenblatt), "V. G. Byelinski" (V. G. Belinsky), *Di Tsukunft*, 1905, pp. 129–35.

49. F. Rozenblat (Frank Rosenblatt), "N. A. Dobrolyubov" (N. A. Dobroliubov), ibid., pp. 179–85.

50. Ibid., p. 181.

51. F. Rozenblat (Frank Rosenblatt), "D. M. Pisarev," ibid., pp. 261–67, 344–48, 401–405, 453–57.

52. Ibid., p. 267.

53. On Chernyshevsky in the United States, see Steven Cassedy, "Chernyshevskii Goes West: How Jewish Immigration Helped Bring Russian Radicalism to America," *Russian History*, 21, no. 1 (1994): 1–21.

54. On Tucker and Dole, see Michael R. Katz, "English Translations of *What Is to Be Done?*," *Slavic Review*, 46 (1987–1988): 125–31. According to Katz, little is known of Skidelsky. On Tucker, see also the entry on *Liberty* magazine by Herbert B. Gutman, in Joseph R. Conlin, ed., *The American Radical Press 1880–1960* (Westport, CT: Greenwood Press, 1974), pp. 373–79. Gutman quotes a contemporary who says that Tucker's translations of Russian works were from French translations. See p. 377. Gutman's entry is reprinted from the reprinted edition of *Liberty* (Westport, CT: Greenwood Reprint, 1970).

55. For example, *Workmen's Advocate* in the 1880s (in one case, coincidentally, right next to an article by Abraham Cahan), and its sequel publication *The People* in the 1890s ran frequent ads for Tucker's translation. Tucker's own *Liberty*, naturally, ran many ads for the translation after it came out in book form.

56. See M. P. Alekseev, "N. G. Chernyshevskii v zapadnoevropeiskikh literaturakh" (N. G. Chernyshevsky in Western European literatures), in V. E. Evgen'ev-Maksimov et al., *N. G. Chernyshevskii (1889–1939): Trudy nauchnoi sessii k piatidesiatiletiiu so dnia smerti* (Chernyshevsky [1889–1939]: Transactions of the scholarly session on the fiftieth anniversary of his death) (Leningrad: Izd. LGU, 1941), pp. 242–69. The account of the meeting appears on p. 268n3. See also S. Pollak (Simon O. Pollock), "Nikolay Gavrilovitsh Tshernishevski" (Nikolai Gavrilovich Chernyshevsky), *Di Tsukunft*, March 1892, pp. 2–12. Mention of the meeting appears on p. 2.

57. The book itself does not identify the translator, and the account that emerges from the Reyzen *Leksikon fun der yidisher literatur* and the Niger-Shatski *Leksikon fun der nayer yidisher literatur* is baffling. In the entries on Michael Zametkin and Adella Kean Zametkin, the Niger Shatski *Leksikon* says that the Zametkins collaborated on the translation that came out in 1917 and that it was published under the editorship of Fornberg. The source given for the claim that the Zametkins did the translation is Reyzen's entries on the Zametkins in his *Leksikon*. But, while Reyzen mentions the translation in each of those two entries, he nowhere gives a date or any other publication information. To confuse matters even more, both the Reyzen *Leksikon* and the Niger-Shatski *Leksikon*, in their entries on Fornberg, attribute to *him* a translation of Chernyshevsky's novel; Reyzen gives no further information, and Niger-Shatski give the date 1917. Though Reyzen never gives any publication information on the translation, it is probable that all the references in his work and in the Niger-Shatski work are to the same book, since the Yiddish title *Vos tut men?* (literally, "what does one do?") is used consistently and since this was not the most common way of rendering the title in Yiddish. In the *Morgenshtern* version, for example, the title appeared as *Vos tsu thon?* (literally, "what to do?"), and in many scattered references in the press it appeared as *Vos zol men tun?* (literally, "what should one do?").

58. S. Pollak (Simon O. Pollock), "Nikolay Gavrilovitsh Tshernishevski" (Nikolai Gavrilovich Chernyshevsky), *Di Tsukunft*, March 1892, pp. 2–12. I cannot establish with complete certainty that the "S. Pollak" listed as the author of the article on Chernyshevsky and Simon O. Pollock were the same man, but all evidence points to that conclusion. Simon O. Pollock was extremely active in Jewish immigrant affairs. The *Concise Dictionary of American Jewish Biography* (Brooklyn, NY: Carlson Publishing, 1994), p. 493, gives his full name as Simon

Oscar Pollock, his dates as 1868–1934, and his place of birth as Minsk. The Library of Congress catalogue gives his year of birth as 1866, but gives no year of death. *Who Was Who in America*, 4:758, gives his year of birth as 1868 and the year of his arrival in the United States as 1890. It mentions, too, that he attended law school at Moscow University, something quite rare among Jewish immigrants. His name appears in advertisements for his legal services in virtually every Yiddish newspaper published in New York, sometimes in the same issue as an article by "S. Pollak." A letter Pollock wrote to Louis Boudin in English indicates that he was part of Boudin's larger intellectual circle. See letter to Boudin, December 22, 1906 (on the occasion of the death of Boudin's wife), in Boudin, *Catalogued Correspondence*. The letter was written on letterhead for the law firm of Pollock and Abrahams, New York, and signed Simon O. Pollock. Pollock was the author of a book in English, called *The Russian Bastille* (Chicago: Charles H. Kerr, 1908). In a notice for this book in the *International Socialist Review*, 9 (1908–1909): 544, the reviewer identifies the author as the counsel in the extradition case. Mark Vil'chur also speaks of the extradition case and names the attorney, but spells his name *Pollak*, as it is spelled in *Di Tsukunft*. See *Russkie v Amerike*, p. 134.

59. See Lavrov, *Istoricheskie pis'ma*, pp. 65–66; *Historical Letters*, p. 141.

60. *Di Tsukunft*, March 1902, p. 3.

61. Ibid., 1905, p. 456.

62. A. Litvak (Khaim Yankel Helfand), and Y. B. Salutski, *Dos revolutsyonere rusland* (Revolutionary Russia) (New York: Bund, 1917).

63. A. Litvak, "Di trayb-kreften fun der revolutsye" (The driving forces of the revolution), ibid., pp. 77–96. The portrait appears on p. 79, and the description of Chernyshevsky as a literary hero appears on p. 81.

64. Cahan, *The White Terror and the Red*, p. 412.

65. Dr. Kh. Zshitlovski (Dr. Chaim Zhitlovsky), "Dos program un di tsielen fun der monatshrift 'Dos Naye Leben'" (The program and the goals of the monthly *Dos Naye Leben*), *Dos Naye Leben*, 1908, pp. 3–16.

66. Ibid., p. 15.

67. Ibid., p. 16.

68. Adela Kien Zametkin [Adella Kean Zametkin], "Fun a froy tsu froyen," *Der Tog*, April 20, 1918, p. 12.

69. "Keyn mol nit shpet tsu lernen" (Never too late to learn), "Fun a froy tsu froyen," ibid., May 18, 1918, p. 12.

70. Laura Z. Hobson, *Laura Z: A Life*, pp. 24–25.

Chapter 8
"We Are Americans"

1. Cahan, *The Rise of David Levinsky* (New York, 1917; rpt. New York: Penguin, 1993), p. 473.

2. John Spargo, "'The Spirit of the Ghetto.' A Review," *The Comrade*, 2 (1902–1903): 55. Spargo is reviewing *The Spirit of the Ghetto*, by Hutchins Hapgood.

3. Cahan, *Bleter fun mayn leben*, 2:118–22; *The Education of Abraham Cahan*, pp. 238–41.

4. See Reyzen, *Leksikon fun der yidisher literatur*, 4:108; and Niger and Shatski, *Leksikon fun der nayer yidisher literatur*, 8:330.

5. See, for example, an ad in *The Worker*, May 5, 1901, p. 4, for the services of "Morris Hillquit, Attorney-at-Law," and "Henry L. Slobodin, Counsellor-at-Law." See the ad in *New York Call*, June 24, 1910, p. 5, for the services of "Henry L. Slobodin, Attorney and Counselor at Law."

6. Goldman, *Living My Life*, 1:26–28.

7. Moses Rischin, ed., *Grandma Never Lived in America: The New Journalism of Abraham Cahan* (Bloomington, IN: Indiana University Press, 1985), pp. 329–31.

8. Emma Goldman to Peter Kropotkin, May 5, 1913, in Candace Falk, with Ronald J. Zboray, et al., eds., *The Emma Goldman Papers: A Microfilm Edition* (Alexandria, VA: Chadwyck-Healey Inc., 1990), reel 7.

9. For biographical information on Tucker, see the article on *Liberty* magazine by Herbert G. Gutman, in Joseph R. Conlin, ed., *The American Radical Press 1880–1960*, 2:373–79.

10. Joaquin Miller, "Sophie Perovskaya, Liberty's Martyred Heroine," *Liberty*, August 6, 1881, p. 1; "Michael Bakounine," ibid., November 26, 1881, pp. 1, 4; the article on the Nihilists is printed under the regular first-page feature, "On Picket Duty," ibid., April 15, 1882, p. 1.

11. N. G. Tchernychewsky (N. G. Chernyshevsky), *What's To Be Done? A Romance*, May 17, 1884–May 1, 1886.

12. The work by Stepniak was *A Female Nihilist*, and it began running in *Liberty*, December 13, 1884.

13. Lincoln Steffens, *The Autobiography of Lincoln Steffens* (New York: Harcourt, Brace and Company, 1931), 1:314.

14. See Chapter 2.

15. Hutchins Hapgood, *The Spirit of the Ghetto*, ed. Moses Rischin (Cambridge, MA: Harvard University Press, 1967), pp. 79–81. The drawings for Hapgood's volume were done by Jacob Epstein (1880–1959), born in the New York ghetto to immigrants from Poland (and later a distinguished sculptor in London).

16. Ibid., pp. 109–10.

17. Ibid., pp. 218–20.

18. Ibid., pp. 222–29.

19. Ibid., p. 39. Spargo, in his review of Hapgood's book, criticized him for the sentence containing the word "reactionary," but he appears to have understood "reactionary" in the sense that was normal in the socialist movement, that is, "ultraconservative," and not in the sense in which Hapgood apparently was using the word.

20. Ibid., p. 40.

21. Ibid., p. 42.

22. Ibid., p. 231.

23. Ibid., p. 232.

24. Ibid., pp. 232–33.

25. Ibid., p. 235.

26. Under "Interesting People," *American Magazine*, 74 (1912): 67–74, Cahan is billed in the subtitle as "A Jew who wields tremendous power over his

people" and described in a caption to his photo as "the most influential man on the East Side in New York." The article on Cahan was written by Joseph Gollomb.

27. Winchevsky, *Stories of the Struggle* (Chicago: Charles H. Kerr, 1908).

28. M. Winchevski (Winchevsky), "Why he did it," *The Comrade*, 1 (1901–1902): 76–78.

29. Winchevsky, "The Knout and the Fog," *International Socialist Review*, 8 (1907–1908): 589–92; *Stories of the Struggle*, pp. 73–81.

30. Simon O. Pollock, "The Singer," *The Comrade*, 2 (1902–1903): 29–30.

31. Pollock, "The Singer. A short story, adapted from the Russian," *The Young Socialists' Magazine*, November 1918, pp. 7–8, 13.

32. See, for example, Catherine Breschkovsky (Ekaterina Breshkovskaia), "The Internal Condition of Russia," *The Comrade*, 4 (1904–1905): 34–36. Charles Kerr, the Chicago-based publisher of the *International Socialist Review*, brought out a pamphlet about Breshkovskaia in 1905, and *The Worker* included a review of it right beneath a review of Cahan's *The White Terror and the Red*. See "Current Literature," *The Worker*, March 12, 1905, p. 4. An unsigned article in the *International Socialist Review* after the February Revolution of 1917 includes a picture of Breshkovskaia as she was greeted by a group of workers and soldiers in celebration of the revolution. See "The Russian Revolution," *International Socialist Review*, 17 (1916–1917): 709–14. Abe Cahan wrote a series on her in the *Forward*, beginning in January 1905.

33. Pollock, "Ekaterina Breshkovskaia and the Russian Revolution," *The Worker*, December 25, 1904, p. 4.

34. Pollock, "The Russian Bastille," *International Socialist Review*, 7 (1906–1907): 533–45.

35. See Chapter 7, n. 58.

36. Deutsch, "Marching Through Siberia," *The Comrade*, 4 (1904–1905): 36–37; review of *Sixteen Years in Siberia*, under "Current Literature," *The Worker*, May 1, 1904, p. 4.

37. Milch, "New Movements Amongst the Jewish Proletariat," *International Socialist Review*, 7 (1906–1907): 354–63, 398–407, 480–88, 599–607.

38. Ibid., p. 354.

39. Ibid., pp. 355–56.

40. Ibid., p. 605.

41. A large number of Cahan's journalistic pieces from this period are collected in Moses Rischin, ed., *Grandma Never Lived in America*.

42. "The Diabolical Massacre of Jews in Kishinev," in ibid., pp. 43–49.

43. Ibid., p. 46.

44. "Nestor of Nihilism," in ibid., pp. 475–77.

45. "Revolution Threatens Russia," in ibid., pp. 503–10.

46. Quoted in ibid., p. xxii.

47. "The Russian Jew in America," *Atlantic Monthly*, 82 (1898): 128–39.

48. Ibid., p. 134.

49. Alexander Berkman, *Prison Memoirs of an Anarchist* (New York: Mother Earth Publishing Association, 1912), p. 5.

50. Ibid., p. 11.

51. Ibid., p. 8.

52. Ibid., pp. 9–10.

53. Ibid., p. 41.

54. Spargo, under "Views and Reviews," *The Comrade*, 2 (1902–1903): 212–13.

55. A. M. Simons, "Kropotkin's 'Mutual Aid,'" *International Socialist Review*, 3 (1902–1903): 544–49.

56. Prince Peter Kropotkin, "The Sacrifices We Often Forget," *The Young Socialists' Magazine*, March 1913, p. 2; and W. Morris Duff, "Russia and Prince Kropotkin," ibid., January 1915, pp. 9–10.

57. "The Young Giant of Russian Literature," *The Worker*, August 11, 1901, p. 3.

58. Eugene Limedorfer, "Gorky and His Philosophy," *The Comrade*, 1 (1901–1902): 43; Maxim Gorky, "Twenty-six and One," ibid., pp. 50–61.

59. Henrietta Roland-Holst, "Gorky as a Proletarian Literary Critic," *The International Socialist Review*, 6 (1905–1906): 705–11.

60. Cahan, "The Younger Russian Writers," *Forum*, 28 (September 1899): 119–28.

61. Cahan, "The Mantle of Tolstoy," *Bookman*, 16 (December 1902): 328–33.

62. Khaim Aleksandrov, "Tshekhov un Gorki (A literarishe paralel)" (Chekhov and Gorky [A literary parallel]), *Arbayter Tsaytung*, 24 September 1899, p. 4.

63. "Maksim Gorki. A bletil fun zayn lebensbeshraybung" (Maxim Gorky. A page from his biography), *Forverts*, December 6, 1902; Y. Entin, "Gorki's 'Meshtshane'" (Gorky's *Burghers*), *Forverts*, November 10, 1903, p. 4; Y. Entin, "Di perzonen fun 'Meshtshane'" (The characters in *Burghers*), *Forverts*, 12 November 1903, p. 4.

64. In 1901, two novels were published, in English translation, in the United States, both translated by Isabel F. Hapgood. They were *Foma Gordyeeff* (New York: C. Scribner's Sons, 1901), and *Orloff and His Wife; Tales of the Barefoot Brigade* (New York: C. Scribner's Sons, 1901). The *Readers' Guide to Periodical Literature* lists nothing by or about Gorky published before 1901.

65. "The Story of a Russian Terrorist," *The Comrade*, 4 (1903–1904): 56. The article is reprinted from the British publication *Free Russia*.

66. William English Walling, "The Evolution of Socialism in Russia," *International Socialist Review*, 8 (1907–1908): 42–46.

67. One can find an occasional remark in his writings that identifies him as a Jew. For example, in an article on Alexander Berkman and Jim McNamara in *Di Tsukunft*, Boudin actually uses the phrase "we, Jewish socialists." See L. B. Budin (Louis Boudin), "Fun Aleksander Berkman biz Dzhim Meknamara" (From Alexander Berkman to Jim McNamara), *Di Tsukunft*, 1912, pp. 54–56. The phrase appears on p. 54. Brothers James and John McNamara were members of an iron workers' union seeking recognition from a management association. James bombed the Los Angeles Times building in October of 1910 as part of this effort. They were the subject of a much publicized legal case, on which Emma Goldman was a frequent commentator. James eventually pleaded guilty to the crime, and John pleaded guilty as an accessory.

68. Boudin, *Government by Judiciary* (New York: W. Godwin, 1932).

Chapter 9
American Realism

1. Cahan, *The Rise of David Levinsky*, p. 475.

2. Abe Cahan, "Der idisher theater un di amerikaner romanen" (The Yiddish theatre and American novels), *Arbayter Tsaytung*, April 29, 1892, p. 4.

3. Cahan, "Realism," *Workmen's Advocate*, April 6, 1889, p. 2.

4. Ibid., p. 2.

5. Abe Cahan, "Gute un shlekhte romanen" (Good and bad novels), *Arbayter Tsaytung*, December 29, 1893, p. 4; and "A guter roman" (A good novel), ibid., January 5, 1894, p. 4, and January 12, 1894, p. 5.

6. Ibid., December 29, 1893, p. 4.

7. Ibid., January 12, 1894, p. 5.

8. Abe Cahan, "Kritishe studyen iber zshargonishe mayster-verk" (Critical studies of masterpieces in Yiddish), *Di Tsukunft*, 1896, pp. 53–59, 153–60, 178–87, 223–29.

9. Abe Cahan, "A por verter vegen kritik in algemeyn" (A few words on criticism in general), ibid., pp. 53–56.

10. Ibid., p. 54.

11. Ibid.

12. L. Budyanov (Louis Boudin), "Tendents in literatur" (Tendentiousness in literature), *Arbayter Tsaytung*, April 11, 1897, p. 5; and April 18, 1897, p. 4. The second installment bears the title "Tendents un literatur" (Tendentiousness and literature).

13. Chernyshevsky, *PSS*, 2:10. See Chapter 2.

14. For an excellent summary of the Yiddish theatre in America, see Sanders, *The Downtown Jews*, pp. 277–326.

15. Hapgood, *The Spirit of the Ghetto*, 135–49.

16. Steffens, *The Autobiography of Lincoln Steffens*, 1:318. Cited in Sanders, *The Downtown Jews*, p. 312.

17. Abe Cahan, "Vos heyst realizmus?" (What does "realism" mean?), *Forverts*, December 8, 1903, p. 4.

18. Abe Cahan, "Romantizmus un realizmus" (Romanticism and realism), ibid., December 14, 1903, p. 4.

19. "Y. Gordin's naye pyese—dem realizmus' nayer erfolg" (J. Gordin's new play—realism's latest success), ibid., December 13, 1903, p. 1.

20. Yankev Gordin (Jacob Gordin), "Realizmus un romantizmus" (Realism and romanticism), *Di Tsukunft*, 1904, pp. 165–69.

21. The reference to cobblers and boots suggests that Gordin was familiar with nineteenth-century Russian literary debates. Dostoevsky introduced the image of boots in a satire he published in 1864. His target was Nihilism. In one section of the article, he lampoons the literary sentiments of Pisarev and Varfolomei Zaitsev, Pisarev's fellow contributor to *Russkoe Slovo*. Because Pisarev and Zaitsev had emphasized utility as a dominant category in the evaluation of literature, Dostoevsky ironically adopts their point of view and says, "You may

accept as a rule that boots are in any case better than Pushkin, because one can get along very nicely without Pushkin, but one cannot get along without boots. Pushkin, therefore, is mere luxury and rubbish." See Dostoevskii, *Polnoe sobranie sochinenii v tridtsati tomakh* (Leningrad: "Nauka," 1972–1990), 19:109. Dostoevsky had in mind not only the general tenor of Nihilist utilitarian aesthetics (from Pisarev, who of course was committed to destroying aesthetics altogether) but perhaps two specific passages from Zaitsev. Zaitsev wrote that "any craftsman is as much more useful than any given poet as any positive number, no matter how small, is greater than zero." See Zaitsev, *Izbrannye sochineniia* (Moscow: Obshchestvo Politkatorzhan, 1934), 1:216. And he wrote, "There is no floor-polisher, no goldsmith who is not infinitely more useful than Shakespeare." See *Russkoe slovo*, 3, no. 2 (1864): 64. A number of years after Dostoevsky's article appeared, Mikhail Saltykov-Shchedrin, who was the principal object of Dostoevsky's squib of 1864, gave the classic form to the sentiment Dostoevsky had derided, as he has a character in a dialogue say, "Every cobbler is a hundred times more useful than Pushkin." See Saltykov-Shchedrin, *Sobranie sochinenii* (Moscow: Khudozhestvennaia Literatura, 1965–1974), 10:102. These references may be found in Dostoevskii, *Polnoe sobranie sochinenii*, 12:284, 311–12.

22. On the Cahan-Gordin feud, see Sanders, *The Downtown Jews*, 301–26.

23. Georgii Plekhanov, *Sochineniia*, ed. D. Riazanov (Moscow: Gosudarstvennoe Izdatel'stvo, 1923–1927), 14:36.

24. K. Frumin, "Der 'Bund' un zayne gegner" (The "Bund" and its opponents), *Di Tsukunft*, 1903, pp. 275–83, 335–41, 556–59, 613–19. K. Frumin was the pen-name of Y. Blumshteyn, a Bund activist living in Berne, Switzerland, at the time. And Filip Krants (Philip Krantz), "Kishinev, pogromen un der 'Bund'" (Kishinev, pogroms, and the Bund), ibid., 1904, pp. 54–59.

25. "Gorki als sheliekh fun der rusisher revolutsyon" (Gorky as envoy of the Russian revolution), *Fraye Arbayter Shtimme*, April 8, 1906, p. 1.

26. "Maksim Gorki als dikhter un sotsyalist" (Maksim Gorky as poet and socialist), *Forverts*, April 12, 1906, p. 4.

27. Yankev Gordin (Jacob Gordin), "Maksim Gorki" (Maksim Gorky), *Di Tsukunft*, 1906, pp. 327–30.

28. Ibid., p. 330.

29. "Der dzhongl. A realistisher roman fun dem leben in 'peking-toun' fun dem fleysh-trost. Fun Opton Sinkler" (The Jungle. A realist novel of life in "Packing Town" about the meat trust. By Upton Sinclair). The first installment appeared on June 3, 1906, and the final installment appeared on August 16 of the same year.

30. L. Budyanov (Louis Boudin), "Der dzshongl" (*The Jungle*), *Di Tsukunft*, 1906, pp. 457–60, 521–28.

31. Ibid., p. 457.

32. Ibid., p. 528.

33. *Di Tsukunft*, 1907, p. 4.

34. L. B. Budyanov Budin (Louis Boudin), "Leben un kunst" (Life and art), ibid., pp. 23–29.

35. Ibid., p. 26.

36. Ibid., p. 24.

37. In *The Development of the Monist View of History* (1895), one of the earliest places where he commented on art, Plekhanov quoted at length from Taine's *Philosophy of Art* (1865) in order to present Taine's view that the "first cause" of a work of art is "the general condition of minds and manners" of the era in which the artist lives. See *K voprosu o razvitii monisticheskogo vzgliada na istoriiu* (On the question of the development of the monist view of history), in Plekhanov, *Sochineniia*, 7:61–326. The quotation from Taine appears on pp. 208–209. The passage Plekhanov quotes may be found in Taine, *Philosophie de l'art* (Paris: Hachette, 1913), 1:7–10. In *Essays on the History of Materialism* (1896), Plekhanov again reproduced a long passage from the *Philosophy of Art* to call attention to Taine's view that "a *work of art is determined by the general state of minds and the predominant morals*" of its age. See *Beiträge zur Geschichte des Materialismus* (Stuttgart: Dietz, 1896) (the work was originally published in German). The passage in question appears on p. 215 and reads, "*ein Kunstwerk [wird] durch den allgemeinen Zustand des Geistes und der herrschenden Sitten bestimmt.*" I have quoted from the Soviet English translation. See Georgi Plekhanov, *Selected Philosophical Works in Five Volumes* (Moscow: Progress Publishers, 1974–1891), 2:156. Emphasis in original. And in *Letters Without Address*, Plekhanov had quoted from Taine immediately before giving the description of art quoted above. See Plekhanov, *Sochineniia*, 14:34–36. In "Life and Art," Boudin reproduces or paraphrases the very same material from the *Philosophy of Art* as Plekhanov had presented in *The Development of the Monist View of History*.

38. *Di Tsukunft*, 1907, p. 27.

39. Plekhanov, *Sochineniia*, 14:36.

40. In *Letters Without Address* Plekhanov says that one of the tasks of a materialist criticism is "the evaluation of the aesthetic merits of the work under investigation." See ibid., 14:189.

41. *Di Tsukunft*, 1907, p. 27.

42. "Di 'tsukunft,'" *Fraye Arbayter Shtimme*, January 19, 1907, p. 4, and January 26, 1907, p. 5.

43. Yankev Milkh (Jacob Milch), "Marksistishe literatur-kritik" (Marxist literary criticism), *Di Tsukunft*, 1907, pp. 157–62.

44. Ibid., p. 162.

45. Ibid. There is circumstantial evidence to suggest that Milch, too, may have derived his ideas in part from Plekhanov. Taine proposed more than one version of the factors that produce art. The most celebrated, of course, is *la race, le moment, le milieu*, as he presents it in the *History of English Literature*. The English translation of Taine's *History* gave the list as "the race, the surroundings, and the epoch." See Taine, *History of English Literature*, trans. H. Van Laun (Brooklyn, NY: Library Publishing Company, 1871), 1:12. In the *Philosophy of Art*, Taine used the phrases *condition d'existence* and *circonstances régnantes* to suggest the *milieu* of a culture. See Taine, *Philosophie de l'art*, 1:9. Milch, when he comes to translate *milieu* ("surroundings" in the English) uses the Yiddish expression *arumringlende umshtenden*, "surrounding circumstances," something that does not appear in Taine's original or the English translation of Taine. This is an exact translation of the phrase that Plekhanov uses (*okruzhaiushchie usloviia*) in *Let-*

ters Without Address to explain how a given individual in society has one particular set of tastes and not another. See Plekhanov, *Sochineniia*, 14:11, 20.

46. Tsvion (Zivion), "Dos folk un di kunst" (The people and art), *Di
Tsukunft*, 1908, pp. 688–92. The quoted passages appear on p. 688.

47. Saul Raskin, "Proletaryer-kunst" (Proletarian art), ibid., 1914, pp. 313–
20. Raskin was not the first, or the last, to write about Meunier in the American
radical press. John Spargo had written about him in *Comrade*, and a few years
after Raskin's article, the *Young Socialists' Magazine* would run a piece on him.
See John Spargo, "Constantin Meunier, Painter and Sculptor of Toil," *The Comrade*, 2 (1902–1903): 246–48; "Constantine [sic] Meunier, the Sculptor of Modern Belgian Labor," *Little Socialists' Magazine*, March 1918, pp. 2–4, 14.

48. Sh. Rabinovitsh, "Plekhanov als filosof un literatur kritiker. Plekhanov als
fanatiker fun marksizm" (Plekhanov as philosopher and literary critic: Plekhanov
as fanatic of Marxism), *Di Tsukunft*, 1918, pp. 704–708.

49. *Pechat'* in Russian means both "print" and "the press." The statement is
from the supplement to a speech on party organization that Stalin gave in April
1923. I. Stalin, *Organizatsionnyi otchet Ts. K. Partii, Zakliuchitel'noe slovo* (Or-
ganizational report of the Central Committee of the Party, concluding remarks)
(Moscow: "Krasnaia nov'," 1923), p. 32. An official English translation of this
speech was issued under the title "Reply to the discussion on the Central Committee's Organisational report," in J. V. Stalin, *Works* (Moscow: Foreign Languages
Publishing House, 1953), 5:227–40. The quoted passage appears on p. 240.

Conclusion

1. "Yiddish Forward Fetes Its 95th Anniversary," *Forward*, September 18,
1992, p. 1.

2. Hobson, *Laura Z: A Life*, pp. 10–11; Adella Kean Zametkin, *Der froys
handbukh* (Jamaica, NY: 1930).

3. Ibid., p. 23.

4. There are two ample studies of the New York Intellectuals: Alan M. Wald,
The New York Intellectuals (Chapel Hill: University of North Carolina Press,
1987); and Alexander Bloom, *Prodigal Sons: The New York Intellectuals and
Their World* (New York and Oxford: Oxford University Press, 1986).

5. Howe, "The New York Intellectuals: A Chronicle & A Critique," *Commentary*, October 1968, pp. 29–51. The quoted phrase appears on p. 29.

6. Bloom, *Prodigal Sons*, p. 14. Bloom cites an interview with Bell for the story
about the street-corner speeches.

7. Wald, *The New York Intellectuals*, p. 212.

8. Bloom, *Prodigal Sons*, p. 14.

9. Mike Gold, *Mike Gold: A Literary Anthology*, ed. Michael Folsom (New
York: International Publishers, 1972), p. 70.

10. Cited in James T. Farrell, *A Note on Literary Criticism* (New York: Vanguard Press, 1936), p. 30n3.

11. Philip Rahv, "The Literary Class War," excerpted in *Essays on Literature
and Politics, 1932–1972*, ed. Arabel J. Porter and Andrew J. Dvosin (Boston:
Houghton Mifflin, 1978), pp. 281–83.

12. "Editorial Statement," *Partisan Review*, 1, no. 1 (February–March 1934): 3.

13. "Problems and Perspectives in Revolutionary Literature," ibid., 1, no. 3 (June–July 1934): 3–10. The quoted phrase appears on p. 5.

14. Daniel Bell, letter to the author, April 13, 1994.

15. William Phillips, letter to the author, September 15, 1994.

16. Phillips, "How 'Partisan Review' Began," *Commentary*, December 1976, pp. 42–46. The quoted material appears on p. 42.

17. Quoted in *V. I. Lenin o literature i iskusstve* (V. I. Lenin on literature and art) (Moscow: Izdatel'stvo "Khudozhestvennaia literatura," 1969), pp. 652–53. Emphasis in original. The final sentence literally means, "He deeply plowed me over again completely."

18. Lenin, *Polnoe sobranie sochinenii* (Moscow: Izdatel'stvo Politicheskoi Literatury, 1975–1982), 6:89. Lenin uses the word *pechat'*, which means both "print" and "the press."

19. Ibid., 6:172–73.

20. Quoted in *V. I. Lenin o literature i iskusstve*, pp. 630–33.

21. See Chapter 9, n. 49.

22. *V. I. Lenin o literature i iskusstve*, p. 90.

23. Joseph Frank tells this story in *Through the Russian Prism: Essays on Literature and Culture* (Princeton: Princeton University Press, 1990), p. 80.

24. *Commentary*, December 1976, p. 42.

25. Frank Lentricchia, *Criticism and Social Change* (Chicago: University of Chicago Press, 1983), pp. 10, 19.

26. Fredric Jameson, *Marxism and Form: Twentieth-Century Dialectical Theories of Literature* (Princeton: Princeton University Press, 1972), p. 416.

27. Paul Bové, *Intellectuals in Power: A Genealogy of Critical Humanism* (New York: Columbia University Press, 1986), p. xiii.

28. The newspaper was called *Kol Mevaser* (Voice of the herald), and it was published in Zhitomir, Ukraine, from 1862 to 1871. On the aims of its editor, see Alexander Orbach, *New Voices of Russian Jewry: A Study of the Russian-Jewish Press of Odessa in the Era of the Great Reforms 1860–1871* (Leiden: E. J. Brill, 1980), p. 204.

29. Cahan, "The Russian Jew in America," *Atlantic Monthly*, 82 (1898): 133.

30. Irving Howe gives this figure in *World of Our Fathers*, p. 551.

31. For the later years of Cahan and the *Forward*, see Sanders, *The Downtown Jews*, pp. 437–53.

Index

ABOUT THE AUTHOR

Steven Cassedy is Professor of Slavic and Comparative Literature at the University of California, San Diego. He is the author of *Selected Essays of Andrey Bely* (1985) and *Flight from Eden: The Origins of Modern Literary Criticism and Theory* (1990).